The Charioteer

JEMAHL EVANS

First published in 2021 by Sharpe Books.

For Tim and his tales of Tashkent and the Silk Road.

CONTENTS

About the same time there came from India certain monks. When they had satisfied Justinian Augustus that the Romans should not buy silk from the Persians, they promised the emperor that they could provide the materials for making silk. Never again would the Romans seek business of this kind from their enemy the Persians, or from any other people whatsoever.

Procopius of Caesarea.

Calliopas Porphyries stood beside his lead horse and whispered soothing words in its ear. A stocky old African with tight silver curls and trimmed beard set against his black face. He still looked formidable with a barrel chest, narrow waist and muscular arms, but there was no denying his age. Cal did not know the team of horses. He had not raced properly in twenty years and needed the animals to trust him. It was cold and dark in the bowels of the hippodrome. The crowd's roar dimmed inside the subterranean stables where the charioteers waited for their turn to race. Cal kept all his weight on his right leg as he calmed his team, and looked down the line at the other pilots. They all looked so young to him, little more than children, and all of them viewed him as some kind of living legend.

'A living legend barely able to walk,' he said to himself. 'I am a fool.'

'I am going to beat you, old man.'

A guttural voice spoke to him from the shadows in broken Greek. Cal turned to see a dark-haired youth with a trimmed beard and dressed in horse hide leathers. The boy was smiling grimly at the old man.

'You are the Bulgar?' asked Cal.

The youth nodded. 'I bear you no ill will, Charioteer, but I will break you on the spina.'

'People always say that,' said Cal, and climbed into his chariot turning his back on the Bulgar pilot.

The other pilots watched the confrontation in silence. All of them knew that the real match was between the African and the Bulgar. After a pause, staring at Cal's back, the Bulgar turned away to his own quadriga.

In the old days, there would have been twelve chariots and four teams of racers: Blue, White, Red and Green. Only the Blues and Greens remained now and festivals rarely happened in the capital. The rest of the Empire remained utterly addicted to the sport, but Constantinople suffered from the Emperor's distrust of the politics the teams had played in the palace. This rare event had been unexpected and rushed; only eight teams of horses could be found by the patrons of the Blues and the Greens for each race. The Blues had promised Cal their best team for the grand opening, but the old charioteer was not sure about the animals they had provided for him. The horses looked skittish and it made Cal nervous.

The fat eunuch who organised the start of the races had a worried look on his sweating red face as he stood before the racers with a young slave boy at his side. The pilots all moved their quadrigas and teams to the shutters ready for the first trumpet call.

'Are you ready?' the eunuch looked to Cal and the other racers who all nodded back in silence. 'Get up there and tell them we are ready for the start,' he said to the slave.

The boy took off as the pilots all waited in silence by their shutters for the call.

Cal was nervous, his hands felt clammy. I am too old for this foolishness, was all he could think as they waited.

The high pitched peal of the trumpets cut through the rumble of the crowds even in the depths of the hippodrome. The wooden shutters opened and Cal cracked his whip. The four horses, snorting and stamping their hooves in excitement, leaped forward at his command pulling the quadriga out into the deafening roar of the hippodrome crowd. He blinked in the sunlight and pulled on the traces to drive his chariot once around the circuit for the spectators to see. The other shutters had opened alongside him letting out the contestants and their teams. The crowd went wild at the sight of the pilots as they drove around the track slowly, lapping up the applause as they moved to the start. Cal could hear his name being called by both sets of supporters. Normally, the shutters would open to start the race, but this first race of the day was given a lap of honour instead: a lap of honour for Porphyries the Charioteer.

The great Hippodrome of Constantine had a track one hundred and fifty feet wide that circled a central spine. The spina was adorned with an ancient Egyptian obelisk, and a great bronze pillar of entwined snakes brought from Delphi to decorate the Emperor's spectacles. Seven statues to Calliopas Porphyries stood along the spina. He had won every honour for both teams, Greens and Blues, and the fanatics of both sides adored him. That was unique in itself, normally the supporters were partisan in the extreme but they all loved Cal. They shouted out to him as he went past, throwing garlands at his quadriga. He bowed at their cheers, showing the famous humility they adored.

It feels like another life, thought Cal as he looked up at one of the statues. Did I really look that young, that muscular? He shifted his weight onto his good leg. I have to win again, just this one last race and I am free.

The long stretch was nearly five hundred meters, making a full circuit over a thousand in length. A race was nearly ten miles over twelve laps, and the pilots and their teams were the most highly trained and rewarded athletes in the whole empire, brought specially to the capital for this spectacle. There would be crashes and personal duels as the chariots rattled around the track at full pelt. Cal was certain that the bloodthirsty audience enjoyed the accidental smashes more than their team's victories.

Cal could see the Bulgar ahead, leading his own team on the presentation lap, bowing and smiling at the crowd's adulation. The Greens had brought the man from Antioch as soon as the emperor had announced the race. He was famous, unbeatable in the provinces, so the Blues had come to the African charioteer

3

and begged him out of retirement. Cal's dire financial predicament had given him little choice but to accept.

Cal pulled up into his starting place, drawn by lot, on the far outside of the teams – closest to the spectators but with a further run around the circuit if he stayed on the outside. He would have to move up and inside to win. The Bulgar was in the middle of the pack; Cal caught him looking over and grinned back to the man's fury. The barbarian turned away and leaned over to talk to one of his Green teammates in an adjoining quadriga.

He is going to be trouble, thought Cal, but he smiled and waved at the crowds who were still screaming his name.

One of his team mates leaned over from his own chariot – a blonde Frank called Silas – and spoke to Cal in cultured Greek.

'They are going to try and break you up on the spina,' he said. 'When the horns blow, I shall stay back and let you cut ahead. Then I will hold your outside line and block.'

The old charioteer smiled grimly. 'Thank you, friend, I will owe you some wine when this is all over.'

'As long as you do not give me your son-in-law's vintage,' Silas said. 'How does a man buy a shipload of Cretan vinegar?'

'With somebody else's coin,' Cal told him. 'Most of it mine.'

The four trumpeters perched high up in the central spina, lifted their horns and blew out another high clear tone that cut through the noise of the crowds. Everyone quieted and turned to the track. All the prayers and rituals were completed; the next time the trumpets blew would start the race. Cal could feel the familiar knot of excitement building in his belly. He was old but still strong and nimble; as fit as a normal man half his age. He kept telling himself that.

'Saint Anthony grant that it is enough to beat the Bulgar and win the prize,' he said quietly. His patron was known for supporting lost causes. Once his granddaughter's debts were settled, Cal could relax back into his retirement. It was just one more race; one last time around the track.

The four trumpets blew again.

The pilots all shouted and cracked their whips and the teams leaped forward in one movement. Cal saw Silas pull back and to the right to let him cut inside and ahead as he had promised. He needed no urging to take that path and drove the quadriga at full pace towards the first turn. The Blues had provided him with a team of animals and a well built chariot; it was only his skills that mattered now.

The first three laps were uneventful although the crowds did not care. Cal moved up and past the slower pilots until he was fourth behind the Bulgar who had taken the lead from the start. Silas the Frank was still to his rear and right, blocking any Green chariot on the outside from getting at him.

'This is far too easy.'

As if the saints had heard his hubris, there was a scream over his shoulder. Cal risked a glance and saw Silas's white face as he was pitched screaming out of his chariot. The driverless quadriga crashed into another as the team veered wildly off course. The crowd roared its appreciation of the smash. That was what they had come for. Cal cracked his whip and drove on, not watching as the Frank was crushed by the hooves of the following teams. Slaves rushed into the track to drag away Silas's prone body. Cal looked ahead: there was only the Bulgar and one other Green to beat. What happened behind mattered for nothing.

He yelled and screamed at his horses, driving them faster and faster as he chased the leaders down. Sand thrown up in the air by the chariot wheels stung at his face, making him squint. At the turn, the second Green pilot took a wide line as the Bulgar cut on the inside. Cal sighed, he knew what they planned but had to spring the trap. He guided his team right up against the central spine, tight on the turn and just behind the Bulgar. The bouncing axles of the chariot were hammering at his bad knee, shooting pain up his back but he fixed his teeth grimly and ignored the throbbing. The pilot on the wide line had pulled in just behind him. Cal was boxed in between the two Green quadrigas.

The pilot behind tried to pull alongside the great Porphyrius and cut him into the spina wall, but the old charioteer was wise to that ruse. Cal yanked his reins pulling his team back and out to let him through. As the team swept past, Cal whipped at the snout of the Green's lead horse with his whip. He caught the animal with the leather right on the nose, making it rear up and pull away from its traces, tipping the chariot in a screaming tangle of wheels and leather. Cal whipped his own animals on, ignoring the crash and cries as the Green pilot's chariot smashed into the outer wall of the hippodrome to the glee of the onlookers.

You need to try something better than that old trick, thought Cal, watching the Bulgar. What have you got barbarian?

The Bulgar looked behind as he slowed his team on the turn. Cal could see him cursing at the sight of the old charioteer still on his tail. There were four quadrigas stilling the race with only three laps to go, but only Cal and the Bulgar mattered to the crowd. It was their struggle that had the spectators transfixed. The wreckage of the four broken chariots and their animals were now obstacles for the remaining teams to avoid. Cal and the Bulgar raced ahead of the other two pilots, soon lapping them from behind. That only added further obstacles for Cal as he strained everything to catch the Bulgar. He heard the trumpets blow again through the roar of the crowd as they reached the last lap, and he pushed his rattling quadriga wide to overtake the Bulgar, screaming at his team and whipping them to go faster and faster. He was pulling alongside the Bulgar; foam was flying from their horses' mouths. The man snarled at him, whipping at Cal's team. The old charioteer whipped back at the Bulgar's horses, and tried to reach over to grab at the traces as they both slowed on the final turn.

Cal missed his moment, grasping only at thin air, and the Bulgar shot forward like ballista bolt to the finish with the famed Calliopas Porphyries trailing in his wake. The trumpets blew again as the Bulgar crossed the line in first place.

'Oh, shit, shit, shit,' said Cal. 'I lost.'

He drew his chariot alongside the Bulgar to congratulate him, and the man was gracious enough despite having tried to kill him during the race. Cal disembarked and limped back to the stables alone. There were more races to come, but that had been the African's last chance to save his granddaughter. A girl handed him a cup of cool spiced wine as he made his way back into the dark underground chambers of the hippodrome.

'How on earth did I lose to that barbarian?' Cal asked himself. 'He would not have got close to me once. How on earth am I going to repay Calista's debts?'

There was an imperial guardsman in shining mail armour waiting for him in the stone cell where he had let his belongings before the race.

'Yes?'

'Narses wants you.'

***

The crowds swarmed to the great hippodrome for the races. Festival days had been few and far between for years in the capital, andrumours that Porphyrius the Charioteer was to race once again had thrilled the city. The announcement a few weeks earlier from the palace had been a surprise to the population. However, nobody asked why the Emperor had suddenly ordered the festivals to start up again; it was too welcome a distraction for them to question. They gathered in their tens of thousands outside the tall building, chanting and singing, pouring inside with their badges proudly displayed and blue and green flags waving. The crossroads outside the massive track was a writhing sea of race supporters. Food vendors, wine merchants, and bookmakers plied their trade to the hordes as they queued to enter.

Cosmas the Rat perched himself on the base of Justinian's Column right outside the hippodrome. The sundrenched obelisk was set on the crossroads in full view of the bathhouses and palaces of the aristocrats and Emperor. It was the perfect place for him to educate the crowds. Race supporters dressed in green or blue rushed past him to get to their seats in the hippodrome for the first race and he smiled. They would hear his words this time and, if the Lord God was merciful, understand his truth. The sailor was a small wiry man in his forties with a long beard, a pointed weasel nose, untamed black hair that was rapidly receding and wild dark eyes. His leathered face burned dark from the sun gave testimony to a lifetime of travel, and his dirty robes to a lifetime avoiding the baths. Cosmas unpacked a small travel stool and placed it on the steps. He could see Brutus the Fruitseller on the other side of the square pointing and laughing as Cosmas stood on his stool.

'Please let the fruit be fresh this time, oh merciful Christos,' Rat whispered a quick prayer and turned to the crowds hurrying to the races. 'And let there be no cow pats or goat turds today.'

He looked down on the race-goers in their blue and green rags, both literally and figuratively, and started to preach.

'You are all doomed,' the scrawny man called down to the swarm. 'Sinners, all of you are partaking in pagan rites that are offensive to the Lord God.' He ducked as someone threw a half-eaten apple at him. 'I have been to the ends of the world, to the Indies and Ethiops, to the frozen wastes in the far north. I have seen the true firmament in the heavens and the Pillars of the Sky.'

'Bugger off back there then,' shouted Brutus the Fruitseller.

'What is he wittering on about?'Cosmas heard someone say as they passed.

'Same old, same old; we're all doomed, the world is flat, and only Cosmas the Rat knows the truth.'

'The man is a fool.'

'Cosmas the Fool they should call him not Cosmas the Rat.'

The Rat listened to the voices receding and turned back to the others waiting to enter the hippodrome. He needed to be more forceful, he decided, if his sermon was to change these poor miserable sinners' lives. It was his duty to God to explain how everybody else was wrong and only Cosmas was right.

'You are perched at your decision, oh sinners,' he called out. 'The dolorous stroke will come soon enough to lay you low.'

This time he could not avoid the barrage of last year's apples, oyster shells, and goat shit thrown at him by a group of young boys. He crouched behind the column as they pelted him, screeching curses back down at them. Brutus was grinning and passing them old pears that stank like rotten eggs when they splattered. The fruit seller had clearly kept back his most fetid wares for them to throw. Brutus' son, a little boy of nine, was the ringleader of the gang.

'You'll pay for this you degenerate little shits,' shouted Cosmas, waving his scrawny fist at them. 'You'll all pay.'

The boys ran off as two soldiers approached Cosmas from behind – from the palace – but the crouching sailor did not notice until their shadows fell over him.

'You are Cosmas of Alexandria?'

The sailor looked over his shoulder and groaned. Normally, he would have taken to his heels before the authorities could get to him, but the snivelling guttersnipes had distracted him. The

Emperor's attitude confused Cosmas. He could not understand why God's own earthly representative could not see his genius, or why he was laughed out of court, or why the bishops and patriarchs of Alexandria, Jerusalem and Constantinople had scorned him. Now they had sent out some roughs to beat him from telling the world the truth. There was a devilish deep conspiracy in the highest echelons of power to suppress the truth. It was bound to stem from the Emperor's eunuch secretary. Cosmas had never liked the man.

'Who is asking?' He said to the palace guards.

'Narses wants you.'

'Think of the Devil.'

Cosmas took to his heels before they could grab him, running for the docks and the warren of lanes and alleyways where he could lose the soldiers. He knew it, the eunuch was behind everything. There was a plot in the highest levels of government to silence Cosmas and the truth. The two imperial guards, startled by their quarry's sudden flight, laboured after the sprinting sailor in their heavy armour, but there were other men stationed by Narses around the crossroads. The Emperor's secretary was not a fool. They all moved to intercept the scrawny Egyptian before he disappeared into the crowds.

Cosmas charged straight down the steps and across the square at Brutus. The alleyway behind the fruit seller's stall led past the gardens of the Basilica Cistern to a small wine shop with a back door. The coarse fruit seller, surprised at Rat's sudden charge and the soldiers rushing after him, stood open mouthed. Cosmas was running straight at him, sandals flapping on the paving.

'What is he doing?' said Brutus to his young son.

Cosmas hitched up his dirty grey robe and vaulted over the fruit stall, flashing past Brutus as the soldiers following crashed into the baskets of fresh apples and pears brought from the stores outside the city. Fruit and vegetables went flying across the cobbles. Brutus screamed curses at Cosmas's back as he ran off down the road towards the baths, with the two imperial guardsmen still in close pursuit.

'You will pay for this, Rat,' shouted Brutus as Cosmas disappeared into the crowds.

The fruit seller and his son turned back to their stall and the goods that had been scattered, trampled on, or stolen in the crash.

'One of these days, I am going to gut that Alexandrian,' said Brutus, picking up a crushed pomegranate. 'We can clean these off and still sell them.'

Cosmas sprinted down the alley, cut through the wine shop despite the owners' protest, and out into another small alley that led back to the hippodrome and palaces.

'That's the wrong direction,' he said.

Cosmas could hear the pounding feet of pursuit and more shouting from inside the shop. He cut down the alley anyway and went into the public bathhouse avoiding any imperial guards. Once inside the baths, he mingled with the bathers waving away attendants and then left by the harbour road entrance. Cosmas gave a quick glance behind for the chase but there was no sign of Narses' men. He sauntered smirking down to the waterfront where he had his lodgings.

'They won't catch me now.'

He turned the corner to his tenement overlooking the ships in the harbour, and barreled straight into the two soldiers that had accosted him at the column. They grabbed him by the scruff of his robe this time before he could run.

'Narses wants you,' the burly guard said again.

***

Theodosius Dagisthaeus, the former Magister Militum per Armeniam, had had six long months to ponder his failures before Petra. It was all somebody else's fault; the vain young boy had decided. He had protested his innocence before the emperor and his eunuch secretary, but all to no avail.

'You set no scouts?'

'You put no troops to defend the pass?'

'You lost an army and a province?'

All of it was true, of course, but Theo had persuaded himself that his staff officers were to blame. They were older and more experienced; they should have explained the situation to him better.

Unfortunately for Theodosius Dagisthaeus, his more experienced staff officers had happily testified to his ignorance, drunkenness, and arrogance. They were just saving their own damned skins, thought Theo.

Theo's letter to the Emperor had put the final nail into the coffin of his reputation. The young aristocrat winced as he remembered the parchment being presented at his trial. It had gone down very badly with the court. Theo had sent it before the defeat, when it looked like he would capture Petra easily and the campaign would be a stunning victory for the new golden haired Alexander. He had fallen short of demanding a triumph like generals in the ancient past, but only just, and when seen against his catastrophic defeat the presumption had appalled the ever-suspicious Emperor. It had only been his grandfather's influence that had seen him imprisoned in a dark cell in the bowels of the palace instead of publicly executed. Justinian, and his equally vindictive eunuch secretary Narses, looked set to have him broken in the hippodrome to send a warning to other officers not to fail. Theo thanked God for his family's influence at court for the thousandth time since his incarceration.

He got up and took a piss in the bucket. The prison had not been too onerous. Theo could hear the screams of the other inmates and thanked the merciful Christos that he had not been tortured. He had been kept fed and watered, but in perpetual solitude with only his disgrace to think on. There were no visitors for him, but no more public humiliations. That was his family's influence again. They had kept him from the axe and would petition on his behalf. Sooner or later he would be released.

'Somehow I shall redeem my reputation,' Theo told himself over and over. 'I shall prove myself.'

The guards that attended him were always silent. Every morning, they would bring food and take away his waste, but mostly he was left alone to ponder his defeat.

The sound of the keys in the lock was a shock. It must be mid afternoon but he never had visitors.

Theo looked expectantly as the door opened. Perhaps his grandfather had finally secured his release. He was going to be freed, free to go home to his mother, free to drink wine again and see the races with his friends.

A thick set palace guard came into the room, holding the lamp up as he looked down at the disgraced officer.

'Narses wants you,' he said to Theo.

2

Cosmas complained every step of the way as the two palace guards dragged him off. He was outraged at the affront to his person, the injury to his reputation, the slurs and smears that would most assuredly hurt his income when he was released. The guards ignored him, just making sure to keep a hold of his arms so he could not escape again. The big one gave a little twist when the sailor's constant whining grated too much – making him squeal aloud with pain. They deposited the still arguing Cosmas into a cold dark cell in the bowels of the palace complex.

'This one is a damned irritant,' said the smaller guard, slamming the stout door shut and plunging Cosmas into shadows.

'Well, this is a strange turn of events for Cosmas the Brave,' said Cosmas as the cell door closed. 'He starts the day preaching God's truth to the masses.' The little sailor peered out of the door grill into the corridor outside. The guards had left and the corridor was empty. 'And ends it in Emperor Justinian's dungeons.'

'This is not Justinian's dungeon.' A voice came from the gloom behind him. 'You can take that as truth from me.'

Cosmas spun around and backed into the door, staring blindly into the dark corner of the cell, blinking in the darkness. There was a man there.

'Who are you, sire?'

A blonde beardless youth, barely more than a boy, in a dirty silk tunic stood up and bowed to Cosmas. Cosmas squinted in the gloom to see his features.

'Theodosius Dagisthaeus at your service,' said the boy.

Cosmas winced. 'Dagisthaeus the boy general? The idiot that lost Petra to the Persians?'

Theo gave a grimace and bowed.

'You lost an army, and a city, and a whole province,' Cosmas continued.

'Technically we got both the city and province back after the event,' Theo said. 'Is that what they tell about me now? That it was my entire fault?'

Everyone in the Empire had heard the story of Dagisthaeus' Folly. The grandson of a Goth general, the boy had been pampered all his life and then given command of the army in Anatolia. He had marched into enemy territory, started a siege, upset local allies, failed to send out scouts, and then seen his whole army ambushed and butchered whilst he was quite literally dictating a letter to the Emperor detailing the rewards he expected.

'I would say that is a fair summation of the tale, although it misses the battles we won before we got to Petra and the ones we won afterwards,' said Theo bitterly.

'It is not so good for me to be imprisoned with you, then, is it?' said Cosmas. 'You being disgraced and all that.'

'This is not the Emperor's prison, as I told you. I have just come from there.'

'What is this place then?'

'This is Narses' waiting room.'

Cosmas nodded. 'The guards said that the eunuch wants me.'

'Yes, they said the same to me when they brought me from the actual dungeons. I would rather not return, if I can help it. You are Cosmas the Brave?' Theo could barely conceal his sneer.

'Cosmas the Brave, Cosmas the Sailor, Cosmas the Truth Teller.' He bowed back to Theo.

'You have a lot of names for such a little man?'

'I have done a lot of things.'

There was no reply to that, at least none that Theo could make without giving offence, so he stayed silent. The aristocrat considered that personal growth. Cosmas did not have Theo's family, education or upbringing, and the young noble was an undoubted snob despite his barbarian heritage, but six months of captivity had taught him more than a smidge of humility. The door rattled again as the bolts were shot and opened wide. Both men looked expectantly as the big palace guard that had brought Cosmas appeared.

'You are both to come with me.' The guard gave Cosmas a pointed stare. 'If you run again, Rat, I shall crush you like a bug. Do you understand?'

'It is a rather mixed metaphor, how does one crush a rat like a bug?'

The guard grabbed Cosmas by the scruff of the tunic, and lifted him up a foot with the little sailor's feet dangling. 'Would you like to find out?'

'No, no.' Cosmas spluttered out a promise to behave, and the guard lowered him back to the floor.

'Ha, Cosmas the Rat, I like that name,' said Theo. 'It suits you better than truth teller.'

The Rat gave Theo a vicious glance as the two of them followed the guard out of the cell and into an unused part of the palace complex. They were taken down a long corridor and up a couple of flights of steps in to a sunlit walkway and manicured gardens. Cosmas and Theo both blinked in the bright light and hurried after the guard to a stone bench outside rich apartments decked in garlands of flowers. A stout old African with tight white curls and muscular frame was already seated on the bench.

Cal saw the guard and the two men following and groaned. He knew Cosmas, the man was a damned nuisance about the city, and the blonde boy could only be the fool general who had lost Petra. He looked the spitting image of his grandfather. Whatever Narses wanted, it was going to be trouble. The guard deposited Theo and Cosmas at the benches and told them to wait. Cal studiously ignored them both but the little sailor poked him in the ribs.

'Did you win?' Cosmas asked the old man.

Cal grimaced and shook his head.

'But you always win?'

'Not this time,' said Cal through gritted teeth.

'Who are you, please?' asked Theo.

'Do you not know?' said Cosmas. 'This is the great Porphyrius the Charioteer. He is famous and he never loses.'

'The one who has all the statues on the spina? I thought he was dead.'

'Well I am not dead,' snapped Cal, 'and I have lost in the past.'

'I meant no offence,' said Theo. 'Are you here for Narses too?'

Cal nodded and gestured to Cosmas. 'The Rat is an idiot and an irritant,' he said to Theo. Cosmas sniffed and turned his back on the charioteer. 'If he is involved, we are in trouble. You are Dagistheus's grandson?'

Theo nodded.

'I knew your grandfather. He used to come to the hippodrome in the old days.'

'All before my time I am afraid, and grandpapa rarely leaves the estate these days. He is drooling in his dotage.'

Cal grunted at that, and a pretty young boy appeared from inside the building and beckoned to them.

'The Praepositus Sacri Cubiculi will see you now,' he said in cultured Latin.'

'The what?' said Cosmas in common Greek.

'Narses,' said Cal and Theo together.

***

The Praepositus Sacri Cubiculi, chamberlain to the great Justinian, said nothing as the three men were brought before him. He merely fixed his cold calculating gaze upon them. They all stood nervously, Cosmas fidgeting with the hem of his dirty robe. The Armenian eunuch was perhaps sixty years old. His long oiled curls were grey and glistening and his thin face was shaved smooth; the skin drawn tight like parchment over a drum. Narses had served the Roman Emperors all his life and had risen high in imperial favour. He was an accomplished general and administrator, and his spies were everywhere throughout the empire. Narses was vindictive and petty, suspicious of everyone in the imperial court, and defensive of his position. Only Justinian himself wielded as much power. Even Belisarius, the Empire's greatest general, was wary of the eunuch's ambition. The imperial court was a nest of vipers, more so since the death of the Empress as senators and nobles dangled their young daughters as a grotesque match for the ageing Justinian.

Narses dismissed the guards from the chamber with a wave of his manicured hand, leaving only the pretty slave boy as witness, and leaned forward at his desk. He smiled at the three of them, like a shark, and nodded at them to sit in the chairs provided. Cal needed no urging, his knee was sore and swollen after the race, and he plopped himself onto a stool. Cosmas and Theo followed suit after a moment's pause.

'You lost the race?' he said to Cal.

'It happens.'

'Indeed it does, but it puts your granddaughter in some predicament, old friend.'

'I am not your friend.'

18

Theo and Cosmas both gasped in shock at Cal's short tempered response. The little Rat's mouth gaped open at the charioteer's insolence.

'Would old comrade in arms be better?' said Narses with a sly smile.

Cal crossed his arms, pursed his lips. Narses sat back on his cushions and beamed at them.

'You are all in a predicament and I can help you,' said the eunuch.

'I have done nothing wrong,' said Cosmas. 'I assure you, magnificence; I was merely preaching the word of God.'

'You were ranting that the world is flat again?'

'It is flat, benevolence,' said Cosmas stubbornly.

Theo looked to the ceiling in despair. If his long dreamed of rescue was tied to the sullen old charioteer and Cosmas the Cretin, he might be better off back in the dungeons. Narses turned to him finally.

'Your grandfather has spent the last six months petitioning for your release. So, I shall give you a chance to redeem yourself. Will you take it?'

'Yes,' said Theo without a moment's hesitation or thought.

Narses smiled again. 'Well that is one side of the triangle.' He turned back to the sailor. 'The Patriarch of Constantinople has declared your idiocy to be heretical. I can condemn you here and now or are you willing to do as you are told.'

'I shall do anything you require, Eminence.'

Narses turned back to Cal. He knew he could not bully the old man into submission like the other two. The charioteer was liable to lose his temper and he had a renowned temper in his youth, but Narses had already trapped the charioteer. The African would have little choice but to agree.

'I have purchased your granddaughter's debt, Calliopas. You owe me, I own her.'

'I can find the coin.'

'You lost the race. The little farm you potter around on in the hills will not pay for it. The family will have to be sold into slavery.'

'You planned this all along. That is why I did not get the good team of horses?' Cal knew Narses.

'If you do as I ask, then the debts will be forgotten and you shall be a rich man.'

'What is it I have to do? I will not kill for you again.'

'When you agree, I shall tell you. It is a matter of utmost secrecy and importance to the Empire. It will involve travel and some time away from the city. As I recall, you were always willing to help out in the past. For the good of the Empire...'

Theo noted a pained look come over the old charioteer's face. There is something dark between these two men, he decided.

'I will do it,' said Cal, after a pause. 'I have no choice do I?'

'Good,' said Narses. 'To warn you, should you fail, I will sell her into the waterside brothels without a second's thought.'

'I would expect nothing less from one such as you.'

Narses beamed back at the response.

'What is this task then?' said Theo. 'If it involves travel, where to?'

'What is that you are wearing?'

Narses pointed to Theo's dirty ragged silk tunic that he had been wearing since his first arrest. The thin material was worn through and stank of the dungeons.

'Well it is my tunic, but I was given no opportunity to change into something cleaner.'

Narses sighed. 'It is the silk. That is why you are here.'

'What, for my dirty tunic?'

The secretary shook his head. 'How much coin do you think we spend on silk every year? Do you have any idea how much of our gold flows into Sassanid Persia's coffers to feed our Empire's passion for the material?'

The three of them all nodded their heads, realising just how vast the amount must be.

'It is a stupendous fortune every year,' said Cosmas. 'I have seen the fleet that travels to the Indies, oh magnificent one.'

'And then the Persians use that gold to pay for armies to attack our eastern provinces, as you found out in Colchis.' Narses waved at Theo. 'We are paying them to invade us in Syria and Armenia whilst our coin and men are needed in Italia and Gaul. All so vain aristocrats can wear a spider's web to a party.'

Theo knew that barb was aimed at him, but did not bite. He wanted his freedom too much to upset the eunuch.

'Now,' Narses continued. 'The very opportunity to kill off the silk trade has fallen into my lap, and you three are going to make it happen.'

'You are going to ban the trade, great one?' asked Cosmas, thinking of all the merchants who would be broken by such a ban and all the others that would make a fortune smuggling it.

'No,' said Narses. 'We are going to make it here in Constantinople.'

'Nobody knows the secret of silk,' said Cosmas. 'They will not trade how to make it in the East. I have tried.'

'I know,' said Narses. 'That is why you are here. You speak Sogdian and Persian and Bactrian and have travelled further than any man currently in Constantinople.'

Theo looked in surprise at that. The Rat did not strike him as the competent sort but Cal merely grimaced. He thought Rat's travels were exaggerated.

'You are going to send a mission to Sogdiana? They will laugh in our faces,' said Cosmas.

'You are not going there to buy it,' said Narses.

'I do not understand.' The weasel-faced sailor looked puzzled.

21

'We are going to steal it, Rat,' said Cal. 'He wants us to steal the secret of silk from the east.'

***

The plan seemed simple enough when the eunuch outlined it to them. The practical detail was somewhat more complex. Two Nestorian monks and a novice had appeared in Constantinople bringing news of the silk industry in the Far East. They had assured Narses, and the Emperor, that the secret would be found in Sogdiana. A separate party was bringing the silkworm eggs from the edge of the world. They would bring it to a city beyond the Bactrian border and the Sassanid Persian's Emperor's prying eyes. Only one of the monks still lived but he and his young novice, accompanied by Cal, Theo, and Cosmas, as well as Theo's personal bucellarii (a small bodyguard), would meet their contacts and bring back the eggs from Sogdiana.

Once he had outlined everything and sworn them to secrecy, Narses dismissed them to an apartment in the palace. Guards were posted on the door and they were told not to leave. Slaves brought them food and wine, and clean clothes for Theo to change into.

'Worm eggs?' said Cosmas, flopping on some cushions. 'I do not believe it. They told me in the Indies that giant talking spiders weave the silk and that the Emperor of the East rides one into battle.'

'You think the world is flat though,' said Cal. He poured himself a goblet of wine and sat on a bench stretching out his leg.

'Open your eyes, Charioteer, where is the curve?'

'You are a sailor, shouldn't you understand how the horizon works?' asked Theo.

Cosmas ignored that point.

'He is only here because he can talk the language of this monk and the barbarians. You provide the muscle with your bucellarii and we are all expendable to Narses, especially me.'

'Why are you here, Charioteer?'

'Because Narses is an evil bastard and for some reason he thinks I shall be of use, or he hopes I will die on the journey. Either way I think he would be pleased.'

'What is it between the two of you?' asked Cosmas. 'He called you a friend but it is tub-thumping obvious you despise him.'

'He is no friend of mine.'

'So what is it?' said Theo. 'We should know if there is some danger to the mission.'

'There is no danger to the mission. It is all in the past, a past I had hoped to escape.'

'What?'

'Nika,' was all Cal said.

3

The three of them left Constantinople in a covered wagon at the dead of night. An escort of Imperial Kataphraktoi provided by Narses kept away prying eyes, and they trundled down the old road to a small estate near the coast. They would rest there whilst the rest of the party was gathered together and a ship prepared.

'The why seems easy enough,' said Cosmas. 'It is the how that strikes me as a problem.'

Cal ignored him, lost in thought, but Theo was bubbling with enthusiasm for his freedom.

'It will not be such a problem,' he told Cosmas. 'We can take a ship to Taurica and from there it is empty steppe all the way.'

'No so empty,' Cosmas said. 'There are tribes there. There are Huns there, Slavs, Avars, and Bulgars.'

'My you are Job's comforter, Cosmas. We shall be fine,' Theo told him. 'You can speak Hunnish?'

Cosmas nodded. 'Some.'

'Then all will be well. We will take gifts for the chieftains and pose little threat to the barbarians. We can barter our passage if there is trouble. I do not plan on fighting our way across the steppes to Serica.'

Cal remembered a Hunnish pilot from the old days. He had raced out of Antioch but had been a dangerous opponent when he came to the capital. He must have been killed at Nika by Justinian's guards. They had slaughtered everyone in the hippodrome that day, nearly thirty thousand people butchered, men women and children. The blood had run thick through the gutters and stained the sand red. He could not bear to go to the hippodrome afterwards. Instead, he had retired to live on his small farm in the hills and bring up his orphaned granddaughter. Now his peaceful life was ruined because Calista had fallen in love with a foolborn wine trader.

I was no innocent in the slaughter, thought Cal. Perhaps this mission is my penance.

The cart jerked as it turned off the paved road onto a dusty dirt track shaking the charioteer from his bitter memories. Theo peeked out.

'There is an estate up ahead,' he said. 'I can see the torchlight.'

'I hope they will have some food for us,' said Cosmas, rubbing his belly.

The estate was owned by Narses and was well appointed with a view down to the coast. They could hear the surf breaking on the shoreline as they disembarked from the cart, stretching their legs after the journey. Narses' slaves met them and showed them to the guest apartments that had already been prepared. The chambers were luxurious: plush furnishings with silken hangings and embroidered tapestries and plump cushions to recline on. Their beds were firm but comfortable and the blankets were made from the softest wool.

'I am hungry,' Cosmas told one of the slaves.

'We shall bring you food, master.' The man bowed and left the room.

Cosmas grinned. 'I could get used to this.'

'Enjoy it while you can,' Theo told him. 'It will not take long for my men to get here and we shall be off again.'

Cal had waited outside breathing in the smell of the sea in the distance. He could see the black expanse of the Euxine Sea below the villa, starlight flickering off the waves. They would have to take a ship to the other side and then ride all the way east towards Serica. Narses had told them that the monk and his novice would arrive in secret later. Persian spies were everywhere, and if word of their mission leaked out the Sassanid Emperor would be certain to try and stop them. The silk trade was too lucrative and essential to the Persian Empire's finances. Narses had rammed that point home to them before they left the palace.

'Silk is more valuable than Cretan vinegar,' Cal said and followed the other two.

'What do you think, Charioteer?' asked Cosmas, as Cal entered. 'Have you ever seen luxury like this before?'

Cal looked around the apartments. They were certainly most luxurious, but he had once been feted by the old Empress herself. Narses' villa was simple and plain compared to Theodora's chambers.

'Yes.'

Cosmas sniffed.

'You were born a slave?' asked Theo. He was fascinated by the famous charioteer.

'In Proconsularis,' Cal said. 'My father came from the south, traded by the desert tribes into Vandal hands. My master took me to Alexandria and then to Antioch.' He paused. 'I did some terrible things on Narses' connivance and my own stupidity and won my freedom, then raced for coin. After Nika I retired, there seemed little point continuing. Is that enough of a history lesson?'

'It must have been hard growing up a slave.'

'Hard enough that I would do anything to stop my granddaughter becoming one.'

'Good,' said Theo, 'because my life depends upon our success.'

'Worry about Cosmas the Rat,' said Cal. 'Not me.'

'That is unfair,' said Cosmas. 'Cosmas the Honest is renowned for his loyalty.'

***

The Nestorian monk and novice arrived two days later. Cosmas had spent the morning crabbing in rock pools on the shore whilst Theo and Cal had rested in the villa. Theo had lived in such luxury all his life and had quickly accustomed himself to his surroundings. Cal by contrast felt out of place and time, convinced the only reason he was on the mission was Narses's vindictiveness. He sat quietly watching the surf break and saying little all day. Around mid-afternoon, Cosmas came running with a bucket back to the estate. Rat was pointing down to the road.

'There is a cart coming,' the sailor said breathlessly when he arrived. 'It must be this monk from the east.' He handed his bucket of crabs to a nonplussed slave who swiftly put them down with a look of disgust.

'So?' said Cal.

'Well, shouldn't we go and meet them. They are going to be our travelling companions.'

'I suppose so.'

Cosmas poked him in the ribs. 'Oh you are far too miserable, Charioteer. We are on an adventure to save your princess from slavery. The poets at court adore this stuff.'

Cal grunted and pulled himself up. 'Come along then, let us see this monk.'

Theo was already waiting at the gates when the covered cart rolled into the courtyard. The armoured escort handed him a wax tablet as the cart stopped. The driver got down and unhooked the coverings to let their passengers out. Cal and Cosmas both peered over expectantly waiting for the two men whose secrets could transform the Empire. The first was a slight boy with a completely shaved head and almond shaped dark eyes, dressed in a long black habit with embroidered hood. He gave a wide smile as he saw Theo and spoke quickly in a strange language to his fellow inside the wagon.

Cosmas frowned. 'White Huns?'

'How in the saints should I know?' said Cal. 'The boy must be the novice.'

Cosmas walked forward speaking quickly in what Cal assumed was Hunnish. The boy turned and smiled again, nodding, and then reached into the wagon. The monk was old, older than Methuselah, dressed in a similar black habit to the novice, with thin wisps of white hair and a lined wizened face. The tiny man was ancient and toothless.

'My god he is decrepit,' said Cal.

'Does it make you feel better about your age, Charioteer?' said Cosmas, glancing back with a sly smile.

'I will break you into pieces, Rat.'

'So you tell me, but I am the only one who can talk to these two. I would say your granddaughter's future depends on my living.' He turned back to the monks and began chattering away to the young boy.

'Well,' said Theo to Cal. 'What do you think?'

'I think Narses has sent us on a fool's mission to die. That way he settles some old scores and gets rid of some problems. In the unlikely event we succeed in stealing the secret of silk, he will reap all the rewards.'

'He will pay us what was promised. You know him well enough to realise that?'

'Yes, he always keeps his promises.'

The two monks were shown into the villa. They had few possessions other than a small satchel each. Cosmas could speak to them in Bactrian, but it was not their own tongue. As far as they could work out the two Nestorians came from lands conquered by Alexander a millennia before. Cosmas explained that there were trading posts and small Christian groups living all along the coastline of the Indies, but these came from further inland. They had come to the Patriarch of Constantinople as the head of the faith. The Patriarch had taken them to Narses, and Narses had taken them to the Emperor. Once all of them were satisfied that the monks spoke the truth, Narses had made his plans for the mission.

'How long until your bucellarii arrive?' asked Cal.

'A few more days, they have to come from near Adrianople. You may as well enjoy yourself like Cosmas. Once we start out there will be little time for pleasures of the flesh. There are slaves here,' he said. 'I can tell you about one...'

'I am perfectly happy, thank you,' said Cal, offended at the suggestion.

'I mean no offence, Charioteer. I merely want us to succeed. I want my life back, my friends, my parties, the theatre and the races. Do you not want the same?'

Cal nodded. 'Yes, I suppose so.'

'Then enjoy yourself, because once my men arrive we will be leaving.'

***

The city of Chersonesus is set on cliffs overlooking the sea. Cal watched from the stern of the dromon as it slowly came into view over the horizon. The tops of the basilica and columns were visible first, and then the red roof-tiles of the town and the stout walls. Beneath the cliffs, behind a stone breakwater, was the western port. The ship's Navarch ordered the lateen sail furled, called down into the rowers pit to take them in, and ordered the helm to steer into their destination.

Narses had sent the imperial dromon to transport them across the sea once Theo's men had arrived at the estate. The warriors were a mixed group of Goths and Italians and even a Briton. Their captain was named Godda, a tough warrior in middle age with bald pate and brusque manner. He had known Theo since the aristocrat had been a baby, as had most of the others. They said little to Cal or Cosmas, only speaking in their Germanic tongue to the blonde aristocrat, but they were nine veterans equipped with metal helmets, mail coats, spatha, lance and composite bow. Their horses had been loaded onto the ship quickly by the Navarch's men, and Cal and the others were soon speeding across the sea to Taurica and the city of Chersonesus. It was a short journey.

'I tell you the world is flat.' Cal could hear Cosmas irritating the poor Navarch again.

'Go away,' the man said brusquely.

'If only you would open your eyes you would see it. The world is flat; the sky is the walls and the heavens the lid. We exist in a bejeweled box made by God.'

'Go away now.'

The Navarch pushed past Rat exasperated, and walked up the length of the ship to stand next to Cal. He said nothing to the charioteer, merely glancing over the sides of the ship as it took the channel into the quays. Cosmas, however, was not going to let the matter drop and followed him.

'Look,' he said to the Navarch. 'I have been further than you; I have seen the edge of the world...'

'If you do not go away, you shall see the bottom of the ocean. Keep him away from me, Charioteer.'

The Navarch turned and stalked back to the helm as the dromon turned in the bay to glide into the docks. Cosmas turned to follow him again.

'Stay,' Cal told him.

'But...'

'Stay or I will pitch you over the side. I am sure that we can find another translator in Chersonesus.'

Cosmas pursed his lips. 'The problem with a prophet is he is never recognised in his own land.'

Cal ignored him and turned back to the city. This was the last bastion of civilization on the edge of the great steppe. There were Roman troops stationed here, and colonists looking for a new life, mostly exiles hoping to hide away from Justinian's spite or poor merchants who traded with the tribes of the interior. Beyond Chersonesus, there was only danger for Romans. The dromon settled up next to the stone jetty and lines were cast to secure it as sailors jumped ashore to tie her up.

'What now?' said Cosmas.

'Wait for the horses to be unloaded and go up into the city.'

'I shall tell the monk.'

Cosmas walked to the rear of the ship. The Navarch studiously turned away at his approach, but Rat ducked into the cabin at the bow instead of going up to the tiller. The two Nestorians had stayed in the cabin for the whole journey whilst Cal, Theo, and the others had slept on deck. The old one seemed sprightly enough, but Cal still feared he would drop dead at any moment. He doubted the boy novice would know the details of their mission.

'My granddaughter's life is dependent on a decrepit old man staying alive as we travel a thousand miles and more into the east. Narses you are a bastard son of a whore.'

Theo appeared on the deck once the ship had stopped. He looks dreadful, thought Cal. The blonde aristocrat gave Cal a weak smile and came to join him. Theo had been seasick ever since embarking. The voyage had been swift, but he had spent most of it whining with a bucket next to him on the deck. His bucellarii had given each other looks of disgust and forced some foul barbarian drink inside him that just made the aristocrat vomit more.

'We have arrived then?'

Cal merely gestured to the town.

'Thank Saint Basil for that,' said Theo.

'Basil?'

'The patron saint of Chersonesus. Cosmas told me about him.'

'I try to ignore Rat, even in the best of times.'

'Yes, well, we are all going to have to get along if we are to succeed, Charioteer.'

'Your men do not seem to like you?' Cal pointed out.

Theo gave a grimace. 'They do not hold me in high esteem, it is true. They think me a fop, a waster, a drunk degenerate who has gone Greek. Had I been born in the old days, they tell me I would have been left in the wilds to die.' He noted Cal's look. 'Oh, do not worry, Charioteer. They are loyal beyond belief to my family.'

'What if your family doesn't like you either?' Cal pointed out. 'What if they want you to die out here? Would they send these men to lose you on the steppe?'

Theo's eyes opened wide. 'No,' he said. 'I am certain that I can trust them.'

But he looked flustered as he went to the bow of the ship to join his bucellarii and help them unload the horses and equipment. Cal smiled grimly.

'A rat, a spoiled brat, and a broken charioteer... The eunuch has a dark twisted humour.'

4

Chersonesus was a well appointed town with a bustling agora and rich churches. Perhaps ten thousand people lived in the stout houses, with a small Roman garrison that nervously watched the tribes to the north. The city had fallen to the Huns in the past centuries, but Attila was long dead and his empire broken up. It was a prosperous colony once more with two ports and a thriving trade with the interior. A great stone wall with strong gates and ballista towers protected the city from all but the most committed assault. Narses had arranged a small domos for them to stay in, and Theo told them a guide had been arranged to take them into the eastern steppe. The boy's bucellarii were still sullen about their golden haired leader, but their moods seemed to be lifting now the voyage was over and they happily settled down in the stables with their horses. Godda and his lieutenant, a broad shouldered warrior with nut brown hair called Beremund, had both served Theo's family for years and seemed efficient enough to Cal's eye. He noted that whenever Theo gave an order, the other warriors looked to Godda or Beremund for a nod of confirmation.

'I am going to take a look around the town,' Cosmas told Cal.

'Stay out of trouble.'

'People rarely go looking for trouble, Charioteer, but it oft comes around none the less.'

'There are other people here who speak Hunnish, you know, we could just hire one of them.'

'But could you trust them?' The Rat smirked. 'Have no fears, I merely wish to visit the Church of Saint Basil.'

Cal did not argue with him, instead he sat in the small atrium of the domos and pondered their journey. Narses had spent a lot of coin and influence on this mission. If it was merely a fool's chase to send them to their deaths, he would not have done that. The two Nestorians must have been convincing when they were interviewed by the Emperor. They were a strange pair. The decrepit old monk just sat smiling at everyone, whilst the young boy only spoke to Cosmas. There was something about the lad that irked at Cal, but he could not put his finger on it. Something that was not quite right about him.

'If it is God's will we shall succeed,' he said. 'Strange Nestorians, Rats, and impetuous young generals notwithstanding.'

'We had better,' said Theo, coming out of the stables. 'Where is Rat?'

'He has gone into the town to visit one of the shrines.'

Theo shrugged. 'He best not start anything with his ranting. The governor is not pleased at our arrival as it is. He thinks it is some ploy of Narses to disgrace him at court.'

'I warned him not to start any trouble.'

'Let us hope he listened,' said the young noble and sat down. 'No wine, Cal? Enjoy yourself while we are here. I am away to the governor again to see about our guide. We shall not be staying in the town for long.'

Cal nodded and called for a slave to bring him some wine, and then he sat snoozing peacefully in the sun.

Cosmas the Rat skipped along the main street of the city. The church of Saint Basil was located in the centre of the town at the basilica. He noted the well ordered streets, pretty fountains spouting crystal clear water, the smiling happy inhabitants of many different races and creeds. Romans, Greeks, Africans and Egyptians from all over the empire mixed with steppe traders and hunters that came in from the Western Gate. Cosmas was not interested in the merchants, soldiers or imperial officials. He wanted to see his patron's church. There was a single tall column in the agora, with a cross set high upon it that could be seen from anywhere in the city. Cosmas followed that, peering over the rooftops, until he turned into a wide paved square. It was bustling with stalls and merchants selling their wares: leathers, furs and pine resin from the steppes, wine and pottery from the empire. A tall white basilica dominated the centre of the square, and shoppers wandered from stall to stall or into one of the shrines to pray. Garrison troops stood, bored, watching over the trade from the steps of the basilica. Cosmas smiled to himself. There were thousands of such settlements on the empire's borders regulating the flow of trade with Rome.

'I could make a fortune here with the right product.'

The church of Saint Basil was set off to the side odd of the agora: a tiny whitewashed building with a red tiled roof. There was a small wooden cross set up above the doorway. Cosmas stepped onto the porch and removed his sandals. The double doors pushed open and Rat bowed as he entered the dark building. Once inside, he was taken aback by the beautifully painted icons on the walls; white eyes flickering lifelike in the candlelight and following him as he moved around the room. He noted that there were areas of broken plaster or where the painting was new and not of the same quality as the older icons of the saints. The city had been ruled by the Huns for nearly a century until Justinian started restoring the empire. Cosmas sniffed: the barbarians had done foul damage to the Christian shrines.

'Pagans and devil worshippers all,' said Cosmas, then he crossed himself. 'I shall perhaps bring the word of God to them as we travel.'

He knelt and prayed for help in his mission to bring the truth of the world to the unbelievers. As an afterthought, Rat prayed that their journey was successful and they brought the secrets of silk back to the Emperor. Then Cosmas got up off his knees, dusted his robe down and left the shrine. Out in the sunlight, he put his sandals back on and wandered along the stalls checking what the different merchants had for sale. Whilst he had no coin to buy (he rarely did), information on the wares available in Taurica would be worth money when he was back in Alexandria, Carthage, or Antioch. Salt, pine resin, furs and hides brought by the steppe tribes and traded for wine and luxury goods from Rome. He listened to the prices, fingered the quality of the produce, stole some figs from a small unattended stall, and then decided to go back to their townhouse.

'Cosmas of Alexandria? Is that you? Yes it is; I knew it was you.'

Cosmas turned and groaned.

'Oh, hullo, Naghi. What are you doing here?'

Naghi the Persian was a petty spice merchant and agent of the Sassanid Emperor. He was a small man with pleasant features, blue eyes and dark blonde hair that gave away his Greek ancestry, dressed in a long brown robe and a wide brimmed straw sunhat. He smiled broadly at Cosmas's question.

'I asked you first,' he said.

'You asked if it was me, I revealed myself and therefore and am still owed an answer as to why you are here,' countered Rat. 'Trade between our empires is forbidden at the moment and I could tell the governor.' Cosmas beamed back at the Persian.

'That is why I am here.' Naghi gave a look of disgust. 'I cannot go to Antioch or Constantinople, and there is nothing here but savages and barbarians trading in coarse goods.'

'Nobody wants your spices? That surprises me.'

'They only want to pay with furs and leathers, what use is that to me? I want gold, but there are still some trades to be made away from watchful eyes. This is a quiet place with little bother from the governor so we came across from Lazica. You're not going to tell on me, are you, old friend?'

'Of course not,' said Cosmas, 'I like to stay away from the authorities if I can help it, not tattle tales.'

Despite that, he could not help but think that the Persian's tale sounded too glib and rehearsed. The man was a spy, Cosmas was certain of that from their past dealings, and he would not be here without the Sassanid Emperor's orders.

Naghi smiled. 'Thank you, where are you staying? There is a taverna by the north dock, if you would pass some time? Wine and women, it's a rough place compared to Ctesiphon but better than nothing.'

'Oh I am staying with friends; perhaps I shall come down later.' Cosmas waved dismissively.

'Friends, Cosmas? That is not like you. Where did you find friends?'

'They are none that you know,' said Rat hastily. 'Friends from Constantinople.'

'Friends from Constantinople?'

Cosmas could feel the situation getting away from him. He did not want to answer anymore of Naghi's questions, but did not wish to seem impolite as that would certainly rouse the man's suspicions.

'Anyway, I must leave. They will be wondering where I have got to. Fare you well, Naghi.'

'May the blessings of Azhura Mazda shine upon you, Cosmas of Alexandria. Come and see us at the taverna.'

Cosmas crossed himself at the Zoroastrian blessing, treating the Persian's words as a curse, and hurried off back to the others. Naghi gave a wide grin as he watched the flustered Rat depart.

Theo's visit to the Governor was not going well. The man was fat, decadent, and lazy; it was like looking in an irritating mirror, thought Theo.

The guide that Narses had arranged to meet them in Chersonesus was late, and the governor informed Theo that he was a Hun and not allowed entry into the city. Despite the early hour, the man's eyes were already glazed from the poppy infused wine that he sipped at incessantly. Realising that there was little point in remaining, Theo took his leave and returned to the townhouse. Once the horses and men were rested after the voyage they would have to leave. There were old ruins at the eastern end of the Taurican peninsula. Old Greek colonies sacked and burned by the Huns and left abandoned a century before. When Justinian's armies had forced the Huns out and colonists returned they were left deserted. The party could meet their guide there and then travel on over the steppes.

'What is the name of the guide, do we know?' asked Cal when Theo returned.

'Anagai the Utiger,' Theo told him. 'The officials know him and said he could be trusted.'

'But not trusted enough to enter the city?'

Theo shrugged. 'No Huns in Chersonesus. Where is Rat?'

'Not back. Are there no Huns in the garrison here?'

'None, they are Akritai here, not proper troops. Poor farmer boys from Greece made into garrison soldiers and of no use should a horde of barbarians turn up.'

Cal nodded. 'So when do we leave to meet this Hun?'

'A couple of days more rest after the voyage. The horses need to settle. We have some supplies brought with us for travel, but I will purchase food for the journey here as well.'

Cal mouth opened to ask something but they were both interrupted by a breathless Cosmas bursting into the room.

'There are Persian spies in the city,' said Rat.

'How do you know?' asked Theo.

'One of them is known to me, a sly slippery scorpion of a man.'

'I shall have them arrested,' said Theo. 'We do not want Persians talking about us.'

'No,' said Cal. 'If we have them arrested, they will know we are up to something. The Sassanid Emperor will peer northwards to see what is happening. I would rather not have his hunters on our trail so let's not rouse their suspicions. Did you give our plans away, foolborn Rat?'

Cosmas sniffed. 'Of course not, he has no idea what we are doing, but he did invite me down to the taverna. If I do not go he will wonder why.'

***

The three of them walked over to the Merchant's Dock at the northern edge of the town. There was a small gate with garrison troops standing bored and aimless, watching the flow of people in and out of the town. Cal and Theo followed Cosmas, all dressed in simple tunics, sandals, and woollen cloaks, and with only daggers at their belts. They raised no eyebrows from the guards as they passed.

'They only close this gate when there is a siege,' Cosmas told the other two. 'It leads down to the waterfront and is used by merchants.'

'I am not sure about this,' said Cal. 'Why do we poke the bear?'

'We do not wish to rouse suspicions, Charioteer,' said Cosmas. 'We go there, have a few drinks, and see what Naghi is up to. Do you two remember your stories?'

Cal grunted.

'I am here in exile,' said Theo. 'Looking for a way back to the court and favour.' He looked to Cal. 'I could do with a wild night anyway.' He licked his lips. 'It has been far too long.'

'Not too wild, I hope.'

The boy seemed insufferably excited about the night out, as far as Cal was concerned, so did Cosmas.

'You will do,' Rat told Theo. 'You,' he turned to the African. 'Need to smile more and grumble less.'

'I will break you, Rat, one day I will break you.'

So you keep saying, Charioteer, but you need me to save your granddaughter; so put a smile on that grizzled-ugly-bear-face that the good lord gave you, and play your part.'

'Why did we not bring some of your men?' Cal looked at Theo.

'Because that would have looked suspicious,' Cosmas said.

'In truth,' said Theo. 'My men are more likely to smash up the taverna and beat this Persian half to death for information. Subtle espionage is not their forte, and so they are best left in the stables.'

'I wish I had stayed at the stables with them,' said Cal.

The taverna was a low single storey wooden house set on the far edge of the cobbled wharfs. Cosmas led Cal and Theo along the waterfront and up towards the building. There was a veritable forest of ship masts and smaller sailing craft in the harbour. Music and singing came from over the boats to them, and the smell of cooking meat was on the air. Cosmas started salivating.

'Roasted spiced mutton,' said Rat.

'You have just eaten,' said Cal.

The slaves at the domos had provided a feast for them that had been rich and well made, and Rat had gluttoned as soon as the plates were laid before them.

'I may as well stuff myself now; we could be eating grass in a week,' said Cosmas.

Cal had no answer to that: it was true enough. They reached the taverna door and paused briefly.

'We are here to find out what the Persian is doing here, no more,' Theo reminded them. 'Do not cause trouble.' He poked Cosmas in the stomach.

'Of course,' said Cosmas. 'Now put a big smile on your face, Charioteer, try not to snarl.'

'One day, Rat,' said Cal, but he fixed a false grin on his face as they opened the door and ducked inside.

The taverna was packed out with sailors and merchants from all corners of the Empire. Lamps and tallow fat candles made the room heavy with oily smoke, and filled the corners with dark shadows. There was a large fire pit in the centre of the main room, laden with boiling pots of stews, and a counter loaded with amphora of wine manned by the staff. The thick heavy-set steward and his slaves were sweating heavily in the firelight as they rushed to serve the packed shop. A young boy was playing a small lira as he sat on a stool behind the fire pit, drawing the bow back and forth and slapping the belly of the instrument to rise up a dance that the sailors all knew and adored. The customers stamped their feet along and clapped with the tune, and even Cosmas was humming along with the music. The only women were brothel workers, dancers, and serving girls, used to such raucous behaviour from their clientele. No respectable Roman maiden would be seen in such an establishment, Theo concluded.

'There is Naghi,' said Cosmas, pointing out the Persian.

They pushed through the crowded room to Naghi's table, sitting down with no introductions. Cosmas smiled and bowed to the men sitting with the Persian, who smiled back and offered some wooden plates for them to take. The table was filled with foods: roasted meat, oysters, flatbreads and jugs full of spiced wine. Even though they had already eaten, the three helped themselves to more at Naghi's urging.

'So you found time to come and visit, Cosmas?' said Naghi. 'Who are you friends?'

'Oh, do you not know? This is Theodosius Dagisthaeus, the former Magister Militum of Armenia.'

Theo nodded at the Persian.

'Dagisthaeus?' said Naghi. 'Not the fool Goth boy who lost Petra to our troops?'

'One and the same,' said Theo, grimacing. 'I am in exile.'

'Strange,' said Naghi. 'I heard you were in one of the Emperor's dungeons.'

'I was for a time,' said Theo. 'Now I wait for my family to beg my return to court.'

Naghi smiled and looked at the stout charioteer. Cal had stayed silent as he sat down merely pouring some wine and sipping at it quietly. He suddenly realised everyone at the table was looking at him.

'Oh, this one is famous, Naghi,' said Rat. 'This is the once great Calliopas Porphyries. I know he is not much to look at now, ugly even some would say, but it is him none the less. Imperator per Circus. The king of the races.'

'Your Latin is awful,' said Theo. He drained a cup of spiced wine and poured himself another. The young officer was already flushed at his first cups of wine in months, and the words tumbled out too quickly.

'Are you really Porphyries the Charioteer?' Naghi asked the charioteer.

Cal nodded. He was used to the different reactions when he was introduced. Mostly it was disappointment that he was not the golden haired Achilles of legend, but a stout old Nubian with a bad knee. Naghi seemed more fascinated than most, his piercing eyes fixing the charioteer with a stare.

'I thought you were dead,' said the Persian after a moment's pause. 'What are you doing with this reprobate?' He slapped Cosmas on the back.

'Regretting every moment,' said Cal, sourly, and poured some more wine.

'He is not much of the conversationalist,' said Cosmas, pulling Naghi's arm. 'So what are you really doing here, old friend?'

'I asked first this time.'

'We are looking for opportunities,' said Theo. 'Something to get me back to court and out of disgrace, and rich if we can.' He drained his cup and poured another. 'Damn this wine is good.'

Naghi smiled. 'Would you like some spices from India?'

'He does have good spices,' said Cosmas.

'You have come from Lazica?' said Theo.

Naghi sat back, still smiling. 'Information is more expensive than my normal wares.'

'Is your Emperor back in Lazica with his army? I want to know.'

Cal noticed that Theo was flushed redder. The boy had not touched a drop of wine since they had met – despite urging Cal and Cosmas to enjoy themselves – this was the first time the old man had seen him drink anything alcoholic, now he understood why.

Two cups and he is already slurring, thought Cal. Oh my god, no, he's a drunk.

Theo had been efficient enough since their journey had started. Cal had assumed it was merely his attempt to redeem his past failures, but now he realised the young officer's problem. The boy could not handle his wine. Away from the grape Theo was pleasant, understood his duty and carried it out properly. A couple of cups of wine inside him, and he turned into a bigger irritant than Cosmas.

The Rat was also looking dumbfounded at Theo, surprised at the young nobleman's behaviour.

'What are you all looking at?'

Theo stood up and belligerently demanded information from the Persians. Naghi demurred and the boy threw a cup of wine in his face. Cosmas ducked under the table as soon as that happened and fists started being thrown, but Cal merely munched at some spiced lamb and flatbread as the brawl exploded around him. Most of the other customers watched on excitedly at the fight, and the boy musician continued playing as four Persians rushed at Theo.

'I said coming here was a mistake,' muttered Cal.

'What has got into the boy?' screeched Cosmas, reaching from under the table at Cal's food.

Cal slapped his hand away and bit into some bread. 'The boy is a drunk, but he seems to be holding his own.'

'Not for long,' said Rat.

Theo had knocked down two of Naghi's men but a third had him in a head grasp as the other Persian punched the boy in the stomach. Cal had decided Theo needed this thrashing, the boy had earned it and the charioteer saw no reason to intervene, but when he noted one of the Persians draw a dagger he finally stood up. A beating was one thing; a stabbing was an entirely different matter as far as Cal was concerned.

'My turn,' he said, standing up and grabbing the knifeman from behind. Cal tossed the Persian rough into the fire pit with ease. The rest of the taverna's customers turned to look at the charioteer with a stunned silence and the musician stuttered to a halt. Naghi cringed back as the charioteer towered over him.

'You can let the boy go now,' said Cal.

The man holding Theo let the young noble free as Naghi nodded nervously at him.

'I shall be taking him home, and we thank you for your hospitality,' Cal continued, and grabbed Theo's tunic. 'Come along, Rat.'

Cal grabbed the drunken, slurring, Theo, bleeding from a cut above his eye, and dragged him out of the taverna. Cosmas climbed out from under the table and apologised to the Persians before following.

***

They rode out of the West Gate three days later under the cover of darkness. Theo was still sporting a black eye. The governor had a squad of garrison troops watching over them as they left – making sure we were gone, thought Cal. Theo sent a man ahead and two to the flanks to scout as soon as they were out of sight of the city. Cal noted one of the Goths, the one Theo called Godda, nod approvingly for the first time at the boy's actions. Despite Theo's reputation, the pampered boy could ride better than most men Cal had seen, and he was obviously skilled with his weapons. He had broken two of the Persians in the taverna with ease until he was overwhelmed by numbers. The thought of freedom and a return to prestige had tempered Theo's natural impulsiveness and rash behaviour.

'Six months in Justinian's dungeons does that to a man,' said Cal, under his breath. 'Let us hope he stays that way and does not do something stupid again. We need to keep him away from wine.'

'What is that, Charioteer?' Cosmas the Irritant asked him.

'A prayer for our success,' said Cal. 'How are the Nestorians coping?' The charioteer was still suspicious of the young boy but had said nothing to Cosmas.

'Dull,' Cosmas said. 'They are from the Indies, but from the eastern parts – very mountainous. I have only travelled in along the coast and up the Indus, these are from further east. The language is difficult and they are monks, so they have not much of interest to say. The boy is cheerful enough, but the older one.' He tapped his head. 'I think his wits are deserting him.'

'That does not bode well for our success.'

They rode through the night with Theo leading the way. As the sun rose it shone directly in their faces as they followed the road eastwards. Theo switched the scouts around and sent two further ahead now it was light.

'Well, he knows what he is doing at least,' said Cal, shifting his sore arse on the hard saddle.

'Spoiled,' said a red-haired bucellarii in pig-Latin. 'His dada did not beat him as a boy. They all told him to thrash him more often.'

Cal nodded. Some of the men knew Latin from their time in Justinian's armies, but unlike their young leader they were still barbarians to Cal's eyes. Still wild, not romanised like the boy. The red-haired warrior was called Llew, a Briton who acted as the party's scout. He had found his way to Italia and been recruited ten years before, and spoke good Greek and some Latin as well as Gothic. The huge Fritigern, said little to anyone, but even Cal was wary of the man's size, had known Theo since boyhood. There was a pair of twins, dark haired and dark eyed, that finished each others' sentences and also came from the family estate, along with a couple of youngsters on their first ever mission. Two Italians who had joined the legions under Belisarius and found themselves in Theo's service completed the bodyguard. Cal was finding it difficult to keep track of the barbarian names, but the whole group seemed to know their tasks and were uncomplaining.

Goths, Goths, Goths, thought Cal. He had ridden against Goths in the hippodrome many times. They were all good pilots, but the charioteer had not met one that he liked or trusted in all those years.

'I am a bitter old man with not enough wine left in the cup.'

'Haven't I been telling you that ever since we first met?'

'And you are an irritant.'

Cosmas smiled broadly at the old man. 'People have been telling me that for years as well, it stops them from admitting that I am mostly right.'

Cal was not going to get into that argument. He had seen Theo point out the mathematics of the world's circumference to Rat whilst they were on the ship. Cosmas had watched the aristocrat's workings out intently and then dismissed it as 'obtuse verbiage'.

'How do you know the ancients were not lying, have you been to Susa? I have.' He told a frustrated Theo.

The sailor was convinced that the world was flat and adamant about it, adamant to the point of hysteria, and nothing they could say would change his mind. Cal by contrast did not care if it was round, flat, or square and saw no need to question why.

After nearly four hours of easy riding across Taurica, they came over a rise with a view down to the sea and the ancient Greek ruins. There had been a prosperous town here once, but it had been destroyed by the Huns a century before. Smoke from a single fire rose from the centre of the old town.

'Our guide must be there,' said Theo, and spurred his horse up to meet with the Llew who had ridden ahead.

Cal looked around at their party. The two monks and the Goths seemed happy enough after riding all morning. The young boy smiled at Cal, pointed, and then said something in his language. Cal turned as Comas replied to the monk.

'What are they saying?'

They want to know if we are to take a ship. I told them no. It is a long ride over the steppe instead.

'Why are they doing this? Why bring the silk to us?'

'War, Charioteer, it is always war. There is a new king of the steppe, a new Attila, so they tell me. War is coming to the east. Their people are enemies of the Persians. If we Romans stop paying for silk, the Persians will lose the war.'

It seemed as good a reason as any for Cal.

Theo and Llew appeared ahead of them and waved them on, and the group rode down into the broken ruins. There were shattered arches and solitary columns still standing, bleached white by the sun, fallen down walls and overgrown paving. At the centre of it all, in the old agora, was a small tent and a fire. A short shaggy haired horse was tied to a post, and the dirtiest barbarian Cal had ever seen was squatting and eating from a wooden bowl with his hands. He did not look up as they arrived in the square.

The barbarian still did not look up as they trotted over. Cal noted that his linen tunic and leather armour was poorly made, and they could all smell him from ten feet away. Theo coughed, as if he was trying to get a young maid's attention at a meal, but still the little man said nothing, just calmly finished off his food. When he had gobbled down the last morsel, he belched, wiped his dirty face with his dirty sleeve and looked up; speaking fast in a strange language, but the monks and Cosmas all understood him.

'This is our guide,' said Cosmas turning to Cal. 'His name is Angai the Utiger.'

Anagai the Utiger looked at them all with a wide smile.

5

The man's horse was different, that was the first thing that had struck Cal about the Utiger. Roman horses were taller and thinner, more muscular and graceful. Angai's animal was short, squat, and shaggy – much like the man – and it was tireless. Their beasts were blown by the end of each long day, but the Utiger's mount seemed untroubled by the wide steppe. The most fascinating thing to the charioteer was the horse's strange saddle. Bindings with pear shaped iron hoops on leather straps fell from it, so the rider could hook his feet up instead of letting them dangle. The stout horse had a rolling gait and wide back, but the hoops allowed the rider to twist and turn, even stand up in his saddle whilst riding along. Cal was amazed, it was such a simple idea, and so obvious, but nobody in the empire had seen it before.

So much for ignorant barbarians, thought the charioteer.

On the first night after meeting Angai, Cal had tried to fashion his own loops from some linen and leather but they were not strong enough to hold, and he almost fell from his animal the next day when they snapped. The Goth bucellarii sneered at his efforts, but the Utiger just laughed and said the word 'Atil' over and over to the charioteer.

'What is Atil?' Cal asked Rat.

'It is a meeting place, so he tells me,' said Cosmas. 'Merchants on the caravan trail east, traders from the steppe; different races and creeds gather there. You will be able to get a saddle with hoops from the market. I am quite excited about visiting.'

'Does that mean trouble?'

'Oh, you are so miserable, Charioteer. Atil will be dangerous, of course it will, but this is a great adventure. Look how flat this land is.' He gestured at the rolling grass steppe. 'If that does not prove what I have been saying about the world...'

'How do you know all these different tribal tongues?' Cal cut Rat off before he started waxing lyrical on the flat earth. 'And yet your Latin is terrible?'

Cosmas looked nonplussed and put his finger on his chin as if pondering the question as they plodded along.

'I have never travelled in the West, it is filled with barbarians,' he said eventually. 'So I have had little need for Latin. Perhaps I shall go there when the Emperor restores Gaul and Britannia to civilization. Young Llew tells me that the Britons still remember Rome, but there is war there with the Saxons. However, to answer your question, these tribes all speak a type of Hunnish so it is just varying the sound of the words. The further east we go the less I will understand or the further south. The Hepthalite Kingdom has many different languages, only some of them are known to me.' He shrugged. 'We have to get to Atil first.'

'You have travelled this way before?'

'No, but others have to bring silk back to the empire and avoid the Persian tax collectors. I had heard of Atil. There are Christians and many Jews there, and Zoroastrians as well as magicians and shaman of the steppe tribes. There will certainly be Persians spies there too. It is a strange place by all accounts.'

'Jews?' said Cal.

'Yes, it is almost a Jewish city.' He looked pointedly at the charioteer. 'You are not a Jew hater are you?'

Cal shook his head. 'I did some shameful things in my youth, Rat, terrible things that I will burn in hellfire for, out of greed and anger. I cannot atone for them, but I will see none of that faith harmed again.'

'You have a dark past, Charioteer, but it is the past.' Cosmas waved his hand dismissively.

'It is the dark things you do that stay with you, poison you.' Cal shrugged sadly. 'I thought we were avoiding Persians after Naghi?' he said, changing the subject.

'They get everywhere.' He touched Cal's hand and spoke in a lower voice. 'If Naghi has a way of getting word to his masters, Atil could be even more dangerous. So do not fret on your past, it is the now we should worry on.'

'How would he do that?' Cal was disturbed by the thought of Persians hunting them as they ventured into the wild unknown. 'We left him behind in Taurica?'

'Did we?' Cosmas frowned. 'I did not see him again after Theo caused the brawl in the taverna. Naghi could easily have left the port without us knowing. It is but a short voyage to Lazica from there.' He gestured vaguely to the south. 'That means that Persians south of the mountains could have known about us a week ago. I have told Theo the same.'

'The Persians do not know what we are doing.' Cal said it firmly but his stomach twisted tight into a knot at Rat's words.

'That is true,' said Cosmas. 'And the boy getting drunk and starting a fight may work in our favour, but...'

'But what?'

'Naghi is a snake, he is clever, and there is only one reason for Narses to send a mission out onto the steppes. He will figure it out eventually.'

'I said we should have left him alone.' Cal glared at the sailor. 'I damn well warned the pair of you. Narses has cursed me with a drunken youth, a foolborn philosopher, and an impossible task.'

'It's all spilt milk, Charioteer.'

Cosmas kicked his animal in the sides to move up and join the two monks. Both gave him a grin as he started chattering away at them.

Cal watched him go with a sour look on his face. What was clear to the old charioteer was that the grass steppe was not some empty desert. There were people and traders throughout the vast plains. Different tribes, and territories, and politics, and their little party was strolling into it all as blind as moles. After five days, they had barely travelled more than a hundred miles from Roman Taurica. Atil was another two weeks riding, according to the Utiger, on the shores of a great sea or lake – Cal was not certain from Cosmas's vague translations. Once they reached the trading post, they would take stock before moving on towards Serica. He sighed; it would be months, if not years, before they came home again; before he saw his granddaughter again.

If I ever actually do, he thought.

Despite the Utiger guide leading the way, Theo still had Llew and the twins riding scout and others watching over the two priests. Both of the Nestorians could ride well enough, but the travel was wearing on the old monk who fell asleep quickly each night. The boy novice said little, just smiled at their questions, and spoke in a quiet voice to Cosmas. Otherwise the two monks kept themselves to themselves. Cal still couldn't put his finger on what irked him about the boy.

The bucellarii kept their horses corralled and watched over them at night, but the Utiger merely hobbled his animal with leathers and left it to graze freely. Cal dismounted and handed his animal over to Ademar, one of Theo's men. He wished he could speak to the Utiger, using Cosmas as interpreter made any conversation difficult, but the man's knowledge about horseflesh intrigued the old charioteer. He wanted to try the saddle with hoops.

The campfire was set up quickly each night, but fuel was scarce on the steppe. The bucellarii scavenged what they found as they rode scout, but there were no trees to keep a fire burning through the night. Once a hot stew of salt pork and biscuit had been prepared and served, the fire was doused. The nights were cold after the heat of the day. All of them were burned red by the sun, but Theo suffered the most. His pale face had turned the colour of a strawberry and he wore a floppy cloth hat with a wide brim to protect his skin. That drew snorts of derision from his men. The huge one they called Fritigern was merciless in mocking the officer, but Theo ignored the barbs.

'Are you faring well, Cal?' Theo sat with the charioteer as everyone gobbled down their rations.

'Well enough but we have a very long way to go.'

Theo smiled. 'Half the world according to Rat.'

'You are just as excited about this journey as Cosmas.' Cal was disgusted by their enthusiasm.

'I am excited about redemption when we return.'

'What do you think of the Utiger?'

'My men are keeping a watch over him, but I think he can be trusted. I am more worried by the old monk. I fear Brother Timothy is too old for this journey.'

The ancient Nestorian was frail, but he and his young companion were uncomplaining as they rode each day. The pair stayed mostly silent around the campfire as the bucellarii chattered away boisterously. The young boy was shy and helpful, always smiling, but Cal still did not trust him. Cosmas told him the lad's name was strange so they called him Petros, a Greek version of his own. Cal found himself irritated by the lad whenever they were together. He pondered it as he huddled down with his blankets after food and tried to sleep. Theo had arranged for the bucellarii to watch over them, but Cal could not get comfortable on the hard earth, tossing and turning. He heard a noise and turned to look. There was a shadow crawling away in the darkness. It was the young monk.

Where is he going?

Every night, at about the same time, the boy sneaked off. Cal had watched him go for the last three nights. This time he decided to follow. The watching Goth guard said nothing as Cal got up and walked into the darkness after the monk.

Perhaps he is just going to take a piss, but why wait till the same time every night, why does he always wait till we are almost asleep?

Cal had some vague notion of the boy leaving markers or messages for any pursuit – perhaps he was a Persian spy – something was just not right about the young monk. Then he saw why. The young boy looked around, and squatted lifting up his robe and revealing pale buttocks in the starlight. There was a gush of piss and a little gasp of relief.

'By all the saints,' whispered Cal to himself. 'He is a she.'

He felt a knife pressed into his back. Rat had sneaked soundlessly behind hm.

'You had to come looking didn't you, Charioteer?' whispered Cosmas. 'I saw you follow her. Now don't shout out else I will gut you like a fish. I have no choice, and I like you old man.'

'You knew all along?' Cal hissed back at Rat.

'Narses told me on the first night and swore me to secrecy.'

'My God, Cosmas, there are Goths and Huns all over, why bring a girl?'

'She is the one who has the secret of making the silk not the old one. I did not understand it all, but Narses was most persuasive. Now you know, but you cannot tell.'

'I will tell no-one,' said Cal. 'If the Goths find out it could cause trouble.'

***

Every day was the same but different: they would wake early and break their fast with dried fruits and salted pork washed down with brackish water, and took to their horses before sunrise. The wide undulating landscape, ever changing, ever staying the same, passed by as they rolled through the knee high grass. Angai took them along paths used by his people, stopping to water the animals and fill their sacks. Cal and Theo both noted signs of other travellers; tracks in the grass, and the bucellarii were kept on high alert for raiders. When the sun was at its zenith, dry and choking in the hot breeze and baking the men in their scale armour, they would break for food before carrying on in the afternoon.

At nightfall, the Utiger would lead them to a campsite. The Goths would throw off their metal coats gratefully, see to the horses, and start a fire and set to cooking up some warm food for the night. Conversations around the campfire were still muted even after two weeks travel. The bucellarii tended to speak only among themselves or Theo, barring the odd word of pig-Latin to Cal, but the charioteer was starting to know them. Huge Fritigern was a docile giant, but deadly in a fight so the others told the charioteer. Llew the Briton scouted every day with the twins Baros and Bruna. Asta and Marcus were young men on their first mission from the family estate and generally kept quiet around the more experienced soldiers. The last two were Romans: a Greek named Sylvester and Ademar a soldier from Ravenna who had both served under Belisarius. All of them were watched over by Godda and his deputy Beremund

'Why do you care about them?' asked Cosmas. 'They are just soldiers, just biscuit eaters.'

'They are our companions and might just keep us alive, and we are all eating biscuits now.'

To Rat, the Goths were common barbarian fedorati and beneath him. He was more interested in the Nestorians. The two monks would listen as Cosmas chattered away incessantly to them, but they said very little in return. Sometimes Rat would pester Angai the Utiger with questions about their destination, but again their guide said few words in response.

None of them can get a word with all his wittering, thought Cal.

The Rat suddenly looked up from his one-sided conversation with the Utiger and burst out laughing. He pointed to Cal.

'Our guide wants to know if you are a demon, Charioteer.'

'What?'

He has never seen anyone from Africa. Romans he knows, Goths he knows, Huns, Avars, Goturks, Alans and Persians.' Cosmas waved at the others around the fire. 'But you are new. So he wants to know if you are a demon or a spirit. Or if you are just another man.'

'Tell him he is no pretty picture himself,' said Cal.

'I told him you were from a land far to the south, and the greatest charioteer in the world, but just an ordinary man.'

'What did he say to that?'

'In faith, he seemed unimpressed. I think he was hoping you were a demon, and he thinks little of chariots but he tells me that there are races at Atil.'

Cal crossed himself. 'They are pagans?'

The Rat nodded. 'I doubt we shall meet many of the faith. These poor people are misguided in their ways and far from the true path of the word. But the grace of God will come to these lands one day. Perhaps we shall be the catalyst for that. Patriarch of the Pagan Steppes,' he said half to himself. 'I would like that.'

'You are delusional,' said Cal. 'How fare the Nestorians?'

'They are happy enough.' Rat tapped his nose and winked at Cal.

Cal grunted and pulled his woollen blanket around his shoulders. The revelation that the young Nestorian Petros was actually a girl named Padma still troubled the old man. The bucellarii may be taking Theo's orders at the moment, but the charioteer still did not fully trust them even if he enjoyed their bluff company. Cal feared Theo could get drunk on the trail, cause trouble and see his men desert him on the plains. There was certain to be wine in Atil.

'You should get some sleep, Charioteer, and stop fretting,' Theo told him. 'If we have a good day's ride tomorrow we shall be close to the trading post.'

'Then what?'

'We will need to speak to people there.' Theo smiled. 'The monks know our ultimate destination, but the path to get there is ours to choose.'

'Everyone is a philosopher.'

The next morning they were up and on the trail once more. As the sun rose higher, Cal saw that Angai was leading them towards a low valley running eastwards. The sun was in Cal's eyes but he could see men down there. There were riders on horses; he could see the glint of metal in the sunlight.

'Men!' shouted Cal. 'Horsemen.'

Theo's scouts came galloping in shouting at their leader. Cosmas started questioning the Utiger in Hunnish, and Theo ordered everyone to have their weapons ready. Most of the bucellarii moved to the front to face the riders with Godda and Theo, whilst the twins nervously watched their flanks. All had their recurved bows and arrows to hand.

'He says not to loose our arrows, they are his people,' called Cosmas to Theo.

They all pulled their horses up to a halt as the newcomers swept up the valley towards them – perhaps thirty of them in all. At two hundred meters, the Huns split, with half circling around them to the left and the rest going to the right, until they were riding around the Romans with their bows at the ready. The bucellarii had grim faces and their own weapons to hand. Cal looked nervously at Angai and Cosmas. The former had a wide grin on his face and started calling out to the Huns. Rat did not seem so sure of himself.

At Angai's shout, two riders broke of the encirclement and trotted up to the Romans nonchalantly and started jabbering away at the guide. He started chattering and gesticulating wildly, as Cosmas watched on intently trying to follow the conversation.

'What is happening Rat?' asked Theo, moving his horse alongside Cosmas'.

'I think there has been a wedding, or there is going to be a wedding, and our man has been expected or perhaps not invited.'

'What about us you cretin?' snapped Theo.

Rat looked hurt. 'Local politics are about us; the more we can find out the easier our journey becomes, and the more profitable on our return.'

'So?'

'They will take us to Atil. The wedding will be there, I think. Nobody breaks the peace of the town, tell your men that. The steppe tribes all respect that; if we break the truce none of them will help us. Worse, they might just kill us all out of hand.'

For the rest of the day, they were shadowed by the Utiger riders as they followed a dried up streambed. Theo's men kept their hands on their weapons and there were mutterings in Gothic. Cal recognised the grumbling without understanding a word; the soldiers were unhappy travelling with Huns. The landscape changed as they rode east and down from the steppe: small lakes and marshes and a tangle of streams now crisscrossed their path. They reached a river fed by the streams, as great as the Tiber, wide and slow moving. Angai turned to the south keeping on the higher ground as they followed the course. As they crested a rise, they could see the wide delta emptying out into the Caspian Sea below them. On a small island in the delta, with pontoon bridges connecting it to the different shores east and west, was a huge stockade settlement of low mud huts and tents. The Utiger turned on his horse to the others and pointed at the town.

'Atil,' He said.

6

Atil was not what Cal or the others had expected, even Cosmas seemed shocked. It was large, well ordered and well built. The town itself was twice the size of Chersonesus, with citizens from all over the steppe and from the lands to the south and north. It positively thronged with travellers and different faiths. Angai told them that there were temples to the Zoroastrian sun god, and others to eastern deities, two synagogues, and even a rude Christian church that had been founded a few years before and many Christians. All lived peacefully together under the King of Atil. Rat told them that the king had wives from each faith and race so that none could claim favouritism. Any disputes were settled by a council of the faiths. Two Christians, two Jews, and two Zoroastrians were selected from their communities along with a Pagan shaman to serve on the council with the king – another pagan. It was a rich town, well ordered, and very well defended.

'I did not expect anything like this,' said Cosmas to the others, with an excited grin on his face. 'The markets must be teeming with opportunity.'

'We are not here to source new products for Rome,' Theo told him.

'Yes, yes, of course, but still...'

Perhaps fifteen thousand people lived in the settlement on a permanent basis, with more visiting the markets. Barbarians in mail coats guarded the gated entrance to the city, and they questioned Angai before waving them all through. There was large open space set aside for caravans and travellers to camp inside the walls, but with its own gate and stockade that set it apart from the rest of the town. Other travelling merchants and traders were set up in the compound, and the main markets were along the river where boats from all over the Caspian Sea docked. The Rat had gone to see what was for sale as soon as they were settled down.

'Find out if there are Persians here,' Theo told him. 'And don't cause any trouble.'

Cosmas nodded and skipped off to the stalls with a big smile on his weasel face.

'You actually trust him not to cause trouble?'

Theo grimaced at Cal. 'No, but he is the best we have, and he is the only one who can talk to these people.'

'He is also the only one who can talk to the two monks,' Cal pointed out. 'If we lose him the mission would fail.'

'Yes, I know,' said Theo. 'It is annoying, is it not?'

Cal grunted and settled down for a snooze. It had been a long journey and he needed the rest. If Cosmas caused any trouble he would let Theo deal with it all. The two monks sat down beside him as the bucellarii pitched their camp. The young girl disguised as a monk smiled shyly at the charioteer, but Cal did not respond. She worried him almost as much as Rat. Instead, he watched as the bucellarii settled down around the campfire and started cooking food under Godda's watchful eye. Strange traders from all directions gathered in Atil to sell their wares. The old charioteer could hardly believe that such a large town existed on the barbarian steppe. Certainly few people in the Empire knew about it other than merchants and travellers. He wondered if Rat had found any deals.

Cosmas skipped along the stalls by the river, spread out along the banks with boats and steppe traders hawking their wares. He fingered the silks and linens and asked prices, whistling at the cost. Atil was a veritable bazaar with rare goods that could make him a fortune back in the Empire. Fine jewellery made out of amber and copper, beautiful glass bracelets and strings of pearls. There was silk, of course, there was always silk. Silk was the reason this place existed after all, but the town had outgrown the one single commodity: there was a slave market, and horse and cattle merchants. Food stalls sold millet, watermelons, peaches, plums, salted beef, and dried fish galore. Amphorae from the Empire filled with Cretan wine, or olives from Thessalonica brought the long way from Persia. There were artisans in the town turning the local raw materials into beautiful works of art for export: potters, weavers, smiths, and glass blowers. Cosmas had seen strange tattooed men from the north with furs, steppe traders with their shaggy horses, brown faced black-haired Bactrians. Then, set back from the river he saw a wooden cross rising above the flat roofs. There was the small Christian shrine Angai had mentioned, little more than a shack.

It would be remiss of me not to pay my respects, thought Cosmas.

It was a hovel not a temple. No painted icons or jewelled crosses inside like the shrine to Saint Basil in Chersonesus. Rough wooden planks hammered together to keep the elements off, and a simple low table as an altar inside. A young boy sat just inside the doorstep with a bored look on his face holding a wooden cup. Cosmas tipped him a couple of bronze coins that rattled as they spun around the cup. The boy picked up the imperial follis and sniffed one, then bit into it. Seemingly satisfied, he nodded for Cosmas to proceed inside. The Rat slipped off his sandals and entered. There was a small altar, just a rough wooden table, but with a tiny icon of Christ on the cross. Cosmas lit a tallow candle from a lamp and kneeled before the rude altar. He offered a brief prayer for success on their mission. Then he turned back to the boy, who was waiting by the door.

'Where is the priest?' he asked in Greek.

The boy just stared at him uncomprehending.

He tried again in Hunnish, and the boy nodded and stood up, pointing outside.

'The priest is outside?'

The boy nodded excitedly and started speaking quickly. Cosmas frowned as he tried to keep up, but followed on as the lad tugged at his robe and turned to leave.

Cosmas put his sandals back on, and followed the boy along a dirt path away from the river to a small brick built building behind the shrine. The boy pointed and knocked on the door. Rat was intrigued; he had not expected Atil to be so large or populous and now there were Christian shrines here. Whoever this priest was, he was a prophet amongst the barbarians.

The door opened to reveal a white bearded, bald headed, old man with a stooped back and yellow teeth. He spoke quickly to the boy who pointed at Cosmas.

'He says you visited the shrine,' said the man in Greek. 'Are you a Roman?

Cosmas nodded. 'From Alexandria.'

The man's face lit up. 'Traders?'

'Travellers, what are you doing here?'

'Come in, come in, and I shall tell you my tale.'

'Well, that is an invitation I cannot refuse,' said Rat glibly, and followed the man inside.

The domos was only one room with mud walls. A small bed covered with furs and cushions for sleeping, a clay hearth with a little fire smoking away, and faded patterned rugs laid out on the earth floor. The man gestured for Cosmas to sit.

'I was born in Neapolis,' said the man. 'During the reign of Emperor Zeno.'

'Is this going to be a long tale?' asked Cosmas.

'As long as it takes, but it is worthwhile, if you seek the truth?'

Cosmas nodded and settled back on a cushion as the man fumbled in a trunk and brought out a small clay amphora, a wooden gourd and two cups and a dish. He placed them on the rug in front of Cosmas but did not open the gourd or offer any other refreshment.

How rude thought Rat, but he said nothing to the priest. The man had been living with barbarians, after all.

'I was born in Neapolis,' the man said again. 'My family were exiles there having fled Roma when Odoacer came. From Neapolis we went onto Pelesium and settled there during the reign of Emperor Anastasius. It was a well appointed place and we prospered despite our exile.'

'I know it,' said Cosmas. 'Oh, but...'

'Yes,' the old man nodded sadly. 'The city was burned by the Persians and I was carried off into slavery, barely more than a boy.' He paused as the words sunk in. 'My master in Ctesiphon was a Christian, kind enough, and eventually I earned my freedom from him. I travelled throughout the east preaching the word until I came here ten years ago and stayed.'

'So why stay here? It is rather out of the way.'

'I never settled in Persia, never knowing what God's plan for me was as I roamed. I came here on a dhow across the Caspian, and I found what I was looking for. God himself had led me to the means to restore my family's fortune. There are many Christians here, but we are poor and they are not generous with the shrine. There is talk of building a newer better church.' Cosmas heard a note of bitterness in the man's tone. 'But now the Good Lord brings true Romans here to me who can take me home and my fortune.'

'Well, we are travelling on, as I said,' Cosmas blurted out hurriedly. He did not want to get dragged into another situation. Theo and Cal would not thank him for causing trouble, and there was something about this old man that did not sit right. 'Anyway, what fortune? You said you were all poor.'

The man smiled as Cosmas spluttered, and uncorked the small amphora. He poured out some black slick balls, a dark substance that smelled of the sea.

Cosmas sniffed at it suspiciously. 'What is this?'

'Wait.'

The old man opened the gourd and poured out two cups of a milky liquid.

'Kumis?' asked Cosmas. 'Fermented donkey milk?'

The man nodded again and spooned up some of the black substance.

'Fish eggs,' he said. 'Taste them and then drink the kumis.'

Cosmas did as he was instructed and a wide smile slowly spread over his face. The black balls gave off a delicate flavour of the sea in his mouth as he rolled them around with his tongue. It was salty with a hint of fish, but not overpowering. He bit into one, popping it delightfully, and releasing a burst of fresh flavour.

'Now the Kumis,' said the man.

Rat gulped his Kumis down in one go. He did not normally enjoy the spirit, but the sensation of the fish eggs popping in his mouth from the alcohol was quite delightful.

'Where does this come from?'

'From all around here,' said the man. 'They harvest and salt it every year and gulp it down like porridge. The Bactrians buy some, the Persians too, but it needs olive oil to travel far and Roman amphorae to carry it in. The potters here cannot make the quality of vessel needed to transport. It is a local secret, but can you imagine what they would say in Rome, or Constantinople, or Antioch if they had this?'

Cosmas could easily imagine. The rich would pay their weight in gold to have this adorn their dinner tables. The Kumis could be produced locally to serve with it. They could call it a Scythian delicacy, barbarian fashions were always in vogue with the feckless aristocrats in the capital. It would mean organised caravans across the steppes between Chersonesus and Atil and then ships to Constantinople, but it could be done. The profit margins would be worth it if they could purchase in bulk and the eggs did not spoil. It would be like shipping gold.

'I can see that you understand,' said the man. 'All I ask is you take me with you, back to the Empire, back to Rome and give me my share.'

Cosmas nodded, he understood. The poor priest simply wanted to go home.

'I have friends here with me,' said Rat. 'I will go to them and ask. I can offer no more.

The man gave him the gourd and the amphora. Let them taste it, let them see. I can get more.

'What is your name?' Cosmas realised he had not asked.

'Romulus Flavius,' said the man. 'I was named after my father.'

Something niggled about that name but Cosmas did not inquire further. He could see an opportunity when it presented itself and this was golden. He had forgotten about the silk, forgotten about the Persians. The fish eggs and kumis was everything any and every merchant dreamed of. It was a new product with one source which only he knew about, and a market that was begging for new goods. The Rat arrived back at the merchant corral to find Cal sleeping and Theo looking bored.

'Did you find any Persians?' asked Theo as Rat arrived.

'Better,' said Cosmas.

'What have you done?' said Cal opening an eye.

'Found manna from God,' said Rat.

He sat down at the fire and crossed his legs, pulling out the gourd and amphora. 'Get me a dish,' he said to Theo. The noble nodded and pulled a wooden bowl from one of the tents. Cal had sat up by now, his interest piqued by Rat's display. They both watched as Cosmas poured out a black slick mess of small balls.

'What is it?' asked Cal, sniffing at the black mess.

'Fish eggs,' Cosmas told him. 'Try some, and then swill it down with the kumis.'

Cal scooped up a spoonful and put it in his mouth. A wide grin spread slowly across his face.

'Now try the kumis,' said Cosmas, passing him the gourd.

Cal took a great gulp of kumis and swilled the taste of the fish eggs around. The strong milky liquid would normally take his breath away, but it made the fish eggs pop in his mouth. He almost giggled with delight.

'We could make a fortune in Constantinople,' was all he said once he had swallowed.

'I know,' said Cosmas. 'We would have to transport the eggs in amphorae across the steppes to Taurica, and then take another boat to the capital, but the rewards would be astronomical.'

'Do we not have enough to worry about with the silk?' said Theo, standing over them.

Cal passed him the bowl of fish eggs. 'Try some,' was all he said.

Theo took a spoonful and had the same reaction as the charioteer.

'That is delightful.'

Cosmas told them all about Romulus and his little shrine down by the boats, and his promise to take the old man back to Rome.

'What was his name?'

'Romulus Flavius.'

I am certain I have heard that name before; he looked at Cal who shook his head.

'Can we take him with us, please?' Rat asked as if the old priest was a pet dog.

Theo frowned. 'We have to get the silk first, friend Cosmas. We will come back this way on our return and take him back then. Tell your friend Flavius that. Narses would not thank us if we brought back another product for the aristocracy to spend gold on, but no silk making in return. Let us see what happens in the meantime. If can go back with both we shall be heroes.'

The Rat huffed and puffed for a while more, but he could see that the young nobleman was fixed in his purpose to get the secret of silk. At the least, he had the knowledge to bring this new find to the Empire one day.

'I will have to go back to Romulus and explain it to him.'

He could see that Cal agreed with Theo. The charioteer's granddaughter would not be helped by the fish eggs. Glumly, Rat wandered back to the shrine to inform Romulus Flavius. As he followed the path along the river wharfs he noticed a new Persian dhow moored on the wooden pontoons.

'Oh shit,' he said, turned around and bumped into someone.

'Well met, again, Cosmas of Alexandria. It must be fate that sets us on the same road.'

The Persian spy Naghi was standing right before him, and with a wide smile on his face.

7

The problem, as far as Theo could see it, was their lack of numbers. The journey from Chersonesus had been easy enough. The Utiger guide knew the route, and it was well travelled by other traders in both directions. However, further into the steppe hostile groups were known to attack even the largest caravans. Merchants regularly banded together on the road for protection in groups of over a thousand men, but they were still attacked by raiders. Theo had only his bucellarii and Cal (he discounted Rat and the two priests as useless in a fight), but joining with another party was a clear risk to their mission.

'Which is the greater danger?' he asked himself. 'The tribes or the traders?'

Cal and the monks were sitting snoozing in the sun. His men were resting or on guard. Even inside the corral Theo kept a watch up. He did not trust the other merchants or whoever the authorities were in this strange place. Godda had seemed happy and Beremund had nodded approvingly at the command. The old warriors were hard to please, and both had beaten Theo often enough as a child, so the mild smiles of satisfaction were high praise indeed.

If Godda had been at Petra with me, perhaps I would not have been such a drunken fool, he thought.

He was pleased he had his bucellarii with him, no matter how surly or sneering they were, but Cal had been correct. If he failed, it was not simply Narses and the Emperor that he would have to answer to – his own men would stake him out on the grass and leave him for the wild beasts of the steppe. There were old tales of his people before they had become Roman, some of them were still barely more than barbarians, and he had humiliated his family once already. They would not be so forgiving a second time.

He noted their Utiger guide returning to the compound and heading straight towards their camp. The man seemed excited, coming to Theo and speaking fast in his strange language. Cal and the young monk sat up and started to take notice as the Utiger babbled away. Without the Rat to translate, Theo had no idea what Angai's words meant. The language was unlike the Gothic spoken by his men, and completely alien to his Latin or Greek.

'Where is Cosmas when you need him?' he said.

The man gestured towards the river and said something. There was urgency in his voice, an insistence that Theo could understand even without language. Angai tapped his head and shrugged at the Roman officer.

'Where is Rat?' Theo repeated to nobody in particular.

'He want you go to chief.'

The young Nestorian monk they called Petros spoke quietly in broken Greek to Theo. All of them turned and looked in surprise. Other than Cosmas, the two Nestorians had barely interacted with the rest of their party. Theo had assumed that they could only speak their home tongue.

'You speak Greek?' said Theo, stating the obvious.

'Cosmas the Brave, he teach some.'

Cal shook his head in disgust. The Rat was a born troublemaker. As long as the girl was kept to herself, kept her toilet hidden, then he had been able to ignore the situation. If she could talk to people, sooner or later she would give herself away. Cal silently cursed Cosmas but a wide grin came over Theo's face.

'You will have to come with us,' said Theo to the monk. 'Wherever Rat is he will find us later, but we cannot snub the city's leaders.'

'I cannot.' The girl looked terrified.

Theo grabbed Petros' robe and looked earnestly into her brown eyes. 'You have to,' he said. 'Our whole mission depends upon it.'

That is overstating it somewhat, thought Cal, but kept silent. The young aristocrat was making their argument. Petros looked shyly up at Theo and nodded. Cal saw the look; he had seen it before on his granddaughter's face when she met her foolborn husband.

Oh, Lord God, you have a dark sense of humour.

Theo did not see the glance the young monk gave him, turning to his baggage instead and pulling out his best armour and clothes.

'What are you doing?' asked Cal.

'I have to look my best for this chief,' said Theo. 'He must see the full magnificence of Rome embodied in us. We have some gifts that should buy us passage onwards. This boy can translate, and it makes us less reliant on Rat in future.'

'I am coming,' said Cal. He did not want to let the girl go unaccompanied.

'Why?' asked Theo.

'Because I am the greatest charioteer in the world,' said Cal, standing up and wincing at his gammy knee.

'Then you can carry the casket of presents,' Theo told him. 'I need to get dressed.'

Theo looked splendid once he had buckled up his gleaming mail coat and fixed a crested iron helmet on his head. He tied his spatha to his belt and snapped down the faceguard on his helm.

'You look as though you are dressed for parade, Magister Militum?' said Cal.

'Display the power and glory of the Empire to the Barbarians and then buy them off,' said Theo. 'It is the Roman way. Are we ready?'

Cal picked up the casket to carry and Petros nodded.

'Lead on then,' said Theo to the Angai the guide.

Petros translated for Angai, and the Utiger smiled and nodded and led them into the town to the chief's stronghold.

The citadel of Atil was on an island in the river delta with pontoon bridges to the different banks. Theo could see the wooden stockade and earthen walls were patrolled by well armed men. There were guards at both ends of the pontoon bridge, but they waved the Utiger and his companions through with no questions. Angai was well known in this place it seemed to the young Roman. At the end of the pontoon was a double gate, twice a man's height and wide enough for two carts to pass through at once. Theo noted the stone foundations as he passed through. The warriors all wore coarse mail armour. Atil was a rich place, well defended, any army would find it nigh on impossible to besiege with the river and wetlands. Whoever ruled here was a power on the steppe.

'This is a King's stronghold,' said Cal.

'Yes,' agreed Theo.

The citadel itself was mostly wood and earthen fortifications. Behind the stockade wall was a great bank of earth piled up to strengthen the wooden face. There were archer platforms and watchtowers at each corner all manned with men, and another similar gatehouse on the eastern wall. The space inside had stables and a smith hammering away at his anvil. There was a well, and squat square barrack houses that would not be out of place in a Roman fort. Angai nodded at Petros, saying a few words, and the young monk turned to Theo and Cal.

'He say great dominus live in hall. You have gifts?'

'Yes,' said Theo nodding at the casket Cal carried.

The Utiger led them to a long brick building with a flat roof.

'It is the Dominus's hall,' said Petros.

The guards at the doors questioned the Utiger again, but Angai spoke quickly and waved at Theo in his gleaming armour and the boy priest and old charioteer carrying the casket. One of the guards burst out laughing at the sight of them, and at Angai's words, and opened the doors to let them enter the hall.

I hate it when people laugh at me but I do not know why, thought Cal as he passed the grinning guard.

Inside was a dark entrance hall lit by oil lamps. There was noise from the hall coming from behind a heavy reed curtain – conversations and singing. Cal blinked as his eyes became accustomed to the gloom, almost bumping into Theo who had stopped dead in front of him. There was a man pouring out cups a dark hot liquid and offering it to the two Romans.

'Take drink,' said Petros. 'It is welcome.'

The young priest led the way, drinking from the wooden bowl and passing it to Theo with another coy smile. Theo took it, not noticing the girl's blush.

I really do not like how that situation is unfolding, thought Cal.

The young warrior supped at the cup, grimacing at the bitter flavour and then passed it to the charioteer. A steaming dark brown liquid – Cal swilled at it –and quickly swallowed his gulp. He had tasted worse broths in the circus, but it was still unpleasant.

Once they had all drunk the tisane, the curtain was drawn back and they were allowed to enter the main hall. Inside was full of people, men, women and children. A long low table stretched the length of the hall covered by a blue woollen cloth, and filled with food and drink on wooden platters. All around were people reclined on cushions, talking and eating, and drinking from fine earthenware cups and fired clay dishes. There were meats and breads, more of Cosmas's fish eggs, and the room was swimming in kumis. At the centre of the table, surrounded by his flunkeys and reclining on an old leather couch, was a fat old man with long white beard dressed in silk robes and dripping in gold jewellery. He gestured for the Romans to approach him and started speaking in a low rumbling voice. Theo and Cal both looked at the young monk for translation.

'He welcomes and asks for gifts,' said Petros.

'Straight to the point,' muttered Cal. 'Typical.'

'Tell him that I have brought fine crafted jewels from Rome itself,' said Theo. 'Sent by the Emperor Justinian in recognition of his power and magnificence. The glory of heaven shines upon him. The light of God's representative on earth hath blessed him.'

Petros looked dumbfounded for a moment at Theo's lofty speech, and then said a single sentence quickly to the headman. The fat old chief nodded and looked at Cal.

'Step up, Charioteer,' hissed Theo.

Cal stepped forward and laid the casket at on the table in front of the headman. Theo had taken a key out of his purse, and leaned down and unlocked it, and flipped up the lid to reveal an exquisite single golden diadem with three pearls set above the forehead. There was a gasp from the audience at the sight. It was a stunning piece, made by the Emperor's craftsmen. The headman leaned forward and plucked it up in his grubby digits. He smiled, plonked it on his head, and gestured for the three of them to be seated at the far end of the table. A small boy led them to places with cushions and brought a pitcher of kumis and wooden platters for them to eat.

'The chief offer hospitality,' said Petros. 'We must drink and eat or he be upset.'

Theo looked at the wineskin. He could smell the kumis. He took it from the slave boy and poured himself a cup of the milky liquid. He had not touched a drop of wine or beer since Chersonesus. Not since the brawl with the Persians. He had promised himself he would abstain but if the mission required it.

***

The dhow's cabin was finely furnished like a Sassanid decadent's boudoir, thought the Rat. The gentle sound of waves lapping at the bow made him want to piss, but Cosmas reclined on the cushions with a cup of Bactrian wine in his hand ignoring his full bladder. Naghi sat opposite him with a plate of fish eggs and glass carafe of wine.

'It is better with the kumis than the wine,' said the Persian.

'I agree,' said Cosmas. 'Can you think of the fortune I could make.'

'We could make.'

'He wants to go back to Rome not Persia, Naghi, but am certain I can cut you into the deal somehow.'

'Come now, Cosmas, you would not try and corner the market yourself?'

'What market? You cannot get past the borders to sell it in the Empire, other than little dead end pisspots like Chersonesus.'

'But I can fill this ship full of the eggs and have them waiting for you on the border. From Lazica you could ship directly to Constantinople. That is far easier than across the steppe to Chersonesus. At the same time I could open the market in Ctesiphon.'

'I do not think that Emperor Justinian is going to raise the trade restrictions on Persia any time soon, friend Naghi,' said Cosmas, pouring himself some more wine. 'I have no passion for smuggling these days, and I can take it overland to Chersonesus and ship direct to Constantinople without troublesome customs inspectors asking too many questions. I can bring oil and amphorae with me from Greece in time for the harvest and fill them up to take back.'

Naghi raised an eyebrow and Cosmas hurriedly continued.

'Of course, I see no reason why we cannot both share. As you say, there will be customers in Ctesiphon and the satraps all over Persia who will want the fish eggs.' Rat smiled softly. 'As I said it is God's bounty.'

'And that of Azhura Mazda?'

'Whatever,' said Cosmas, crossing himself. 'You sell exclusively to the Persians and I sell to Rome.'

'I will also need amphorae and olive oil to transport them?'

'I am certain that you can find those without my help, I will bring my own overland.'

'Then when can I meet this contact of yours to seal the deal?'

'Tomorrow, hopefully,' said Cosmas. 'I should be getting back to the others, they will be wondering where I am.'

'Oh, you are still with the crippled old charioteer and disgraced general?'

Rat cursed internally. He should not have revealed that.

'One provides the coin, the other the amusement,' he said glibly.

The Persian spy grunted at that, but did not stop Cosmas from leaving once the arrangements were made for the next day. The two of them shook hands and the Rat headed back to the caravan compound on the outskirts of Atil. Theo's Goths were there, with the horses and tents, eating some pungent stew and muttering in their guttural Germanic language, but Theo, Cal and the young monk were missing.

'Now, where have they got to?' said Cosmas.

He pondered quizzing Godda or one of the other Goths, but he did not know Gothic and their Latin was worse than his. He wandered back to the gates of the compound, still wondering where the others had got to, when some running children caught his attention. They all seemed to be heading out of the city in a great rush. He grabbed one grubby little urchin.

'What is happening?' He asked in Hunnic.

'There is going to be a race,' said the child. The Roman emperor has sent his pilot as a challenge to our champion.'

'Oh, Lord God,' groaned Cosmas. 'What have they done now?'

8

The Atil chariots were not imperial quadrigas fit for the hippodrome. There was no carriage or side rail, just a wooden crossbar fixed to the yoke at the front for the pilot to grasp. Two rough planks were strung between the wheels above the axle with animal sinew for him to stand on. The wheels and axle themselves were well made, Cal concluded, which was the main thing. The only metal on the machine was two thin strips of iron binding around each wheel rim – no bronze axle cap, just a wooden peg holding the wheels in place. The two horses harnessed between the yoke at the front were short scruffy animals like Angai's pony. Cal looked them over. They were not old, or broken, and better than the nags Narses had seen him hobbled with at the hippodrome back in Constantinople.

'Good animals,' he said. 'And the chariot is sturdy enough.'

'Are you sure?' said Theo doubtfully.

'Do we really have any choice?'

'No.'

The Hunnish watchers explained the ruled to Petros, who then relayed them back to Cal and Theo. The race would be along the river to a white stone and back to the city gates where a finish post had been set up. They would have to do two circuits of the course, with the first back to the post declared the winner. The local champion was a small wiry man with greasy dark hair and dirty face. He grinned at Cal, a broken toothed smile, and the charioteer smiled back. The chariot might be a wreck, the horses' barely broken donkeys, and the track a wild course through the wilderness, but for Cal it felt like his childhood in Africa. He had raced small chariots like this around his home town for training as a boy, and for the first time on the mission

Cal actually felt of use. He climbed into the chariot and stood waiting for the start of the race.

'You had better win,' Theo told him.

'I always win.'

'Losing is why you are here,' Theo pointed out.

That brought the charioteer back to the present. This was not some dusty ravine in Africa with his fellow slave boys racing for cups of wine; this was his granddaughter's future.

The fat headman of Atil had been carried out of his hall and through the town on a cushioned litter, bringing crowds of townsfolk along with him. He reclined with a cup of kumis on his litter to the side of the two chariots, chattering away to his grovelling courtiers about the display. The Atil champion stepped into his chariot after a few words with the headman, and nodded that he was ready. Everyone in the crowd looked to Cal.

'Are you ready?' asked Theo.

'Yes,' said Cal, and nodded to the headman.

The chief raised a grubby white cloth with his hand, and they watched and waited in anticipation. Then he dropped his pudgy hand to start the race, and both pilots screamed and whipped their pair of horses up into a burst of energy, dragging the rude chariots along with them in a rattle of dirt and dust that sprayed the spectators at the starting post.

Cal felt the sudden jerk as the horses took off; a familiar pull and rush of air as he cracked the reins. It brought a wide smile to the charioteer's face. The Atil pilot had gone straight into the lead, moving about twenty metres ahead of the African as he raced along the dusty riverbank. A crowd of children and youths ran after them, or had already taken position along the course, shouting and screaming encouragement at the two racers.

'Well that does not bode well,' said Theo to Petros, as the two chariots sped off along the riverbank with Cal trailing behind the local pilot.

Cosmas was just coming over the pontoon bridge as the two chariots took off. He could see the stocky frame and tight white curls of Cal dressed in his leather kilt and shirt and a small barbarian in the other vehicle disappearing off into the distance upriver.

'What on earth have they done? They warned me not to cause a scene and they go and do this.'

He saw Theo and Petros standing near the Chief of Atil, and pushed his way through the crowd to get to them, tugging at Theo's arm as he arrived.

'What on earth happened? Did you get drunk?'

Theo was relieved to see Rat. Cosmas' absence had concerned him as well as the young monk's broken Greek. Now he could speak properly to the chief and explain that no insult had been intended by their embassy.

'I had barely a sip of kumis,' Theo told him. 'The charioteer went wild with one of the chief's men and threatened to beat him into a pulp.'

'That does not sound like Cal? He's a grump, I grant you, but not often a brawler.' He gave Theo a sly wink. 'That is more your turn.'

'Not this time. The man grabbed at young Petros, here, and Cal took offence.'

That stopped the Rat's brevity. He started babbling away to the young monk in her Hunnish tongue, and then in a quieter tone at the answers. Theo did not understand the conversation, but he could see the worry on Rat's face.

'What is it?'

'They are not racing for our right to pass. It seems that one of the old men at court took a fancy to our translator.'

'What?'

'He is not racing to prove his honour, as such. He is racing to stop Petros from falling into the old man's clutches.'

'We cannot let that happen to the boy.' Theo was outraged.

'Ah, yes, well, there is something else that I should tell you.' He leaned over to whisper in Theo's ear. 'The boy is actually a girl, well a young woman really.'

Theo was stunned into silence, he had not expected that. He looked at the pretty young monk and then back to Cosmas and back to the girl again.

'Oh I hate you, Rat. What have you done?'

'Not me, it was Narses.' Cosmas looked around. 'Best I explain after the race.'

'Best you do,' said Theo grimly. 'And best you hope that the African wins this race for yours and her sake.' He gave the girl a reassuring smile and she blushed. 'I am going to let Cal beat you next time.'

'He always wins,' said Cosmas glibly.

'No, no he does not.'

'Almost always.'

***

The broken ground was like a hammer on Cal's knee; bouncing, bouncing, bouncing, every jolt shooting agony up his leg into his groin. The barbarian pilot was still twenty metres ahead of the old charioteer, but that did not concern Cal. He wanted to know what line to take on the wild course; he watched intently as the man led the way along the riverbank, following along in his wake. His team was fast, he could feel them responding to his twitch of the reins or flick of his whip, and the machine was well made if crude in construction.

I can win this, he reassured himself. I am Porphyrius the Charioteer. I am Porphyrius the Great.

They raced along the riverbank, whipping past stunted trees and brown grass to their left, with water and mud to the right. The track was well worn and baked hard in the summer sun, flatter than the Via Ignacia with its deep ruts and potholes back home in Greece, and as flat as the sand in the hippodrome. Cal could see he was gaining on the barbarian, as he tried to take a tighter line behind him, but Cal noted every landmark and obstacle on the route as they raced along. He would wait until the second lap to try and take the lead. He treated it like a new course in Antioch or Alexandria, not a wild ride on the steppe. The barbarian looked behind a couple of times at him, grinning that Cal was still trailing. After nearly a mile of rolling along the riverbank, Cal could see a tall rock bleached white by the sun and weathered by the wind ahead of them. It looked like a single column of marble glistening in the sunlight.

That must be the marker, thought the old man.

The barbarian raced down to the rock column and turned sharply, jerking his chariot around rather than a smooth turn. Cal realised why at the very last minute: water and mud just beyond the rock made the turn treacherous. He yanked his reins to the left as hard as he could, dragging his pair of horses into the tight turn, and sliding around the white rock in a shower of dust and pebbles. Then he whipped the animals up into a gallop again to try and catch up with the barbarian.

'Now I have you.'

The route back was slightly different, avoiding the drops that they had come over on the first half of the course as they raced back to the town. Cal was gaining on the barbarian, but the man kept his team stubbornly ahead of the old man. More and more children lined the route as they came closer to Atil, with Cal only a few metres behind the lead chariot; breathing in the dust and being hit in the face by grit and stones thrown up from the barbarian's wheels.

Theo and Cosmas saw the two chariots approaching as the crowd raised up a great cheer.

'He is still there, he is still there,' shouted Cosmas bouncing up and down and grabbing hold of Theo's cloak. The aristocrat brushed the Rat off.

'He is still losing,' he pointed out.

Cosmas fixed Theo with a patronising smile. 'He is Porphyrius the Charioteer, young man. You never saw him in his prime, and even as an old man Narses had to fix the race.' He waved at the two chariots. 'This barbarian doesn't stand a chance.'

'Best you are right.' Theo was still fuming that he had been duped about the young monk's identity.

'I wonder if I can get a bet on?' Cosmas looked around.

As Cal and the barbarian turned around the post set up before Atil the old charioteer took a wider line, whipping and geeing the horses up as he came out of the turn and tearing the chariot forward in a rush. The crowd screamed and yelled louder than the hippodrome itself, and the old man cockily waved at them as he slipped into the lead, giving a quick glance behind at the barbarian pilot.

'I told you so,' said Rat to Theo.

'That is only the first lap.'

'Pessimist,' said Rat.

The crowd had moved further along the course now, all the way down to the white rock marking out Cal's route. He took the same line as before, making spectators jump out of the way to avoid being crushed under his wheels as he flashed by. His knee was throbbing in agony, his back ached, but he felt utterly exhilarated behind the reins. At the white rock, he skidded around spraying watching children with dust - who screamed their delight in response. Cal grinned as he whipped the team up to speed again. The barbarian had only just started his turn behind and had gone too wide; he was slowing down, stuck in the mud. By the time the cursing pilot had his chariot moving again Cal was fifty metres or more ahead. There was no catching the African as long as his chariot held together.

'Look,' shouted Cosmas as Cal came into sight along the riverbank with the barbarian way behind. 'It is not even close. I should have wagered.'

The relief on Theo's face was palpable. Losing the monk could have finished their mission and Narses would not have been forgiving. As Cal crossed the finish line, Theo finally yelled in triumph along with Rat like spectators in the circus. Cal pulled the chariot up before the headman and stepped down, almost falling as his knee gave away. Cosmas, Theo and Petros quickly joined him. Theo held Cal up to stop him from collapsing.

'Tell him I have won and we have right to pass onwards to Samarkand,' Cal gasped out the words.

Cosmas waxed lyrical in the Hunnish tongue, quickly having the headman and his courtiers laughing at the beaten barbarian pilot who was just drawing his own chariot up, and smiling at Cal and the other Romans.

'He agrees,' Cosmas told them. 'We can go on to Samarkand and the boy is free.'

'Tell him also,' Cal gasped for breath. 'Tell him that I am Porphyrius the Charioteer, the greatest the world has ever seen or ever will see. Does he acknowledge my victory?'

'Don't you think that's more than a trifle vain, Charioteer?'

'Just do it, Rat.'

Cosmas relayed the old man's words to the court and they nodded and the headman pulled out the diadem that Theo had gifted him earlier. He threw it to Cal who deftly caught it in one hand and tucked it in his jerkin.

'You have earned it, Cal,' the Rat told him. 'But you insulted him at the end.'

'This diadem will pay off Calista's debt when we get back home.'

The headman's litter bearers picked up their chief and carried back through the gates and over the pontoon bridge into Atil's citadel with courtiers in attendance. The rest of the crowd started to disperse now that the excitement was over. The teams and chariots were taken away, leaving the Romans unsure of what to do next, and then Naghi the Persian appeared.

'Well, well, that was exciting, Cosmas. Well met again, Master Dagisthaeus, Master Charioteer.' He bowed deeply at the Romans. 'Did I hear you say that you were going on to Samarkand?'

9

The weather turned suddenly after the race as dark clouds like mountains rolled in from the Caspian Sea. A downpour of biblical portions fell on the rough trading town in only a few hours, turning the streets of Atil into a quagmire; slick mud up to the knees along the river wharfs. The dusty sun-baked steppe was transformed into a miserable wetland swamp, leaving all the travellers huddled on their boats or hiding in their tent sat the merchant compound. The locals seemed used to such sudden changes of weather, retiring to their small squat homes for the duration of the storm.

Cosmas slipped and slid along in the mud as he hurried back to the compound and his companions. The streets were empty as people sheltered inside from the storm, and he pulled his cloak around him to shield from the cold blasts of wind. The compound gates were unguarded in the rain, but the twins stood sentinel at the Roman tents with grim faces and water dripping down their chins. They did not welcome Rat as he arrived at the pavilion. Cosmas pulled open the flaps and stepped inside.

'Close the doors, it's damnably cold,' shouted Cal.

'Tents do not have doors.'

'Don't split hairs.'

'I have always wondered how hairs are split,' said Cosmas tying the tent flaps closed. 'You would need a very sharp knife.'

'Sharper than your wit.'

Theo's tent was the biggest in the party. He had used it on campaign in Lazica and it had been brought by his men from Greece. Some of the others had gathered there with the poor weather. Godda was the only Goth warrior present, as well as Theo and Cal. The girl was there still in her boy monk act, but the old monk Timothy was sleeping. He slept a lot, thought the Rat.

'Well?' asked Theo.

'Can I at least get dry?'

'No.'

Rat sighed, threw his wet cloak to the floor and sat down on some cushions, still pouring himself a cup of hot wine before answering.

'There is to be a wedding, but it works in our favour.'

'How so?'

'Angai's sister is to marry a great chief of the Goturks; a tribe to the East. He is the new King of the Sogdians and the steppe, so I am told. The headman of Atil is their uncle and he has arranged the alliance. It is why they wanted a Roman diadem.' He nodded at Cal. 'There will be a great caravan across the steppe to deliver her to him. We can join them. It will take us all the way to Tashkent.'

'I thought we were going to Samarkand?' asked Cal. 'Where is Tashkent?'

'We meet the others in Tashkent,' said Petros slowly, nodding. 'They wait for us there.'

'Samarkand was merely a decoy, Charioteer,' Rat said. 'Naghi and the Persians can spend their time searching the caravans and trails in Bactria, whilst we are going in a completely different direction.

'That is quite clever,' said Cal.

'Thank you,' said Rat. 'I thought so too.'

'What of the Persians?' asked Theo. 'Before you become too smug.'

'They are still here, the dromon could not leave with this weather so bad, but I am certain they will be gone as soon as the weather turns. The fish eggs will make him eager to get back to

Persia to open up the market and make arrangements for the egg harvest.'

Naghi had not pressed Cosmas for details of his journey after Cal had revealed Samarkand as their next destination. There was only one reason for a Roman mission to be travelling east over the steppe to the ancient city – silk. The Persian spy was certain to take that information back to his masters, and they were certain to put obstacles in the way of them returning out of mere spite, but if they found out the real reason for the mission…If they realised that it was not just a caravan of the material they planned to bring back, but the means to produce it that Theo and the others sought? Then the Sassanid Emperor would move heaven and earth to stop them stealing the trade.

'At the moment they think we have gold and plan on buying a caravan of silk to bring back over the steppe,' Cosmas explained. 'Other Romans have done it before and Samarkand is known to our merchants.'

'So they will not cause trouble?' asked Theo.

'Oh they do not like our merchants cutting them out of the trade, but I have given Naghi the fish eggs as well to sweeten him. By sending them to Samarkand we should avoid further complications.' He paused. 'So we take the caravan to Tashkent.'

Cosmas explained that there would be hundreds of people travelling together: Angai and an honour guard of Utiger warriors as well as his sister and her attendants. Merchants and travellers from all over the steppe had all joined the great caravan, seeing an opportunity to pass over the steppe in such numbers that the bandit tribes and raiders would be scared off.

'It sounds too good to be true?' said Cal.

'Oh you always have to complain, but there is one problem.'

'I knew it.'

Cosmas sniffed at him and turned back to Theo.

'What is the problem?' asked the aristocrat.

'Well, there are other tribes who don't so much like the idea of an alliance between the Utiger and these Goturks. The risk is they will try and stop the caravan and take off the girl into captivity.'

Theo spoke to Godda and explained the situation to him. The Gothic warrior was blunt in his assessment: Rat's plan was better than travelling the steppe in a small party.

'Godda agrees with Cosmas,' Theo told them after the brief consultation.

'I have always thought he was a man of good sense and refined judgement,' said Rat.

The Goth sneered at Cosmas and said something to Theo who giggled.

'What is it, what did he say?'

'It would not translate.'

The Rat's lips pursed at that but he did not press the point. There was going to be a grand celebration as soon as the weather turned, and people from all around would gather to bid the princess on her way. It would be a great party.

'I think that perhaps we should keep ourselves out of trouble after the race,' said Theo. 'We are supposed to be travelling in disguise but we seem to be declaring our presence to everyone we meet. Every merchant is a spy and there will be many in this caravan.'

'Not every merchant is a spy,' said Cosmas.

'You are,' Cal pointed out. 'Naghi is.'

'Nevertheless I think it best we stay here,' said Theo.

Cal and Petros both nodded: the charioteer because his knee hurt too much for a party and it would annoy Cosmas; the girl because she would agree with anything that Theo said. She was infatuated with the blonde aristocrat, Cal could see that. He prayed it would soon pass and she did nothing that would endanger the mission, but the girl reminded him of his granddaughter. Calista used to sneak out of the windows to go and meet her future husband. The last thing that Cal wanted was romantic complications in the group, but girls and boys think of only one thing at that age.

'But there is going to be a party?' Cosmas was distraught at missing the engagement; there was a whine in his voice.

'It will do you no harm to miss it,' Theo said.

'You don't know that.'

***

The great caravan stretched out for as far as the eye could see, winding its way over the dusty plains. Hundreds of people, thousands of animals – horses, mules, donkeys, even camels, strung together in long teams carrying goods bound for the strange kingdoms of the east. Four wagons with solid wooden wheels as tall as Theo trundled up front, each one drawn by twenty heavy set oxen, carrying Angai's sister and her attendants. The Utigers had brought an escort from Atil provided by his uncle, and all of the merchants had their own guards. There were perhaps three hundred men, well armed and trained, guarding the caravan – including Theo's paltry group of Goths, as well as all the merchants and animal handlers who carried weapons. It was an army on the steppe. The travel was slow, rolling along at the snail's pace of the wagons, but everyone understood it was safer than braving the plains in a small party.

'Slow and steady wins the chariot race,' said Cosmas when anyone complained about the pace.

'No it doesn't,' said Cal. 'You need to be fast and aggressive.'

'It was a figure of speech'

Theo galloped along the length of the caravan, letting his horse have its head, and throwing up dust in a clatter of hooves. Both of them, man and beast, were exhilarating in the rush of power and speed as they thundered past the merchants and porters. The caravan was like an army on the march to Theo's soldier eye. Angai had Utiger outriders on the flanks, and scouts ahead and behind watching out for enemies. They would be well warned if there was an attack.

'Here he comes,' said Cosmas, as Theo rode up.

'You have an irritating habit for stating the obvious.'

Cosmas's incessant babble was driving Cal slowly insane.

'Ah, did the grumpy old man have a bad night? Perhaps you should go for a nap grandsire. The girls in the wagons would welcome you and your rheumatic leg.'

'I am well enough, thank you.' Cal could feel himself blushing.

The charioteer was still suffering with his knee. After the race, Theo had had to carry him back to the compound in Atil. His knee had swollen up to the size of a melon, and every step was an agony; shooting pain up and down his leg. They had been fortunate that the caravan had taken two weeks to assemble, because Cal had been unable to walk for a week.

'Once I would have been up and about the next day,' the old charioteer had grumbled. 'Now I am crippled.'

Cosmas was merciless in his mockery of the charioteer, even when Cal pointed out that he had actually won the contest. Theo dismounted and walked alongside them, leading his horse by the reins.

'Well?' asked Cal. 'What is happening up front?'

'We will travel east until we reach another sea and then follow that around. One of the tributaries takes us all the way to the city of Tashkent. I think it is the Jaxartes River they mean, but it is a long time since I read my Ptolemy.'

'How long?'

'Oh, at least ten years.'

'Not since you read Ptolemy, how long till we get to Tashkent?'

'Oh, it is perhaps a thousand miles over the steppe,' Theo told him. 'It will be weeks before we reach the next sea.'

'Slow but safe,' said Cosmas. 'There are traders from all over in the caravan and the trail is well travelled.'

Theo nodded. 'Mostly it is Angai's people, but there are others with us, no other Romans, but Persians and Bactrians. They all seem to be merchants avoiding customs officials, but...'

'I do not think we can assume all Persians are spies,' said Cosmas. 'Naghi is certainly, but men who try to avoid customs officials tend not to work for the government.'

'Even if they are spies, what can they do?' said Cal. 'We are in the middle of nowhere.'

'We do still have to get back from Tashkent,' Cosmas pointed out. 'But I may have an idea there; we shall see when we get to our destination.'

Neither Theo nor Cal wanted to press Rat on his ideas. Both could see months of travel stretching out ahead of them. Theo was eager to complete the mission, but the charioteer just wanted to go home to his granddaughter.

The grassy steppe that they had travelled through since Taurica changed after they left the shores of the Caspian Sea. It became drier, dustier, and they choked on the clouds thrown up by the hooves of thousands of animals. The summer storms had passed, and the hot baking sun scorched the earth brown leaving only stunted shrubs and twisted trees as they passed. The Utigers knew where the waterholes were in the arid wastes, but for such a large party making sure the animals were fresh was the first priority, often leaving the humans on rationed water if there was not enough. Day after day of unchanging landscape, bare rocks and dusty desert, throwing up clouds from the hooves of their animals as they passed.

'I note that the young princess gets enough water to wash her hair,' said Cosmas, as they sat around the campfire. It had been six weeks of travel since Atil, and it was grating on them all.

'I note that you whine constantly,' said Cal.

'There is only a few more days and we will reach the next sea. Everyone can wash their hair then,' said Theo.

'Salt water,' Cosmas said.

'There are rivers feeding it. I spoke to Angai and he explained.'

'How did you speak to Angai without me?' Cosmas seemed affronted.

'Petros, here helped me, well Padma is her real name. I am teaching her Greek.'

The girl dressed as a monk beamed at Theo.

'We are supposed to be keeping her identity a secret,' said Cal.

'Oh we did,' said Theo, looking at the girl. She looked back at him, and the two of them burst out laughing at some private joke.

'Oh, Lord God, you are cruel,' muttered Cal.

'Well, what did Angai say?' asked Cosmas.

'We shall rest on the shores of the sea for a few days to refresh the animals and ourselves, and then follow it around the northern shore. Some will divide from us and head south to Samarkand.'

'The Persians?'

Theo nodded. 'Which means our little ruse for Naghi will soon be exposed.'

'What then?' asked Cal.

'We travel on to Tashkent with Angai. At least another two months travel at this pace.'

'Slow but safe,' said Cosmas.

'Not so much,' Theo told them. 'There are people set on stopping the wedding. We are passing near their territory now. They could attack us, if they can gather an army big enough.'

'We shall be safe,' Rat insisted.

Two days later they came over a rise and saw the inland sea, the northern shore stretching off and around to the east; the western shoreline going directly south. In the summer sun, with barely a cloud in the sky, they could see for miles and miles. There were small islands dotted along the coastline, but the land around was still arid desert akin to Cal's African homeland. Angai led them down to a fresh water spring with enough water to feed their herds of animals and people. The merchants pitched their tents and fires were set up. Some of the mule porters and merchants ran down to the beach to swim and wash in the sea, and a festival atmosphere came over the camp as they settled down to rest. Angai told them they would wait at least a week before moving on.

10

Half of the caravan departed south for Samarkand after three days camped along the shores of the inland sea. Most of the merchants with their long camel trains and teams of porters and animal handlers were heading for Samarkand in search of the silk caravans from the east. Angai's Utiger tribesmen, the wagons and the women, a few hardier merchants, and the Romans would all take the northern road. Cal and Cosmas watched the southern column slowly move off in a long winding line.

'Why do we not go that way if it is easier?' asked Cal.

'To the south is Kwarezem,' Cosmas replied. 'There are towns there, and forts, and soldiers; Bactrians, Huns, Turks, Persians and Hepthalites but they are constantly at war. It is easier to get to Samarkand that way, but far too much attention is paid by different the kings to the merchant caravans. They will travel that way to the oasis towns.' He waved at the departing train. 'But they will pay for it in excess tariffs. We shall go around the northern shore to the Jaxartes River and then follow that south to Tashkent.'

'It is bare desert,' said Cal, looking east along the northern shore.

'Angai assures me that there is water enough on the route for our party.'

'There had better be.' Cal did not feel convinced. 'I am going down to the sea.'

'Why?'

'I want some pebbles.'

'I think they have pebbles in Tashkent already?'

Cal did not answer him, walking instead down to the sea shore alone. There was a small stream that emptied into the sea snaking across the flat sandy beach. Cal followed it up the shore until he found what he was looking for. As the stream dropped to the beach from the dry steppe there was a pool with flat rounded pebbles at the bottom.

'Perfect,' said Cal, and waded into the water. He picked up one of the pebbles and hefted it; the stone fitted snugly in the palm of his hand. 'Good weight and size. These will do just right.'

He took out a flax cloth and began filling it with pebbles about the same size. Once he had about thirty of them, he climbed out of the pool and sat in the sand drying off his feet. Then he took out a leather sling he had fashioned himself in camp. It had been years since he had used one, but he had no sword or skills as a soldier. He could not wield a bow and arrow and had no time to learn, but as a boy he could hit a moving target at thirty paces with a slingshot. With a bit of practice he would at least have some means of defence if there was a battle.

'I should have thought of it before now.'

Cal had not left the Empire in his lifetime, Vandal Africa did not count, and indeed he had not even been near the borders where barbarian raids were commonplace. The charioteer had spent his life in the races of Antioch, Carthage, Alexandria and Constantinople and his retirement in Greece. Other than a small dagger, he had never had to think of barbarian dangers. They were a story Roman matrons told the children to make them behave. Gaul, Britannia, Hispania, the lost provinces were all so far away, and Attila and the Huns so very long ago. Now, he was in the middle of the Sarmatian steppe with a disgraced fop and a fool who thought the earth was flat. He needed something better to defend himself than just his wits.

'Let us see how much I can remember.'

He took one of the pebbles out and slipped it into the pouch of his sling, and hooked his finger into the hoop he had made at one end. Then he picked out a target perhaps twenty paces away, stood with his feet wide apart, and started spinning the sling around his head. Cal swung the sling slowly at first finding his rhythm, and then faster and faster whirling it around and around. When it was whistling in a circle above his head, Cal released the loose end of the leather, keeping his finger hooked in the loop. The pebble flew out of its pouch straight and true, thudding into the dune and sending up a spray of sand.

'That was easier than I expected.'

For the next thirty minutes, Cal swung pebbles at the dune. Mostly, they went in the right direction, some hit the target dead on, a few went flying wildly out of the back or side of the sling when he released them. As one went straight up in the air, and the charioteer had to quickly step to the side to avoid being crowned as it fell back to earth, there was a peal of laughter from behind him.

Cosmas had followed Cal down to the beach, curious as to what the old man was up to. He had kept his distance and watched from a dune as Cal fished the pebbles out of the pool, and started practicing with his sling. Rat was intrigued and amused: that the charioteer was able to use a sling was no surprise (most Roman boys were), but he doubted it would be of much use against a Hunnish bow. When the last pebble almost hit Cal on his head, Rat could not conceal his mirth.

'What are you doing, Cal? Do you think to scare away the Huns with a child's toy?'

'It is no toy,' said Cal sourly at the sight him. 'You have heard the tale of David and Goliath.'

'Oh yes,' said Rat cheerfully. 'But David was not a grumpy old man with a bad leg, and the Philistine was not a Hun with a horse and bow.'

'I am not so grumpy or old that I cannot break you, Rat.'

'So you keep saying, but you would have to catch me first, and...' he gestured to Cal's swollen knee. 'What is this for, Charioteer? You are not a warrior. That is not why Narses sent you.'

'I do not know why he sent me. Other than the race in Atil, I have felt next to useless on this mission,' Cal admitted. 'You know the route and can translate the languages. Theo has his Goths and the girl. I do not understand why Narses sent me, what use am I?'

'Narses is a snake,' said Cosmas. 'He wanted you out of the way and this was the means to do it.'

'Why did he want me out of the way, that is what concerns me. He had better not have harmed Calista.'

'Oh you know him better than that. He is a snake, but he will keep his promises.'

Cal nodded. That was true of the imperial secretary. He kept his promises. Cal remembered that from the old days.

'I am not sure he thinks we will succeed,' Cosmas continued. 'And, well, it would be convenient for him if you and Theo did not return – at least not empty handed. I have few who will speak for me or miss me. Being a truth teller about the nature of things does not win you friends among the powerful. There is a conspiracy in the highest echelons of power to suppress the truth of the world's flatness, you know. If we come back with the silk all is well for Narses. If not, well then, we are all expendable.'

Cal understood that as well, excepting the conspiracy and world's flatness which he dismissed as the Rat's foolishness. Theo's family had supported Narses and the boy's failure was an embarrassment for the eunuch. Cal was privy to dark secrets about the secretary's past and the Nika Riot, and Narses would not miss either of them should they be lost on the steppe. With

Cal, it would trim a loose thread that the imperial secretary had left dangling for decades.

'The Nika Riot was a very long time ago,' said Cosmas reading Cal's thoughts. 'Before the plague and famines. The Empress is dead and Justinian is old, nobody cares anymore.'

'And yet,' said Cal. 'Here I am in the middle of nowhere because of it.'

They returned to the camp and settled down for the rest of the day. Theo and his men were out hunting with the Utigers. The young noble had come into his own now that he had stopped drinking wine. Instead, he drank clear water from springs on the steppe that Angai showed him or weak kumis that had barely fermented. Godda, Beremund, and the rest of the bucellarii seemed impressed by Theo's transformation into a responsible officer and leader, and the Utigers were all impressed with the Romans' tall horses. Despite the long distance still to travel, Theo was feeling far more confident about the journey than his companions. The barbarians were well organised, for barbarians, and well equipped, and Angai was loved and respected by his people. The Utigers and Goturks were powerful tribal confederations that could protect the travellers, and both were worth cultivating as Roman allies. Theo could taste his redemption on the tip of his tongue. As long as the Charioteer and the Rat did not cause complications their mission would be a success.

Miserable old men, thought Theo as he rode back to the camp. They should be enjoying the adventure instead of complaining every step of the way.

The young girl was waiting for him. Theo grinned when he saw her. Padma still kept to her monk's habit, and in the confines of the caravan concealing her toilet was more difficult, but she and the young noble were fast becoming inseparable. Theo had been teaching her more Greek than Cosmas had managed, whilst she had been teaching him some phrases of the Hepthalite Hunnish language in return. When they reached Tashkent he would be able to act as a Roman ambassador of sorts. Theo pulled up and dismounted.

'Did you catch?' The girl asked.

'We found a herd of strange antelope,' said Theo. 'Deformed snouts, but the Utigers insist that they are good eating. There is enough meat for a roast today, and the Utigers will smoke some for the journey.'

Godda and the others had enjoyed the hunt as much as Theo, but it had been a salutary experience for the Goth warriors. All of them had sneered at the steppe riders' hooped saddles when they had first seen them, but in the twisting turning hunt on the steppe the value of the hoops had been proven. Llew and Asta had both been pitched from their mounts in the chase, but the Utigers sat stable on their horses laughing at them with their strange saddles. Godda and the others all wanted the saddles with hoops – a point they made quite forcefully to Theo. He was going to have to pay for them to have new saddles made in Tashkent for the Roman animals, but back in the Empire the hoops would be an innovation that could transform the army.

With the fish eggs and the silk and now the hoops, we have a fortune in our hands and my political redemption, Theo decided. He hooked his arm in Padma's and strolled back to the others whilst his men saw to his horse.

Cosmas saw the two of them approach the campfire and nudged Cal.

'Love's young dream,' he giggled.

'Don't give them ideas,' said Cal. 'We have enough trouble without Cupid's arrow causing more.'

'Was the hunt good, Theo?' Cosmas asked innocently as the couple arrived. 'Did you catch what you were looking for?'

'Antelope enough to feed us all, The Utigers tell me they taste good. I cannot wait for my first bite.'

'I wager you cannot,' said Cosmas with a salacious smirk at Cal. 'We all like our first bite. What think you, Charioteer?'

'I think that God put you on earth just to annoy me,' said Cal.

***

Cal had grown up on the edge of the great desert in Libya. His father had been traded over the sands, and had terrified a young Cal about the hellish journey that brought him to the slave market in Carthage. The charioteer did not relish the idea of dying of thirst on some sandy desert dune. When they finally broke camp three days later, he was relieved that the pace had picked up. Angai drove the wagoneers to push their animals harder, and there was a genuine sense of urgency over the whole party.

'There are enemies nearby,' Theo told him in explanation. 'Scouts came in last night. It is best that we move on quickly.'

More trouble, thought Cal.

Three days later that trouble became apparent to everyone in the caravan. As they crawled along the sea shore, dust clouds to the north gave warning of an approaching horde. Angai quickly had his sister's wagons halted and corralled with the remaining merchant camel train and Romans. Everyone was taking out weapons. Cal felt foolish with his bag of pebbles and leather sling, but still made sure he had a stone to hand.

The Utigers gathered together in three bands, with Angai leading the central group of horsemen and two flanking units covering him. Theo kept his Goths close as they followed behind the Utiger chieftain in the centre, with Godda barking orders at the men as they dragged on their mail coats and got their weapons ready.

Cal could make out figures in the swirling sand as the dust cloud drew nearer – horses and men –there were hundreds of them.

'Oh shit,' said the charioteer. 'Shit, shit, shit, shit, shit.'

The force that had arrived in a thunder of hooves was perhaps five hundred strong. Angai and his Utigers were outnumbered but not by much, thought Theo. Shaggy steppe horses and riders with bows and lances. Most were dressed in leather armour and barbarian trousers, but some had mail coats and helmets. The sun glinted off their iron lance heads as the enemy drew up opposite Angai's three divisions. The two armies began taunting each other as emissaries were sent out by the newcomers.

Theo gathered his bucellarii to him; all finally armed in metal and on their tall horses. The others all went to the corral with the wagons and women. Once he saw that Cal, Cosmas and the monks were safe, Theo led his men over to Angai.

'You cannot speak to them,' Godda pointed out in Gothic.

'Yes, but we know who our friends are and who are enemies are.'

'It would have been better for us to stay with the wagons and protect them.'

'Stay with the women? That is not like you.'

'We have a mission, Dominus. Do not forget that.'

There was a hint of a threat in that statement, but Theo brushed it off. If he had told the men to wait with the women, the bucellarii would all have been complaining about that whatever Godda said.

Angai noted their arrival and smiled and nodded as Theo's group of Goths took up a position at the side of his division. If nothing else, thought Theo, we have earned some trust with Angai and his people. Then he looked to the front, the Utiger emissaries were already returning from their short discussion with the enemy.

'I do not know who we are fighting for, who we are fighting against, or why we are fighting in the first place,' said Theo to Beremund. 'Only that we must fight.'

'That is what it is to serve Rome,' said the broad Goth to his lord.

As the emissaries returned to Angai, the Utiger host let out a great scream that was matched by the horsemen on the opposite side. The sound of the shouting hosts boomed around the dusty plain. Theo and the Goths joined in the wailing, yelling at the tops of their voices along with the Utigers. Then a horn blew from someone – Theo was not sure if it was friend or foe – and the central division of the enemy host moved forward at a trot.

11

Theo had fought mounted archers in Lazica. The Sassanids were masters of the art, but they fought in organised divisions with officers and banners and generally on a small field somewhere where everyone could see everybody else. This was a wild race, swirling clouds of dust, flashes of enemies and friends fighting in the mêlée; arrows flying through the choking orange sky; men falling among the horses, screams and shouts. There were horn calls in the madness, but none of the Romans knew the commands. The bucellarii kept close to their dominus, hacking at any enemies that came near Theo with their spathas or stabbing down with their long spears at men on the floor. They crested a rise and the fighting cleared around them. Theo turned his horse and looked back. The dunes were full of battling warriors but there was no telling which side was which. The barbarians had all merged into an unidentifiable mass of struggling men. He counted his own men; there were two missing. Sylvester the Italian and Asta the young retainer from his family's estate had both been lost in the rush. Theo's stomach turned over in guilt, he had known Asta all his life. The aristocrat prayed that the two were merely missing in the mêlée.

'It seems you were correct,' he said, turning to Godda. 'We should have stayed with the wagons.'

The old warrior nodded and pointed back to the wagons. 'That group is going for them, Dominus; we can still make a difference.'

A small party of fifty barbarian attackers had gone around the melee in the dunes to assault the caravan where the princess, and Cosmas, Cal and the monks, were hiding.

'We can be of more use over there,' said Godda.

There was urgency in his voice and Theo agreed with his judgement. He should have listened to Godda earlier; it would have saved two of his men's lives.

'Back to the wagons to help them,' he shouted at his bucellarii.

Godda smiled with grim satisfaction and looked over at Beremund, who nodded. It had taken Theo some time but he had come to the correct decision. The Romans formed a tight wedge around their dominus as they rode around the dunes to get back to the caravan, loosing arrows at enemies as they went – or at least Theo hoped they were enemies. The bucellarii would hit the attack on the wagons in the rear at full pelt and cut through them to save the princess.

'Follow me!' screamed Theo as his horse pounded over the sands.

Cal could see that a group of attackers had broken off from the chaos in the dunes and swept around the battle to come straight at the wagons. Angai had left a few guards with his sister, all well armed and in mail coats, and the other merchants and porters were all grabbing weapons of sorts, but they were too few against a determined assault by real warriors.

'Stay with the monks,' he told Cosmas, and weighted a stone in his sling.

'Gladly,' said Rat, and scarpered back to the two Nestorians. Padma was standing watching the battle with terror in her wide brown eyes, but Brother Timothy was sitting on the ground hugging his staff with his eyes closed as if in prayer. The fool is napping whilst the barbarians swarm, thought Cosmas.

'Get down,' he shouted at Padma. 'A stray arrow can still kill.'

The girl nodded and crouched down with Brother Timothy, but the old monk did not acknowledge her. Rat joined them on the floor, and they crawled under one of the great wagons to watch the fight unfold. The old monk did not complain as the other two dragged him with them. The four wagons and merchant animals made a compound of sorts, with the wagons forming a wooden wall to face the oncoming enemies. Merchants had stacked their boxes and goods to the sides giving extra defence, whilst the animal handlers had driven most of the camels and pack mules down to the waters away from the battle. It would be winner takes all for them.

Cal stood with some of the Bactrian merchants and Utiger guardsmen as the enemy horsemen tried to go around the wooden wagon wall and into the corral. He swung a stone at one of them, but did not see if it made its mark as he reached into his sack for another. There was a groan from behind as one of the merchants collapsed with a black feathered barb sticking into his chest. Cal ducked down as the oncoming riders unleashed a hail of arrows. More men were falling around him, but the charioteer was unharmed by the first volley.

'Shit! Shit! Shit!'

The raiders burst into the merchants' corral, pushing boxes and baggage out of the way, and cutting left and right at the fleeing traders. Two of them jumped from their horses straight onto the back of a wagon where they were promptly swatted off by Utiger warriors. There were screaming women inside the cart; it must be the princess, thought Cal. One of the defenders fell out of the wagon with a black arrow at his throat, and more riders were appearing.

Cal understood full well how hooves could crush a man, and leaped out of the way of the enemy horses, swinging a slingshot at one as they passed and cracking him in the back of the head. The raider slipped from his mount, stunned senseless by the pebble, and Cal leaped on him smashing him in the face with another stone, again and again until a red mist of blood sprayed up. He picked up the man's spear from the sand and looked around for a new enemy to fight. The old charioteer stabbed at one raider with his new spear, sticking the rider in the side as he sped past and dragging him from his horse with his other hand. There was a wide grin on Cal's face; he had not felt so alive in years. Then he ducked down as an arrow thudded into the wagon just above his head. Nor so close to being killed, he thought. Where the hell are Angai and the others?

Theo watched the raiders attack the wagon corral as his men charged down. Some of the barbarians had burst around the defences and into the compound itself, but more were circling around the corral loosing arrows at the defenders. They had not noticed the Romans approaching from their rear.

'Ready,' called Theo to his men.

Godda nodded beside him

'Now!'

His men loosed their arrows in a single volley, and then holstered their bows and drew out their lances in the space of two hoof beats. Theo did not bother to see where his arrow fell, nor did his men, simply using the training that had been drummed into them all since childhood. The young Roman aristocrat held his spear overhead in one hand as they crashed into the back of the raiders, stabbing left and right at his enemies, and feeling a moment of satisfaction at the suck from their bodies as he drew out the leaf shaped blade.

'Kill them,' he screamed at his men. 'Kill them all.'

The Romans were better armed and trained than this rabble. The barbarians' leather armour was like butter to the bucellarii's spathas and spears, whilst the Roman mail coats were impervious to the enemy weapons. Theo's spear stuck in one man's shield and he let it go, drawing his spatha from its jewelled leather sheath in one movement. Godda was at his side stabbing at them with his spear. The aristocrat could see some had started to flee as his men butchered them with brutal precision. At the front, the raiders attacking the corral were oblivious to the chaos that Theo and the bucellarii were causing. The raiders were still intent on capturing or killing Angai's sister as the battle in the dunes unfolded.

Cosmas and Padma crawled further under the wagon, still dragging the old priest with them, desperate to hide from the attackers. Rat noticed a fat purse dropped in the fighting. It was not his, nor the monk's, but just out of reach. It must be one of the merchants; he would have to go back out from under the wagon to get it.

'That is a most cruel jest, Lord God.' He started shuffling out to get at the purse.

'Where are you going?' shouted Padma, terror evident in her voice.

'Wait here.'

Cosmas crawled from under the wagon and right to the feet of an enemy who stabbed down at him with his spear. Rat rolled to the side as the man stabbed down again. Padma followed the Rat out from under the wagon, and tried to grab at the barbarian as he stuck out at Rat, but the warrior shook her off, punching her with the back of his hand and knocking her down. She had given Cosmas enough time to draw his petty dagger and stab the barbarian. The poor knife bent on contact with the stiff leather armour.

'Bugger,' said Cosmas. 'Brutus always has cheap utensils.' He had stolen the dagger from the fruit seller in Constantinople.

The barbarian tribesman grinned down at the Rat and raised his spear to stick him.

Brother Timothy, still sitting under the wagon, opened his eyes crawled out and stood up, quite spritely. Everyone turned to see what he was doing, even the raider. The old man simply battered the steppe warrior over the head with his staff. Cosmas saw the barbarian's eyes cross and then he collapsed to the ground at Rat's feet. The old Nestorian monk sat back down at the wagon wheel and closed his eyes again, still clutching his staff. Cosmas slit the unconscious barbarian's throat with his bent knife, and helped the girl to her feet.

'Are you hurt?'

She shook her head. 'Are we winning?

'I do not know.'

Cal was enjoying the battle. Once the initial terror had passed, he moved quickly and easily. It was much like being in the circus, perhaps he would have been a gladiator not a charioteer in the old days. His painful knee was forgotten and he wielded the stolen spear like he was a master, stabbing at any enemy who came near him. Three more raider corpses lay around him and his leather kilt and jerkin was splattered with their blood but Cal was unharmed. He could see more men arriving on horseback.

'Come on then you whoresons,' he screamed at them. 'If I am to die today I shall take some more of you bastards with me.'

The leader of the new attack lifted the jewelled front piece of his helm.

'You have never met my mother, Charioteer, and I can assure you that she is a respectable Roman matron from Ravenna.'

Theo had a wide grin on his face that matched the African charioteer's. The Romans had cut through the attack on the compound with ease, beating off the barbarian raiders who streamed away from the wagon compound back across the dunes. There were horn calls, signals from the battle in the sands.

'What is happening over there?' Cal asked Theo.

'That is a good question.' Theo said as he dismounted. 'Where are the others?'

Godda and the bucellarii were swift in mopping up any remaining barbarians in the corral, and the sight of Cosmas and the Nestorians unharmed at the wagons was a relief to both Theo and Cal. Padma rushed straight to Theo, but stopped herself from hugging him, just looking up into his eyes and touching his cheek. She wiped away a splatter of enemy blood from his face, and said something in Hunnish.

'I am unhurt,' said Theo in response.

A wide smile came over her face.

'It is Angai,' shouted Cal. 'It is the Utigers.'

The charioteer was pointing out to the battle in the Dunes and all of them rushed to see. Angai and his warriors were returning, with much smaller numbers, but cheering in victory.

'We won, Charioteer,' said Cosmas. He held up a purse. 'And I found some gold,' and then pointed at Cal's blood splattered clothes. 'I think you need a wash.'

***

It was not a victory. The battle in the sand had been a bloody stalemate that only ended when the attack on the wagons was beaten off by Theo and his bucellarii. The enemies had melted away into the dunes but they had not fled in disorder. That night was a nervous wait with all of them watching shadows in the darkness, terrified of another attack. As dawn broke, Angai left no time for recovery of the wounded or for seeing to burial of their dead. He had the wagons on the move as soon as there was enough light to travel, and it was a much tighter column than before.

The Romans took up position at the rear of the column. There had been grumbles from some of the Goths that their two fallen comrades received no Christian burial, but when Theo and Godda offered to let them go and deal with the cold corpses starting to decompose in the sand the bucellarii politely declined. It put an end to their grumbles and earned Theo more respect.

'You are winning them over,' Godda told Theo.

'By leaving our dead unburied?'

'It was the right thing to do and they know it. Warriors whine like hungry hounds and need a firm hand on their collars. They do not appreciate a weak leader that they can bully.'

Theo said nothing to that, merely nodded and kicked his horse up to a trot so he could ride with the girl. Throughout the day's travel there were alarm calls and shouts from scouts and once a small party of warriors rode out with Angai at their head. Enemy archers hidden in the sands poached at them as they passed. Three of the Utigers had been wounded. One had been left behind to die. The Utigers gave him a small flask of water and his weapons, but took his horse.

'The enemy will come for him,' Angai told Theo. 'He will make them pay, but we cannot carry him nor wait for help. That is what they want.'

The Romans plodded silently along on their horses after that. All still in metal armour, broiling in the hot sun, but the thought of a single wound leaving them alone in the dust fixed them in a single purpose – to survive. Cal and Cosmas fared better in their light clothes, along with the two Nestorians, but all of them were parched with thirst as the day wore on. The glistening salt waters of the sea to their right as they marched seemed to taunt them with the thought of cool draughts to drink.

'I would sell my own mother for a flask of cool water,' said Cosmas.

'Have you not sold her already?' said Cal.

'She died just before we left the capital, Charioteer.'

'Oh, I am sorry.'

Cal felt guilty but Cosmas burst out laughing.

'You are so gullible, Cal. My mother has been dead twenty years, and she was a horrible woman.'

Cal pursed his lips.

That night there was little sleep for any of them, although Rat happily dozed off under a wagon and took no watch. All of the Utigers had expected an attack in the darkness but nothing came that night. The next morning they moved off quickly again, but there was still no sign of the enemy. At about midday, with the sun high in the sky, shouts from the front of the column alerted the Romans that something was happening. Beremund pointed to a dust cloud approaching from the east.

'There is an army coming, Dominus.'

'Get your weapons ready,' Theo told the bucellarii.

All of them quickly took out their bows; whilst Cal grabbed the spear he had taken in the battle in the dunes, and fixed a grim look on his face. Angai pulled the caravan into a corral once more, keeping his mounted force close to his sister's wagons. Now they were all gathered in battles, Theo could see that the fight in the dunes had thinned out the Utigers considerably. Perhaps half of Angai's force had been lost on the journey, and now a new army was approaching.

'Over there,' said Cosmas. 'There are hundreds of them.'

Cal followed the Rat's pointing arm. Hundreds of horsemen were approaching over the dunes, even more fanning out to their sides and keeping to the high ground, perhaps a thousand of them in total. The Romans stared at this new force in despair. There was no chance of survival, there were far too many of them for the Utigers to stand against.

'Say your prayers,' Theo told his men. 'Make your peace with God.'

Beremund took out a golden bull pendant and kissed it, whispering quietly as the others crossed themselves and mumbled prayers.

Well, well, thought Cosmas. The big Goth is a Mithratic heretic.

As despair settled over the Romans, the Utigers suddenly let out a great cheer and wide grins came over the Nestorian faces and the other merchants in the corral.

'What is it?' asked Cal. 'What is it?'

The two Nestorians spoke excitedly to Cosmas and Theo, and Rat turned back to the stout African.

'It is the Goturks,' Cosmas told Cal. 'Their prince has come for his bride. We are saved.'

12

The Jaxartes River was the very edge of the known world, so Cosmas told them. From its mouth the course ran for over a thousand miles to the great mountains that bordered Serica. A wide, winding, slow running river that snaked across a vast floodplain with farms and small settlements littered along its banks. The Goturks had boats with banks of slave oarsmen waiting for Angai's party at the mouth of the river. This was an alliance between two great powers on the steppe. The Utiger princess and her attendants would take to the craft and be transported upriver to Tashkent. Cosmas, Cal and the Nestorians had found themselves a berth on one of the wide flat-bottomed barges along with the princess, but Theo and the bucellarii stayed with the animals and Angai as they rode alongside the river. Every night, the boats would moor up and campfires would be started on the riverbank. Theo would make sure to find them with Godda in tow. Just to make certain that they were all well, so he told Cal, but the charioteer noted that it was mostly the girl he talked to. The rest of the bucellarii pitched their tents with the merchants and animals.

'Even the great Alexander did not dare cross the Jaxartes,' Cosmas told them as they sat around the campfire. 'We are exceeding the greatest conqueror in history.'

'Greeks get everywhere,' grunted Cal.

Theo grimaced at Cosmas's words, and looked up from his conversation with the Nestorian girl. 'Alexander did cross the Jaxartes, I was taught that at school, and he won a battle against the Scythians on the other side. Then he founded a city and left a Greek garrison.'

'There are Greeks on this river, then?' said Cal.

'There were a thousand years ago,' said Theo.

'Haven't you been this way before?' The charioteer asked Cosmas. 'You said you had been to the edge of the world and seen the pillars of the sky.'

'Not this way, and not to Tashkent. We took a boat from Clysma and crossed the seas until we came to the Kingdom of Sindh. I took a boat up the Indus and saw the great mountains. We are on the other side of the pillars of the sky. To the far north, and there are the Hepthalites and mountains in between.'

'What of this Tashkent?'

'It is a city on the trade roads going east. It was ruled by Huns, then Hepthalites, but now it is ruled by the Goturks. The city is the halfway point on the road to Serica.'

In Tashkent the Romans would finally meet their contacts from Serica – Padma's sister who carried the secret of silk for them to take home. Theo would then need to find a way to get back from that far flung city to Constantinople. Cosmas talked of taking a ship from the Indies back to Egypt, but sailing boats across the oceans did not strike Cal as appealing. He could not swim and would rather take his chances with barbarian tribes on the steppe than drown in the oceans.

'Can we not come back the way we came?'

'That would be the most logical course,' Theo agreed, but Cosmas looked troubled.

'What is it Rat?' asked Cal.

'From Tashkent we can travel overland to the south. Through the Hepthalite lands to the seaports in Sindh. There will be other Roman merchants there and we will find a ship home with ease. It is longer in distance but perhaps much safer.'

The Rat had not enjoyed the journey over the wastes, and an ocean journey did not hold the same fear for him as it did Cal and the Goths. Cosmas had taken the monsoon winds to the Indies before and back with little fuss.

'You want me to persuade Godda and the others to take to ship?'

'They would have to leave their horses behind.'

'Then there is no possibility of it happening,' said Theo.

'They are only horses.'

'They love the animals more than their wives,' said Theo. 'I have literally watched Beremund go sleepless for a week nursing a sick foal. They will not leave the animals behind.'

Cosmas fixed a sour look on his face, but that was the end of the conversation. Theo went back to his men on the shore and they all settled down for the night. The next day boats continued the journey upriver. Like his men, Theo was much happier on horseback and had no desire to go sailing on rivers or oceans unless his Emperor commanded it. He had been seasick on the short crossing from Constantinople to Taurica.

'I do not have to worry about that now,' he said.

The Jaxartes valley and floodplain was a thriving community of friendly people that waved as the bucellarii passed by with their Goturk lords. Angai rode with his own companions alongside the bridegroom. Theo had not managed to catch the Goturk lord's name, but he was young and a great warrior according to Cosmas. Angai's sister would lead a pampered privileged life, but she was still a brood mare as far as the Roman could see. He did not want that for himself; although his mother and grandfather had both talked about marrying him off to some maiden full of virtue before the disaster in Lazica. The problem with maidens full of virtue, as far as Theo could see, was that they were utterly boring conversationalists.

'Not the Empress Theodora,' Godda told him with a salacious smirk. 'She was an *actress*.'

'Not the old Empress,' Theo agreed, 'but can you imagine what my mother would say if I brought an actress home to marry?'

'Oh yes, that I can.' Godda's grin grew wider. 'Do you think they have actresses in Tashkent, or are you planning on seducing the lady monk?'

'You are an evil old man.'

Godda just laughed at his lord.

The land they passed was full of small farms and rude settlements. There were stone built towns along the river, nothing of civilization compared to the great metropolises of Rome or Persia, but it was encouraging. Men, women, and children tended the fields together watching and waving as they passed.

'The people seem happy enough.'

'People always smile to their master's face,' said Godda.

'Does that include you?'

'Of course, Dominus, you should hear what we say about you behind your back.'

Theo was not sure if the old warrior was jesting.

On the boats the travel was leisurely and relaxed. The slave rowers worked as a team speeding them upriver. Cal was bored after only a couple of days, leaning over the side of the boat and watching the green lush farmland irrigated by the waters of the Jaxartes as they floated by. The Rat joined him.

'You can go blind if you stare to long at the water, Charioteer,' Cosmas told him. 'The sunlight glinting off the ripples will give you headaches.'

'What is this land called?' Cal gestured to the settlements.

'This is Sogdiana, technically part of the Hepthalite kingdom, but the Goturks rule here and only pretend to obey the southern kings.'

'And Alexander came here?'

'To the southern bank; he may have crossed as Theo says and fought a battle but he did not stay on.'

'And the river takes us all the way to Tashkent.'

Cosmas nodded. 'There is a great mountain range, I have only seen the foothills from the south, but other travellers have told me. Beyond the mountains is Serica and the silk, the source of this river is in those mountains.'

'So these others will have come from Serica, over the mountains?'

'From what I gather from the girl, but she seems to speak to Theo more these days.' There was a hint of jealousy in Rat's voice and Cal laughed. Cosmas frowned. 'Why all the questions on geography, Charioteer, I have explained this before?'

'Perhaps I shall write a memoir when we get back?'

'I did not think you could read and write.'

'You thought wrong.'

'I may write a memoir also. Our journey will prove that the world is flat.'

Cal had no response to that.

Theo and the bucellarii were enjoying their days now that the riding was easy. The land was rich and fertile near the river, with green fields on terraces fed by the waters. The young noble was fascinated by the crops. His family grew grapes and olives at their villa in Greece, but these terraces were something new.

'What grain is that?' asked Theo, pointing at the waterlogged fields.

'I know not,' Godda told him. 'It would rot the roots of the vines at home.'

The crops were laid out in regular lines with women knee deep in water tending to them, their skirts hoisted up to their waists as they bent over. When the column stopped at midday to break in the hot sun, more women brought wooden plates with food and cool draughts of beer for the men. Theo took a platter but declined the ale.

'Even the beer?'

'Best to not,' said Theo regretfully. 'I have fresh spring water in my sack.'

Nevertheless, he looked enviously at his men as they all drank deeply. The food that the women had brought was some sort of grain, soft and brown. He sniffed at it, there was a spicy aroma.

'Barley polenta?' he said.

'Rice,' said one of the women and smiled at him.

Theo had heard of rice before but never tasted it. He picked up a spoonful of the grain and sniffed at it then put it in his mouth. It was spicy and soft, the individual grains were plain and tasteless, but sweetly flavoured with nutmeg and fruits.

'It is good,' Theo told his men.

Theo gobbled the dish down, the grain was filling and tasty, but his bucellarii merely picked at the food, happily drinking the ale instead. There were grumbles when it was time for them to mount up and move on. Theo, jealous at their indulgence, barked at them to hurry up and they were soon following along the valley.

For the rest of the afternoon they rode near dozing in the saddles at the leisurely nature of it all. A direct contrast to the hellish race they had endured from Atil and it lulled them into complacency, but the sound of shouting made Theo look up from his horse.

There was a barefoot young boy on the edge of one of the fields. With dark hair and dressed in grey rags. He was desperately trying to stop his goat from eating the rice plants whilst also avoid a beating from one of the farmers. Theo was still irked that he had not taken ale with his men, and it put him in a foul temper as he watched the scene. The farmer towered over the boy waving his stick, but the lad could only have been ten or eleven years old at the most and he looked tiny in comparison. Theo kicked his horse and led it over the sodden field to the confrontation before Godda or Beremund could stop him.

The two brown faced peasants looked over as Theo approached on horseback followed by his bucellarii. Godda was not going to let Theo wander off unprotected, and if their noble dominus was going to be a fool then he, Beremund, and the other Goths wanted to see.

The farmer with the stick turned back to the boy and his goat, and started waving his stick around menacingly and shouting at the lad in an indistinguishable tongue. Theo grimaced, he had forgotten about the language issue. Their little party had been travelling together for months and had grown accustomed to each other. They could communicate even when they could not talk the same tongue, but Theo had no idea how to speak with the two Sogdian peasants.

'Stop!' he shouted at the farmer. 'Stop, I say.'

The man turned back to Theo and started shouting back at him, pointing furiously to the goat and boy and waving his stick, and then waving it at the bucellarii who had trampled his crops with their horses. When the stick got too close to the young noble, Theo reached out with a gloved fist and grabbed it, twisting it out of the farmer's ham hand with ease.

'I said stop!' He threw the stick on the floor at the farmer's feet.

The man started shouting at Theo, ignoring the warriors at the aristocrat's back, berating him in the strange language.

The commotion had not gone unnoticed by the Goturk column. The Utigers were laughing at the scene and Angai sent a man over to see what was happening. The problem still being that none of them spoke the local language and the Romans still could not talk to the Utigers or Goturks without Rat or Nestorian girl present. Theo realised all of this as he sat dumbfounded on his horse.

'Did you have a plan when you decided to intervene, Dominus?' asked Godda.

'No.'

Godda looked down at the furious farmer and crouching boy – the goat was still eating the plants and the bucellarii's horses had torn up the neatly dressed field.

'Give him a coin and let's be on our way,' said Godda. 'We are making a spectacle and drawing attention to ourselves.'

Theo agreed. He took out a solidus, a gold coin that was a month's pay for one of his men. The glint caught everybody's eye as Theo flicked it up, spinning in the sunlight, and then caught it in his gauntlet. The farmer had stopped shouting at the gold, and looked with new respect at the horsemen.

'I said stop,' said Theo again. He flicked the coin at the farmer who caught it deftly. 'That will pay for your plants.' He gestured to the boy. 'You can leave him and his goat alone.'

The man looked nonplussed for a moment and then nodded and took the coin. He barked a couple of sentences at the boy and then turned on his heel and left. The goatherd looked up at Theo with a fearful look.

'There you go, lad, have no fears. I have bought him off.' Theo smiled down benevolently at the boy.

Pleased with himself, Theo and the bucellarii turned and rejoined the slow moving Goturk column on their horses. The boy took out a scrap of rope and tied it around his goat's neck. Then he shrugged and followed on after them.

'He is following us,' Godda told Theo.

'He will get bored soon enough.'

The boy led his goat alongside the Romans, keeping his eyes down as they plodded along for hours in the afternoon sun. When they set up camp that evening, the boy and his goat sat at the edge of their fire. Fritigern gave him a bowl of flat bread, dried fruits, and a cup of ale.

'We cannot let him starve, Dominus,' said the huge Goth to Theo.

The lad took the food and drink gratefully, beaming a wide smile at the massive warrior. Fritigern smiled back and patted him gently on the head like a puppy. Just before nightfall, Cosmas arrived from the boats where he had irritated Cal so much the charioteer had threatened to throw him to the crocodiles.

'I do not think this river has crocodiles,' Theo told Cosmas, and then showed him the boy and goat. 'Explain to him that he should go home and the farmer will not beat him again.'

Cosmas sat with the boy and chatted away for a few moments in Sogdian, and then burst out laughing. The Rat turned back to Theo.

'He is not worried that the farmer will beat him, he is worried that you will or perhaps worse…'

'Me? Why would I beat him?'

'Well, it seems you did not just pay for the damage to the farmer's crops, you bought the boy as well.'

'What? I have no need of a slave.'

'You see, he has heard lurid tales about the treatment of young boys in decadent noble households, so he is understandably concerned. The whole world knows of the debauched court of Justinian in Constantinople.'

'Well you can assure him that I am not like that.'

Cosmas gave a wicked grin. 'Oh I already have.'

'So why does he not just go home, I have no need of a slave?'

'He has no home to go to. They were glad to see the back of him and his goat, it seems. He is an orphan.'

Theo was left with little choice. He could have abandoned the child on the riverbank, but the boy had already wormed his way into his men's hearts with his big brown eyes and scruffy dark hair. There would be outrage among the Goths if Theo abandoned an orphan on the riverbank.

'Well I suppose he must come with us then,' he said, grudgingly.

Cosmas spoke quickly to the boy who smiled and said something in response.

'The goat too?' asked Rat.

'The goat too,' said Theo, with a sigh. 'At the very worst we can eat it.'

Cosmas explained that to the boy who smiled and nodded and said a few words. The Rat turned back to Theo.

'He says his name is Uba.'

13

The city of Tashkent was on a tributary of the Jaxartes not the main river as Cosmas had assumed. The great boats that had carried the Princess upriver moored up at a stone built jetty and the whole party disembarked. Cosmas and the others rejoined Theo and the Goths on horseback to ride the rest of the way. Angai's sister was to be transported with great ceremony to Tashkent in a processional column. The Romans were placed at the rear once more, as the procession took a long winding ravine northwards from the great river. Cosmas stayed close to the young goatherd Uba, asking questions of the local area and people.

'Information is always the most valuable commodity,' Rat told Theo. 'Narses knows that better than anyone.'

'Has the boy told you anything useful?'

'Not so much,' admitted Cosmas. 'He is a Sogdian. They have had Bactrians, Persians, Alexander, Hepthalites and now Turks rule over them in times past. He knows some words of all of the languages, he could be useful.'

'What of this Istami?'

'He is the rising power on the steppe. The Goturks are strong and the Hepthalites weak. It will not be long before even the pretence of service will be ignored. A war between the Goturks and Hepthalites is coming. This marriage is part of that. It will be an alliance between the Turks and Angai's people from Atil. There will be many different tribes gathered in Tashkent.'

Theo could understand all that, he had been raised in the Roman court, but the last thing they wanted was to be dragged into local politics.

'How soon will this war start, from what the boy tells you?'

'We shall see when we get there, but I would guess in the spring. It is autumn now and the winters are hard. I do not think there will be fighting before then.'

The terrain changed as they moved northwards through the ravine, rocky with little vegetation, and always climbing, covering the Romans in a grey dust thrown up by the thousands of hooves. The procession wound along at a slow crawl, but there was a celebratory atmosphere in the party after the long journey. For two days they followed the ravine until it opened out to a wide plain with great mountains in the distance rising up to the heavens.

'The pillars of the sky,' said Cosmas pointing. 'They are what stop the heavens from crashing to earth.'

'They are just mountains,' said Cal. He had grown up in the foothills of the Atlas Mountains in Africa.

'Bigger mountains than I have seen anywhere in the Empire.'

'It looks just like the mountains of Norica in Italy,' said Theo. 'They can't be that big.'

'It is called perspective, Theo. The pillars are bigger than the Alps,' insisted Cosmas. 'Much bigger. Just you wait.'

'If things go well,' said Theo. 'This is as close as we shall ever get.'

They travelled on in silence for the rest of the day, and camped down alongside the tributary that flowed back to the Jaxartes. The next morning the procession set off again with the Romans at the rear. About midday, they crossed a rocky rise and saw their destination for the first time. A stone walled city rose up out of the plain on the banks of the river where it widened into a small lake. There was a great citadel at the city centre visible for miles, and scores of tents outside the stone walls. Camel trains and merchants had gathered in Tashkent before the winter snows came.

'It is the halfway point to Serica,' said Padma in her broken Greek.

'Only half way?' said Cal in a moment of panic.

'We will meet the others here,' she smiled at the old charioteer. 'My sister will be among them.'

One of Angai's warriors rode over from the head of the procession, speaking slowly to Cosmas and the Nestorians. The man turned away to ride back, but shouted something over his shoulder at the Romans.

'What does he say?' asked Theo.

'We are to camp outside the walls with the other merchants. There is a compound prepared for travellers, but he says there is snow coming. We will need to buy furs.'

'Snow?' Cal looked at the clear blue sky. It was colder certainly, and they were higher, but surely it was too early in the season for snow.

'Once the snows come we are stuck here till spring,' Cosmas told him. 'And the winter comes early to Sogdiana.'

The charioteer sighed. It would be months until he saw his granddaughter again. The old man had already had enough of the adventure; he just wanted to go home now. The girl squeezed his arm, understanding his misery.

'I see my older sister soon,' she said in her broken Greek. 'She comes from Serica. It has been three years since I last saw her. And you will see your granddaughter again, Cal.'

'And you are sure she will be there.'

'I am sure she will come, perhaps in the spring if the snows are early, but she has never let me down.'

They camped down with the other merchants outside the city walls, and Theo gave Cosmas some coin and sent him to find them all furs and clothing for the winter.

'I am not sure that this will be enough,' said Rat, looking at the silver coins in his palm.

'Then haggle.'

The Rat hurried off into the winding streets of the city, taking the young goatherd Uba with him. Tashkent meant Stone Tower, referring to the citadel at the centre of the town and the tall walls surrounding it. Inside, the city was well ordered and prosperous; it had grown wealthy on the silk trade as a meeting place and a melting pot. Rat saw Kushans from the Indies, Sericans, Bactrians, Persians, Sogdians and Hepthalites, as well as the new Goturk overlords who now ruled the town.

'Prince Istami does not live here?' Cosmas asked Uba.

The boy shook his head. 'He travels with his men but he will come here for winter.'

The Goturks were the new rising tribal power on the steppes, Cosmas understood that, but the danger to trade was also obvious to the little Alexandrian. There was a hungry new power on the rise, and a weak empire ripe for plundering nearby. It was a recipe for a war, thought Rat. A return journey over a battling steppe will not be easy, even if we meet our Nestorian contacts here. The Rat was still convinced that travelling over the great mountains was the best option for their return.

'I have never seen the sea,' said Uba.

'Oh it is very big,' Cosmas told him.

They found a merchant inside the town that was happy to trade for the Roman coins and soon hurried back to the others laden down with furs. As they arrived back at the camp a snowflake settled on Uba's nose and the boy giggled.

***

A Goturk warrior stood before Godda barking at him in a strange language, but the tall Goth would not let him pass and was starting to get belligerent himself. The argument was causing a scene on the edge of the traders' encampment. The snow had laid a sheet of white over the land, but it was not yet thick, and the other merchants and travellers outside Tashkent's walls looked over at the confrontation. The problem, again, for the Romans was language. Cosmas could speak most tongues but the Turk speech was new to him, and Uba the Goatherd spoke only a few words of the language. The warrior was gesticulating at Godda and clearly annoyed with the Goth, with his right hand laid casually on the hilt of his curved sword.

'What is going on?' asked Theo. 'You are making a scene.'

'I found this one messing with our horses.'

'What?' Theo turned to the Goturk warrior. 'Cosmas!'

Rat grabbed a Bactrian spice merchant that he knew could speak the Turkic language and arrived in short order at Theo's shout.

'Ask him what he wants?'

Rat asked the merchant and the merchant spoke, respectfully, to the Turkic warrior. The Goturk said one word in response, and the merchant fell to his knees leaving the Romans dumbfounded.

The Goturk warrior took off his helm to reveal a young beardless face and dark hair. His eyes glinted with amusement at the merchant falling on the floor before him, and he smiled at the Romans and started speaking slowly to them. The fur merchant, with his eyes still to the floor, translated for Cosmas, and Rat translated in turn for Theo and Godda.

'This is Tardu, son of the Great Khan Istami. He wants to speak to the Roman general.'

Theo pulled Godda back and stepped forward to face Tardu the Goturk. 'What does he want?'

'He wants to know why you do not bow before him.'

'Romans do not bow before anyone excepting their own Emperor,' Theo said.

'This emperor, is he a good warrior, a good rider?'

Theo paused before answering that one. 'He has never known defeat.'

Tardu laughed at that couched answer and spoke again to the prostrate merchant.

'Only a man who has tasted defeat truly understands victory.'

'Damned barbarian is a philosopher', muttered Godda.

Tardu continued talking and the chain of translation kept up.

'Angai tells me that you are brave men, and that your lands are rich and your emperor is powerful. You are to attend to my father tomorrow. He wishes to speak with you.' Tardu kicked the translating merchant. 'You need not bring this wretch. We have one who can speak your language.'

Tardu looked intently at Theo after these words for a few moments, and then turned away. It was not a request it was a command. Theo understood that as he watched the warrior's departing back.

'What now?' he said to the Rat.

'Now we have to give him the diadem,' said Rat.

The charioteer will not be pleased.

Cal was huddled by the campfire, miserable and aching. His rheumatics were up; his hands red and swollen and his knee was agony. The cold weather made him feel every single one of his sixty three years. The others might be enjoying the mission, but Cal still just wanted to go home. The news that he was going to have to give up his diadem to the barbarians barely bothered him, to Cosmas' surprise.

'Will it be warm in the citadel?' was all he asked.

'Probably,' Cosmas told him. 'There are healers here, Cal. They will have something to help you with the aches.'

Cal just grunted and turned back to the fire.

The Rat watched Cal's back for a moment and then turned to go and find a healer for the old man. Cosmas liked the charioteer and he knew that a potion of poppy infusion could help Cal. There was certain to be someone selling it in the city.

***

'I feel like Priscus visiting Attila,' said Theo.

'You should,' said Cosmas. 'I have been asking questions of the Sogdians about this Istami. Perhaps he is a new Attila.'

'How so, we have heard nothing of him at home?'

'They rule the steppe. Istami and his elder brother have unified the tribes and now control the plains from Serica to Chersonesus.'

'He has an elder brother?'

'They call him Bumin, I do not know if that is a name or a title, but he rules in the east and Istami rules in the west under him. They want to make contact with Rome which is why we have piqued their interest.'

'And Angai told him all about us of course,' Cal felt faintly betrayed by the Utiger warrior.

'The people of Atil care only about trade,' said Cosmas. 'A strong ruler on the steppe makes trade easier and all of them wealthy.' He gestured to the walls of Tashkent. 'It is the same here. The tribes do not live in the town, rarely visit, leaving only a small garrison at best. People can go about their lives in peace. The trouble comes when a new power rises and shakes everything up.'

'The Hepthalites?' asked Cal.

Cosmas nodded. Rat had tried to explain the complex politics of the East to his Roman compatriots at the start of the journey, but had found them with the same dismissive attitude to the world outside the Empire shared by most Romans abroad. They were all now having to reassess that, Rome was just a big fish in a very big sea. For Cosmas, ever fascinated by the new and strange, the barbarian lands offered opportunity and knowledge. For the others it shook their sensibilities. Theo could see the politics of the situation, and Rome's advantage, but he also understood the threat to Rome if a new enemy appeared on the Thracian border.

'Well I shall enjoy the feast at least,' said Cal

Theo and Rat gave each other a quick glance; the poppy infusion had eased the pain in Cal's joints and left him with a happy smile on his face.

'Do not drink too much wine with the poppy juice, Cal,' said Cosmas. 'Else you will sleep and not wake.'

'It is good food I want instead of salted fish or salted pork or hard stale biscuit and beans.'

The Romans pulled out their best clothes for the audience with Istami, at least Theo did. Rat and the Charioteer were clean if nothing else. Theo put on his dress armour, after Uba had polished it up to a shine, and a soft woollen cloak dyed deep red by his mother. He had Godda and Beremund similarly dressed and polished ready for parade.

'We represent Rome,' he reminded everyone. 'I am Magister Militum of the Empire and a direct representative of Justinian in this land. We are ambassadors, so let us try not to start a war.'

'You will not be drinking then,' said Cosmas.

'I will not be drinking,' said Theo. 'If we insult these barbarians I doubt we would leave this place alive, but even if we did the Emperor would not thank us for sending another Attila hurtling towards Rome. Better they go south to the Persians rather than west to us. You have the diadem, Cal?'

'I did win this fair and square,' Cal told him. 'I expect to be recompensed when we return home.'

'If we get home you will be as rich as Croesus.'

'I just want enough to pay off my granddaughter's debt.'

Theo took the box containing the crown off the charioteer and gave it to Uba. He had forced the boy to bathe and fitted him in clean clothes and new sandals. The lad did not complain; he was expected to carry the diadem when they presented it to Istami.

'That diadem has got us halfway around the world,' said Cal, 'in one way or another.'

'We have to get ourselves halfway back,' said Rat. 'Hopefully it will pay for that passage as well.'

Padma and Brother Timothy remained at the compound with the bucellarii. Cal had been keeping an eye on the growing romance between Theo and the young girl. The two of them were spending more time than was seemly together teaching each other their languages. That was the excuse anyway. They always seemed to be laughing to Cal. Young love, thought the charioteer; it causes more problems than hate. Helen of Troy, Cleopatra, love caused them all trouble, and their peoples.

'You are a miserable old cynic, Cal,' Cosmas told him.

'Some people say a realist.'

The Romans were escorted by Goturk warriors through the wide well ordered streets of Tashkent. The city was grown prosperous on the silk trade. There were craftsmen, metal workers and smiths of remarkable skill, masons and woodworkers, spices from the Indies, silks and all manner of trinkets and inventions that passed down the road from Serica. Cosmas informed them of all this as they walked with their escort to the citadel.

All the raw materials from the steppes, all the furs and leathers and the metal ores from the mountains were sucked into Tashkent and transformed into crafted goods that travelled the length of the road. At one end was the Empire of Serica and at the other Justinian's Rome. The Goturks, Bumin and Istami now controlled the middle. The Hepthalite White Huns were a fading power, just as Attila had faded before them.

'What of the Persians?' Theo asked Cosmas as they walked. 'Where do they fit into this?'

They fight the Hepthalites but have lost repeatedly. The rise of the Goturks is something the Sassanid Emperor will want to exploit, but I do not think he wants to send his armies here. It would be too costly and he risks Justinian taking advantage in the west. But Rome cannot fight against the Persians properly with most of our armies in Italia. If the Hepthalites can be crushed and the Goturks contained, The Persians can turn west against us.

'Is this not all highly speculative,' said Cal. 'The distances are vast.'

Theo shook his head. 'The Persian Empire is massive; we have always known that the Eastern satrapies were rarely brought against Rome. There has been a whisper of war keeping the Sassanids busy, and one thing is certain.' They all looked at him. 'Belisarius and our field armies are in Italia. Asia, Syria, perhaps even Egypt are vulnerable if the Persians start a real war. We need to make a good impression on this Istami. These Goturks could be useful to our Emperor.'

'We are just here for the silk,' said Cosmas.

'We are here for Rome,' Theo corrected him. 'We can let Istami know that the Empire is his friend and Justinian will thank us for it.'

14

The citadel of Tashkent was old, built of giant sandstone blocks fitted together so tightly there was no need of mortar. A stone gatehouse and tall walls with battlements and towers guarded the approach to the citadel. It was a mighty fortress surrounded at the centre of the city with a large garrison of Goturk warriors and the locals able to man the walls. It would take a powerful army to besiege and capture Tashkent, Theo concluded. He had taken nearly seven thousand men to Petra and failed dismally, it would take ten times that to assault these walls and the attackers would bleed men.

'I would not want to assault here,' he told Godda in Gothic. 'It is stronger than Petra.'

'Start fires at the base of the walls and crack the stone,' said Godda, he gave a sly glance at Theo. 'And always make sure that you have scouts sent out in case of relief.'

Theo grimaced at the barb. 'As they loose arrows at us, crush us with boulders or burn us with sand?'

'And boil us with water, and they have naphtha here.'

'How do you know?'

'I took a walk around; they have barrels of it stored in the towers. We can thank the Gods that Rome will not send us here to assault the place.'

Theo grimaced again. 'You never know with Narses, but if they have naphtha it must have come from Rome?'

'The Rat and his merchant ilk would sell their mothers, whatever the Emperor's customs officials say.'

Cal and Cosmas ignored the two warriors' Gothic conversation; neither of them knew the Germanic tongue. Rat helped Cal along as the charioteer leaned heavily on the slight Alexandrian and his cane.

'It is the cold that gets to me,' said Cal. 'At home it is just a twinge, here it is agony.'

'The poppy is helping?'

'Yes, but if I take too much I sleep too long and wake exhausted.'

'Do not take too much, else you may sleep forever.'

'It tastes too foul to be habit forming.'

'I would not count on that,' said Cosmas. 'It is a powerful potion.'

The feast was being held in a great hall at the centre of the citadel. Delicate mosaic floors and slender columns built by master craftsmen greeted them. Silken tapestries and painted sheets hanged down from the ceilings, shimmering as people passed by. There were great tables set up before a dais in the centre of the hall, already filled with Goturk warriors and their allies. Coarse drunken steppe tribesmen waited on by the grim-faced Sogdian servants. The arrival of the Romans had started a babble of conversation in the hall as they were brought forward to the dais.

'Not much to look at is he,' muttered Cal.

Istami the Great Khan of the Goturks and lord of the western steppe, was a chubby black haired man in his fifties; short and squat, even seated, and with a wide grin and laughing dark eyes that flashed when he was angered. He beckoned the Romans forward and began speaking to them quickly in his own tongue.

The four of them all looked at each other and then at Cosmas.

Rat merely shrugged. 'I have no idea what he is saying.'

'Get the diadem out,' hissed Theo to Cal.

Cal reached into the bag carried by Uba, and pulled out the jewelled diadem wrapped in a linen cloth. The court all watched intently as he unwrapped the package and revealed the crown.

There was a gasp of wonder from the audience and Angai, seated at Istami's left hand, spoke to the Great Khan in excited whispers.

'He is telling them we are from Rome, ambassadors of the Emperor,' said Cosmas.

The khan beckoned to Cal to rise and approach the dais. The charioteer stood up and stepped forward holding out the diadem and keeping his eyes down. Istami ignored the crown and reached out to rub Cal's head, fascinated by the tight white curls. The charioteer flinched back at first, taken aback by the familiarity, but he had been born a slave, he had enough women, and men, do the same for luck when he was in the hippodrome. They were always fascinated with his hair and surprised at how soft it was. It was still an insult and as a free man Cal would have beaten anyone who dared rub his curls, but in the court of the Great Khan he swallowed his honour. After a few seconds, Istami stopped rubbing Cal's curls and took the diadem from his hands. He held it up for all to see as Cal stepped back and rejoined his comrades.

'What now?' he hissed at Theo.

Istami was talking directly to them but paused at their blank looks and then beckoned one of the Sogdian servants to him. The man cringed at the command from the khan, but turned to the Romans and addressed them in perfect Greek.

'The Great Khan welcomes representatives of Rome to the feast and to his wedding. The Great Khan wishes you to enjoy the feast and thanks you for your gift. He says that the snows are coming now and you are welcome in Tashkent through the winter.'

The slave gestured for the four Romans to be seated at the end of the table with other foreign dignitaries and guests. They bowed to Istami and were shown to their seats by other Sogdian servants.

The rest of the audience and guests turned away from them as other gifts and visitors were presented to the Great Khan. The Romans had been early in the procession, a sign perhaps of their lowly status to the Goturks and the far distance of Rome. There were others from closer that were more important: dark skinned merchants from the Indies with spices and gemstones brought over the great mountains, Sericans with gifts of silk and strange laminated armour from their lords. There was a vast array of steppe chiefs, princelings, lords and ambassadors gathered together for the wedding.

'It is like Trimalchio's feast,' muttered Theo.

'By all the imps in hell, he has found us,' said Cosmas suddenly.

The others followed his glance to the entrance hall.

Standing at the back of the procession waiting to be presented, with his own guards and servants carrying gifts for the khan, was the Persian spy Naghi. As the Romans all looked over at him, the Persian caught their glances, recognised them all, and smiled back at them. Then Naghi turned back to the Great Khan to present their gifts from the Sassanid emperor.

'What now?' asked Cal.

'He has no idea why we are here,' said Cosmas. 'None of them do; we just relax and act like the ambassadors that we are.'

'But when the other Nestorians get here what then?' said Cal. 'There will be Persians dogging our every step home.'

'Perhaps it is time to discuss going over the mountains again...'

'No,' chorused Theo and Cal together.

Godda nudged Theo. 'You are making a scene, Dominus, people are watching.'

Theo nodded and gestured to the others to be silent as the gift giving ceremony proceeded. Naghi was one of the last to present his chests to the khan, filled with amber and gold from the Sassanid Emperor, and then he was seated close to Istami's right hand.

***

The snow was thick in Tashkent, trapping the inhabitants inside their homes. Streets were cleared of drifts by householders, but the ground was hard and icy. After the feast, Theo had managed to take a house in the town arranged by the Great Khan's officers. It had stables for their horses and a walled compound to provide protection. There were other merchants and foreigners in buildings nearby. The foul weather had driven the wealthier travellers into the city to hide from the elements. The merchants left in the caravan park outside the walls were frozen and there was word of disease among them.

Cal point blank refused to leave the buildings once they were ensconced. He bathed his knee in hot water every morning and night, and sipped at the poppy infused wine to dull the pain.

'You can all bugger off,' he told Rat. 'When the spring comes and the passes are free to travel then we can talk about leaving. Until then I am going to sleep and eat and drink and nothing else. Do you understand?'

'We may have to make a fast exit,' said Rat to him. 'We shall have to move out of the house once the Nestorians arrive.'

'They are not going to arrive in the middle of a damn blizzard, now are they? Talk to Theo, I have literally no interest in you until I get some warmth in my bones.'

Godda and the other Goth warriors had camped down in the stables with their horses. There were always a couple of men on guard, but mostly they sat playing dice and drinking. Like Cal, they had no desire to go out into the winter wasteland outside. The whole city huddled down as the snows piled up. Theo found himself with his coarse bucellarii more often; either them or the girl. Sometimes he would play dice with Fritigern or Beremund, but mostly he sat and listened to his men. It was the first time he had really bothered about the warriors that served him and his family. For days as the snowstorms raged they talked of home, of their wives and children. Llew regaled them all with tales of Britannia and wars with the Saxons. His father had been a petty king or chieftain among the Britons before the scout had come to Rome. Theo was embarrassed that he knew so little of their lives.

'You are finally learning how to be their lord,' Godda told him. 'You should have done this years ago.'

'I was spoiled,' admitted the noble.

'We did tell your Dada to beat you more often,' said Beremund.

Theo smiled. 'My father was a gentle man.'

'That Tardu is at the gates of the compound.' Baros, one of the twins who were on guard duty, poked his head into the stable. 'He says he wants to see you, Dominus.'

'He is speaking in Latin?'

'He has the Greek slave with him; they kept saying your name over and over.' He sniffed. 'It was not so very difficult to figure out.'

Theo and Godda both got up and put on their cloaks to go outside, wrapping the furs around them to protect from the cold.

The Khan's son stood in the courtyard of the domos with the other twin as Theo and Godda came out of the stables. Tardu was all smiles and big brown eyes, opening his hands wide at the sight of the Roman general. The Greek slave accompanying him looked relieved to see Theo, and Tardu pushed the man forward to speak to them.

'Dominus,' said the Greek. 'My master wishes to speak with the ambassadors of Rome. He has questions to ask, should you be willing to answer.'

'Of course,' said Theo, quickly. 'We would be honoured to answer any and all questions he has of us. Please come inside the house. It is but a humble place not suited to Rome's embassies but all we have.'

The slave relayed Theo's purposefully diplomatic words to the Goturk, and Tardu smiled and strolled towards the buildings. Theo, Godda and the slave followed on. The others all looked up as the newcomer strode into the house. Rat leaped to his feet, but Cal merely grunted and turned back to the fire.

'Get us some wine,' Theo hissed at Cosmas.

Tardu sat next to Cal on cushions by the fire and smiled at the charioteer, reaching out and rubbing his head. Cal endured the humiliation with barely contained anger.

'What does he want?' he asked Theo.

'He has questions of Rome,' said Theo.

'Then tell him that if someone did that to me in Constantinople, I would break their hand off and beat them to death with it.'

'I am not telling him that,' said the Greek slave.

'Then I will beat you,' said Cal.

Tardu looked in askance, as the Romans all glared at the slave. The poor Greek bowed and muttered something to the Goturk, who whipped his hand away from Cal's head and stood up and bowed to the charioteer. He kicked the slave, but Theo held up his hand and smiled.

'Tell him it is of no matter, different lands have different customs.'

'Arms still break the same way,' muttered Cal.

Theo ignored the charioteer and gestured for Tardu to be seated. The young warrior sat again next to Cal and spoke quickly.

'He humbly begs your apology,' said the Greek to Cal. 'In faith, I have never seen one of them apologise for anything.'

Cosmas brought a small amphora of Bactrian wine that he had bought in the market and some clay cups and set it down in front of them, and then he sat next to Cal and peered at the steppe tribesman. Theo joined them as the Greek slave stood by his master and Godda perched on a bench by the door.

'What does he want to know of Rome?' asked Theo.

For the next hour Tardu quizzed the three Romans on their homeland: the customs, the crops and people, the Emperor and his family. Theo and the others answered honestly enough, but they were more evasive when it came to the Emperor's armies and forces.

'He asks why you are Romans if Rome is not yours?'

'How does he know that?' said Theo quickly.

'News travels,' said the slave glibly.

'Well it is out of date,' said Theo defiantly. 'The eternal city is not the centre of the empire, it is true, but Justinian's writ reaches across the old Empire to the Pillars of Hercules as in times past. Even Gaul and Britannia now bow down to the Emperor's sovereign power once more.'

The Greek relayed the words to Tardu who nodded, and then he pointed to Cal again and spoke to the slave.

'He wants to know if this one is a devil. I have said he is from Nubia.'

'I am from Proconsularis,' said Cal.

'Tell him that this is the greatest charioteer that has ever lived,' said Cosmas. This is Porphyrius.'

'No,' said the slave with wide eyes. 'Are you Porphyrius the Great? I thought you were dead.'

'Well I am not dead,' snapped Cal. 'Everyone thinks I am dead.'

'See, Cal,' said Rat. 'You are famous even at the farthest ends of the world.'

The slave spoke to Tardu – more than a mere sentence of explanation – and gestured to Cal. The tribesman sat upright at the slave's words and a wide grin came over his face. He spoke quickly to the slave who relayed it back to the Romans.

'When the blizzards have stopped the ground will be hard. There will be a race in honour of the marriage.'

'The Goturks have chariots?'

'Oh, no,' said the slave. 'The Sogdians do and the Bactrians. They race around the city for prizes from the merchants. The Khan has tolerated the practice, but with you as the Goturk champion it will bring them honour.' He paused. 'They do not really mean honour as we would. It is more like avoiding embarrassment.'

'Then tell him that Cal will be happy to serve,' said Theo.

'Is nobody going to ask me?'

'You are the charioteer, Cal,' said Cosmas. 'Perhaps Narses knew why he sent you after all. There is none who can match your skill, remember you won in Atil.'

'Tell him,' Theo insisted.

The Greek slave relayed the Romans message to Tardu who stood up and made to leave.

'He will inform his father,' said the Greek. 'You must come,' he said to Theo. 'The Khan will wish to hear of this.'

'You two stay here,' Theo said to Cal and Cosmas. 'Come, Godda.'

The Goth warrior and Theo followed Tardu and the Greek slave back to the citadel.

15

The wedding celebrations consisted of three days feasting in the citadel, with the chariot race arranged for the last day after the ceremony. Theo spent his evenings in the company of Angai and his Utiger warriors as a guest of the Great Khan. He had managed to avoid drinking any of the imported Roman wines or local spirits that the Goturks and Utigers guzzled with abandon without insulting their host, and his rank as ambassador of Rome gave him gravitas in the court of the steppe lords. There were others gathered for the ceremony, not least Naghi and the Persians, but the absence of any Hepthalite envoys was notable.

'The Hepthalites do not want the Goturks ruling the steppe,' Cosmas told Theo the next day, as he sat outside their domos watching the previous day's snow melt in the noon sun.

'Yes, obviously, but it is poor politics not to send an embassy. It means war is close.'

'Why?'

'They see no need for diplomacy. Justinian would have sent an embassy to test the waters and spy whilst he gathered the legions to fight. The Hepthalites do not bother. It is a mistake that I think they will rue.'

'You are an expert on steppe politics now?'

'I grew up in the court at Constantinople, Rat,' said Theo. 'It matters not if it is a yurt on the steppe or a palace in Greece, the principles are the same.'

Cosmas sniffed. 'Well, let us hope we are long gone before the fighting starts.'

Theo agreed with him: it was not their fight, and the Emperor would not thank them if they failed in their mission for silk whilst starting a war.

'What of the wedding?' asked Cosmas.

'Tomorrow night,' said Theo. 'It is to be held in the hall of the citadel.' He glanced down at Rat. 'We have been invited, you will make sure to have washed?'

'Is that diplomacy and politics as well?'

'No, you simply stink like a sewer. Where is the girl?'

'She is in there with the charioteer.'

Theo left Rat lazing in the winter sunshine and wandered into the domos to find Padma. Now that they had arrived at Tashkent, and given her disguise had worn decidedly thin, she had taken to a dress and leaving her cropped head uncovered. The raven black hair was growing out thick, but still looked like a legionary short cut. Theo's bucellarii had been nonplussed at the sight of the boy monk suddenly transformed into a young woman, and he had noted that their general manners and behaviour had improved. Beremund or Godda were quick with their stick should one of the men utter a coarse expletive or salacious comment in front of her.

They are treating her like she is a princess, he thought.

He found Padma sitting with Cal inside their rented house. It had once been the spacious home of a rich Sogdian merchant. All of them had separate chambers with a large hall at the centre of the stone building and a great hearth and tables for meetings. The African was rubbing some ointment into his knee that Padma had found in the markets.

'Does it help?' he asked Cal and pointed to the ointment.

'Not so's you'd notice.'

'Why do it then?'

'I am somewhat of an enthusiast.'

The girl giggled at the old man's words. 'I think he enjoyomplaining.' She looked up at Theo with shining eyes and a wide smile and he beamed back at her.

'What do you call an element that always complains?' said the Charioteer, interrupting the love-struck pair.

Theo and Padma both looked at him. 'I know not,' they chorused together.

'A lament,' said Cal chuckling as the other two groaned.

'Oh that's terrible,' said Theo. 'A mercy you were a charioteer and not an actor.'

'Everyone's a critic,' said Cal. 'I think I shall go and find the Rat and annoy him. The ointment seems to be working today.'

'I told you it would,' said Padma. 'My sister will know better, she is a great healer.'

'Let us hope she comes soon then,' said Cal. 'For my knee's sake. Where is the Rat?'

'He is outside.'

Cal hoisted himself out of the chair and left the young couple alone. He had no desire to be their third chariot wheel. Cosmas was still lounging outside in the sun with his eyes closed.

'Did the young lovers chase you out, Cal?' he said without opening his eyes.

'Sort of,' admitted the charioteer. 'What are you doing?'

'I am contemplating a bath.'

'You need one,' sniffed Cal. 'Do they have bathhouses here?'

'I am told that there is one down by the southern gate.' He opened his eyes. 'It is not going to be as comfortable as home.'

'I think I shall join you. A good sweat will do my knee wonders.'

Cosmas sighed. 'Come along then,' he said sitting up. 'It gives them some time to themselves as well.' He nodded inside. 'She spends most of her time with Theo or Brother Timothy these days.'

'You sound like jealous lover?'

'She is a good conversationalist.' He stood up. 'Now I am stuck mostly with you, and you are an old grump who does not appreciate my wit. Come along then, old friend; let us go for a soak.'

Cal started to chuckle. 'Who told you that you had wit?'

The local bathhouse was a crude affair compared to Constantinople. A slave girl took away their dirty tunics to clean, and they sat in stone baths worn smooth by thousands of people sitting and cleaning themselves over the years. There was no olive oil, only stinking tallow soap which Cal and Cosmas both sniffed at and used reluctantly. Hot water was provided by another slave who poured it over their heads, scrubbed them both down and then ushered them into the steam room. Both of them sat for an hour, ladling water onto hot rocks and sweating out the dirt of the steppe. Afterwards, a slave swilled them down again with buckets of icy cold water that made their skin sting after the heat of the steam bath. Their clothes, cleaned and pressed dry, were returned and Cosmas gave the owner a silver coin.

'Where did you get that?'

'I have some means, but in this case I took it from Theo's purse. I am certain that he would not begrudge us. You know that we are being followed?'

'What? Where?' He looked around nervously.

'Don't look around,' groaned Rat. 'Oh he has gone now. You will never make a spy, old man.'

'Who was it? I did not see him.'

'One of Naghi's men, I think. It was a Persian not a Sogdian or Goturk.'

'That man is going to be trouble, I think.'

'He always is, but we are honoured guests for the wedding. It will send him and his masters in Ctesiphon into a panic.'

That brought a smile to the charioteer's face. 'Well then, it is good that we are clean for the wedding.' He looked pointedly at Rat. 'Especially you.'

***

The great hall in the citadel of Tashkent had been decorated with silken hangings and rich tapestries. Angai the Utiger was seated to the right hand of the Khan, facing the guests as the attendees entered and paid their respects. As the brother of the bride Angai was afforded honour by the Goturks, but the Khan still commanded the hall. Istami sat grinning widely at his new family members and allies, but his dark eyes kept moving, always watching over the guests like a wolf watching sheep. It was an all male affair; the women had been ensconced for three days with the bride making preparations for the ceremony. The Romans were seated further down from Angai in a place of honour for the feast. When the guests were all seated, Istami stood up and spoke at length in his own tongue, but none of the Romans understood the words. Cosmas had had little luck learning the Turkic language, complaining it was too different to the Hunnish to translate.

'What do you think he is saying?' Cal whispered to Theo.

'He is talking about war, look at their grim faces.'

At the end of the khan's speech there was a great cheer from the gathered nomads and warriors, and the Romans and other guests all joined in. There was a great shout and silence settled over the audience as Angai's sister was brought into the hall for the ceremony.

'She is stunning,' gasped Rat. 'I should have tried to make her acquaintance on the journey.'

'Her guards would have cut you down without a thought,' Cal told him.

The Utiger princess was dressed in a sheer silk robe dyed purple, her nipples erect and visible in the cold air, her body lithe and toned. The bride's face was painted white and her eyes were heavily made up with kohl, and lips painted blood red. Cal's jewelled diadem was on her head, worn like an Empresses crown, and intricate patterns had been painted in henna black over her hands and arms. She fair dripped in gold and silver jewels, and smiled at her groom who leered lasciviously back at her.

'Poor girl,' whispered Cal.

'She is going to be queen of the steppe,' said Rat.

'She is still a brood mare with no say in the matter. Istami is twice her age.'

'Your granddaughter married for love, how did that turn out?'

'Will you two be silent,' hissed Theo. 'People are looking.'

The ceremony itself was brief; a priest or shaman of the steppe presided over the couple, tying their arms together with a silken cord before making a great shout to the heavens and raising his arms. Then the couple tried to step on each other's toes whilst still bound together, giggling and laughing with all the men folk cheering them on until the girl finally let Istami step lightly on her toes. Cosmas was chatting excitedly with an Utiger asking the meaning of the ceremony and explaining it back to the other two.

'It is to symbolise who gets the last word in the marriage,' he told them. 'She was wise to submit. A good wife needs to know her husband is the master.'

'You have never been married have you, Rat?' said Cal.

'No, what has that to do with anything?'

'It shows.'

The couple was led off by cheering guests to the bedchamber as the rest of the womenfolk now came into the hall to join their families. Theo noted that the women walked proudly with their heads held high; there was no subservience and even the toughest warriors paid respects to the old matrons.

They are a strange people, thought Theo.

The celebrations continued long into the night. Utigers and Goturks all came to speak with Cal. Angai had told their hosts of Cal's victory in Atil, and all of the tribesmen were eager to meet the black demon who would drive their chariot to victory over the locals.

'I had best win on the morrow,' said Cal.

'You always win,' said Cosmas. 'Have another cup of wine.'

***

There was no hippodrome or circus in Tashkent, but chariot racing was just as wildly popular in the east as in the Roman Empire. There was a track around the stone walls of the city that started at the gatehouse. A single circuit was a two miles, and they would be expected to go around the course three times. Four teams had been gathered, three were local Sogdian racers used to the course, and the last pilot was Cal. News that Porphyrius the Charioteer was to race had brought the crowds out. The walls were packed with shouting spectators and food sellers. It was a fitting end to the wedding celebrations.

'Even this far from home you are famous, Cal,' Cosmas told him. 'You are the greatest charioteer to ever live.'

'Not true,' said Cal. 'Diocles was better.'

'Oh pish. Diocles has been dead for three hundred years. Who do you think this crowd has come to see? It is you, Porphyrius the Charioteer, not Diocles the dead man.'

'The Sogdians are here to watch Istami's champion humiliated.'

'True,' admitted Rat. 'But they are still here to see you.'

'To see me lose.'

'Well, we shall just have to prove them wrong then.'

'We?'

'Well, you.'

Cal grunted and climbed into the chariot, bouncing up and down to test the floor. 'It is solid enough, the wheels are good.'

'And the team?'

The horses were shaggy steppe ponies, just like in Atil, and nothing like the magnificent beasts bred for the hippodrome. The Sogdian pilots' animals were the same, but Cal knew enough of horseflesh to see that his animals were sturdy and strong. He just prayed to Saint Anthony that they were fast enough. He looked back down at Rat.

'They have come to see the Goturks humiliated. I have raced Bactrians before; they are good pilots and know how to race. Do not take victory for granted, Cosmas. I lost my last race in the hippodrome, if you remember?'

'And you won in Atil, and you will win here. Narses was no fool, he sent you because you would be useful.'

Cal grunted as he checked over the Persian chariot: smaller than a Roman quadriga and only two horses in the team. The wheels were well made, and ringed in iron and the machine was light but strong.

'I have raced in worse,' he told Rat.

'I will watch with Theo and the others up on the walls. Fortuna smile upon you.'

'Pagan heresy?'

Cosmas tapped his nose. 'We won't tell the Patriarch about it when we get home, if you win.'

Cal nodded and clicked his tongue at the horses to get them moving as he positioned the chariot at the starting post in full view of the city walls. The Great Khan was set up on top of the gatehouse with his court in attendance, all grim faced steppe warriors like his son Tardu. Theo and the others were further along the walls with the other merchants and Sogdian locals. Cal had walked the course the day before, when the slaves were clearing the track of the biggest snow drifts and packing down a space for the chariots to race. There had been only a light snowfall overnight, settling on the frozen earth. The other three pilots drew their chariots up alongside Cal, saluting to him.

I have to race all three, whilst all three have to beat me, he thought. They will play some tricks, of that I am certain. He glanced at the others. But I know some tricks of my own.

He looked up to the gatehouse where the Great Khan watched on, and waited for the command to race. Istami waited until everyone was in place and raised his hand, then dropped it in a chopping motion. Cal snapped his traces and called out to kick his team out of the starting position. Two of the Sogdians closed him in on both sides as a third with a red cap on his head leaped ahead of them.

He's their champion, thought Cal, these other two are just spoilers to interfere with me.

Cal could see that the two tail locals were trying to box him in, cutting close to his wheels to break out the spokes and send his machine smashing. Cal smiled, and twitched the reins to the side. His chariot veered straight into the chariot on his left, crashing into it in a flurry of snow and ice. The Sogdian pilot had not been expecting the move and the crash of the two machines tilted his chariot up onto one wheel. Cal grinned, reached out of his own chariot and gave the Sogdian a push with his whip. The man's teetering chariot went right over at the slightest touch, throwing the pilot clear as it crashed and bounced along. The horses still running wildly and dragging the wreckage through the snow, throwing up ice into the other pilots' faces. Cal cracked his reins and pushed his team on. The red pilot was still ahead of them, but Cal had pulled clear of the wreckage of the crash and the other trailing chariot.

Cosmas was panting by the time he reached the top of the walls and pushed through the cheering crowds to Theo and the girl. The two of them were becoming inseparable. Rat considered some smutty comment, but decided against it. Theo could be touchy about his honour.

'Do you think he will win?' Theo asked as Cosmas arrived.

'He always wins.'

The first circuit of the city had been uneventful after Cal had crashed the Sogdian vehicle out. The red-capped pilot was still in the lead but not overwhelmingly. Cal was not far behind him, with the last Sogdian pilot trailing just after. Any one of them could still win the race. At each turn the chariots slid around the corner of the city walls, a sharp turn that jerked the pilots, bouncing them around their machines. The dull familiar ache started up in Cal's knee from the pounding of the chariot's wheels over rough ground, but Cosmas's poppy juice kept it from being too sharp. He grinned as he sped past the gatehouse the first time, sending up a spray of snow and ice on the few people gathered there, and cracked his reins to speed the horses up.

Cal wanted to deal with the trailing Sogdian before catching up with the Red Cap. His animals were strong, and they had a burst of speed. The charioteer was convinced he could take the lead, but had decided to have some fun. He pulled on the reins and slowed his chariot slightly, to let the trailing Sogdian come up alongside. The man was grinning; he thought Cal's animals were tiring; he thought he was going to take the lead and push the African back into third place. Cal swept his chariot to the right and smacked the left horse of the man's team on the nose with his whip.

The horse reared and pulled up as the other team horse carried on straight ahead. The leather traces snapped and the chariot pitched onto the side crushing the Sogdian pilot in the crash and dragging his prone body along for a hundred metres. Cal snapped the reins and called out to his team and they leaped forward pulsating power and charged after the Red Cap.

'That was dangerous,' said the watching Theo.

'He is very brave,' said Padma.

'He is having fun,' said Cosmas with disgust. 'He should be trying to win; instead he is intent on breaking the Sogdians. He will still win but it will upset the locals. He is humiliating them.'

Theo glanced over and up to where the Great Khan sat watching, with a smile on his face. Istami wanted the Sogdians humiliated, but there were already grumbles among the crowds on the wall.

The two remaining chariots flashed past the gatehouse on the last circuit of the city. The Red Cap was still ahead but Cal was fast closing on him and the Sogdian's team was tiring.

'He has not paced his team,' said Cosmas. 'And Cal has waited for his moment. Porphyrius the Great wins again.'

'There is half a circuit still to go,' said Theo.

'I have seen enough races in the hippodrome,' said Cosmas. 'I remember Cal in his prime. The gamblers would have stopped taking bets on the race after he crashed the last Sogdian out.'

Cal proved Rat's words true. At the last turn before the finish, he pulled alongside the red-cap charioteer and started screaming at his team, whipping them, cracking the traces, urging them up to a pounding charge. The red-capped Sogdian tried to crash into the chariot in despair as he realised his team was spent, but Cal was expecting that move and merely veered away from the crush. He was two chariot lengths ahead when he crossed the finish line.

16

Cosmas was enjoying their time in Tashkent. The city fascinated him: a melting pot of cultures and peoples, Bactrians and Sogdians mostly, but there were Indians who Cosmas questioned incessantly about their homeland; Persians from Ctesiphon, and Sericans from Kashgar as well as steppe tribesman everywhere. After the race, Theo sent him and Beremund down to the market to find saddles with hoops for the Goths. Cosmas led the tall Goth and Uba through the warren of alleyways and stalls to a Sogdian trader Rat had met previously.

'We want ten saddles,' Cosmas told the trader as Beremund inspected the leather. 'Ten, you understand?' The Rat held up his grubby digits and pointed to the saddles. Uba spoke briefly in Sogdian and the man nodded happily.

'Does he understand?' Cosmas asked the boy.

Uba nodded.

'These are no big enough,' said Beremund in broken Latin.

'What?'

'The saddles too narrow for our horses backs.'

'Does it matter?'

'Of course it matters.'

Rat sighed, neither his nor the Goth's Latin was good but he knew there would be complaints if he just ignored Beremund. He turned back to the Indian trader. The next fifteen minutes was spent trying to explain to the Indian that they needed specially made saddles. Eventually the trader understood and sent a boy back with them to the house to measure up the horses. The price was high but not extortionate, and Cosmas handed over some coins and promised the rest once the new saddles were made. They walked back to the house in silence; conversation was difficult for Beremund and Cosmas was uninterested in the coarse barbarian.

Even the boy seems to be turning into a Goth, thought the Rat.

Uba was flourishing under Theo and the bucellarii. They had cut his hair into a Germanic style with a topknot, and dressed him in a spare tunic and lamellar cuirass. The warriors all sparred with him to train him to the sword and Godda was teaching him to ride. Cosmas's jibes that the lad was too old to become a Goth simply spurred them all on to prove Rat wrong. They turned into a square with a fountain; the Romans' house was down a small road on the other side. There was the usual gaggle of local women and children at the fountain gathering water for their hearths and gossiping, but there were also some strangers in the mix. Four Immortals dressed in mail coats and bearing weapons were chatting and laughing with the Sogdian locals.

'Just ignore them,' said Cosmas to the others.

They moved around the fountain to avoid Naghi's men, but one of the men nudged the others and the Persians moved to intercept them.

'Bugger,' said Rat, as Beremund's hand fell to the hilt of his sword in case of trouble.

The four Persian warriors came straight up to them standing in front of Rat and blocking their way home. Cosmas gave a bow to their leader.

'We are just passing masters, I am certain Naghi would not want any trouble?' he said to them in Persian.

The leader ignored Rat and squared off against Beremund, speaking fast and gesturing to the tall Goth. The sneer on the Sassanid's face was obvious to Beremund, even though he could not understand the Persian language. Uba moved to his side and he smiled down at the boy.

'Trouble?' the Goth asked Rat in his broken Latin.

'They seem intent on it,' Cosmas replied as the Persian continued with his unintelligible diatribe to Beremund. 'He is insulting Justinian and the late Empress.'

'Well, we all know that Theodora was a whore,' said Beremund with a shrug.

'I am not his catamite!' Uba burst out, and started talking to Beremund in Gothic. The tall Goth glowered at the Sassanid and stepped forward.

Cosmas cursed. 'You could have just kept silent, Uba.'

Beremund towered over the Sassanid warrior but the man was dressed in mail, whilst the Goth had no armour. One of the other Persians spoke sharply to Rat who turned back to Beremund.

'Are you challenging him?'

'What?'

'Are you challenging him? They want to know.'

'He has insulted the Emperor the empress and the Goths and this boy. I am not certain I can let it all pass, Rat.'

'Yes, but do we really need to get upset about it?'

'He insulted Theo as well,' said Uba.

'Will you please be silent!' shouted Cosmas at the boy.

'Truly?' Beremund asked the boy. Uba nodded.

'Tell him that if he does not apologise for the insults then I challenge.'

'Really?' That was the last thing Cosmas wanted to do.

'Tell him Uba.'

The boy happily chattered away in Sogdian whilst Cosmas watched on with a sour look on his face.

'I want it understood that this is nothing to do with me. I will not have Theo blaming me for causing trouble in Tashkent.'

The Persians all had wide grins on their faces as the meeting was arranged for the next day outside the city walls. They had got what they came for, thought Cosmas, and typically this brutish barbarian biscuit eater fell into the trap. Theo will be furious.

The slave that the saddle merchant had sent with them was white-faced after the confrontation with the Persians, and once they reached the house he hurried to measure the Roman horses and get back to his master. The other three went into the building to explain to Theo and Cal about the next day's duel. The two of them listened in silence as Beremund, Cosmas and Uba blurted out their explanations.

'Very well,' said Theo when they had finished the tale. 'Naghi clearly wanted this, so we shall teach them all a lesson about Roman arms.'

'It never rains but it pours,' said Cal.

'What else has happened?' asked Cosmas.

'The old man is ill,' Cal told him. 'He woke up this morning in a sweat. The girl is tending to him but he is coughing and cannot keep anything down. He is too old and weak for this adventure.'

That was a more pressing problem as far as the sailor was concerned. The honour of a fool born barbarian was immaterial to their mission, but if something happened to Brother Timothy it could cause problems with the silk.

'Then I shall go and pray for his recovery,' said Cosmas. 'For all our sakes.'

***

'Who do you want as your second?' asked Godda.

'I will take the boy.'

Theo's eyes narrowed. 'Are you certain? What about Fritigern?'

Fritigern was a man mountain that in full armour would terrify the Persians and anyone else.

'No, I think Uba will do well enough.'

Theo made sure that all the men of the bucellarii were in their metal armour, polished until it gleamed, and badges of rank displayed. There were political implications to the fight that Theo understood even if the others were oblivious to them. A Roman and a Persian warrior fighting outside Tashkent would influence how the Goturks viewed both empires. Theo thanked God that it had been Beremund who had taken the challenge. He was the most experienced fighter other than Godda, and was wily enough not to get caught out by Persian tricks.

'What about the Persians?'

'Immortals by the dress. I have fought them before, Dominus, and I am still here to tell the tale.'

Theo shrugged and looked around at the others gathered in the courtyard. His men were all assembled as if they were on the parade ground in Adrianople with Godda at their head. Theo felt a pang of pride as he looked at his men. He trusted that Beremund would not lose to this Persian warrior.

'Are you ready?'

They nodded.

'Then let us go.'

The Romans marched through the deserted streets of the city to the gates, their hobnailed sandals stamping in time on the cobbles like drums in the theatre. Theo was at the head of the small column with Godda, followed by Beremund and Uba. The young boy beamed, proud to be alongside the Goths, and Goturk guards grinned at them as they passed outside the gates. Cal and Cosmas ambled after them, both eager to see the fight, but Padma had remained behind to tend to Brother Timothy.

The news that there was to be a duel between a Roman and a Persian had enthused the local population and the Goturk tribesmen. People had flocked out of the city to see the match, and there was a large crowd waiting. It was clear that the Sogdian locals were supporting the Persians after Cal had humiliated their charioteers. They called out and cheered as the Persians arrived whilst ignoring the Romans. Four poles were set up in a square with cord strung between the staves to mark out the battlefield, and surrounded by spectators. Theo, Beremund and Uba went to one corner with the other Romans, whilst the Persians took up position opposite.

'I cannot see Naghi,' Cosmas whispered to Cal.

'He makes the poison for others to drink.'

'That's true enough, but you would think he would want to see the results of his handiwork.'

'Not if his boy loses. I remember a patron of the Blues who would never watch the races when he had sponsored a pilot. He thought it brought bad fortune.'

Theo walked over to the leader of the Persians. 'You are ready?' he asked in Greek.

The man nodded and Theo went back to Beremund in their corner. The Goth looked in askance to Theo who nodded back.

'They are ready.'

Beremund pulled his closed helm onto his head and drew his spatha, banging it on the oval shield emblazoned with a fading yellow chi rho on a red field.

'Do not lose,' Theo said to him.

'Have no fear, Dominus.'

The Goth raised his sword to salute the Persian warrior, who did the same, and both stepped into the middle of the battlefield. Neither warrior wanted to make the first move; they circled around offering only feints. The crowd started baying for action, not this tentative feeling out of each other's defences. Beremund looked completely impassive dressed head to toe in metal, but the Persian's face, visible in his open helm, flushed red at the crowd's taunts.

'The Persian understands their words,' said Cal. 'Our Goth has no idea what the audience is saying.'

Stung into action by the crowd's insults, the Persian warrior launched a vicious attack on Beremund, hammering his sword into the Roman shield sending sparks up from the iron rim. The tall Goth endured the barrage of blows, parrying with his shield, and then stabbed at the Persian's belly when he had blown himself out. The man stepped back to avoid Beremund's attack but the Goth followed up, his blade glistening in the winter sunlight as he stabbed at the man's face and belly.

Theo could see the difference in fighting styles of the two men. Whilst they were both armed in a similar fashion, the Persian favoured the edge of his sword slashing and cutting at the Roman. Beremund in contrast preferred the sharp point of his spatha, using it like a gladius to stab at the Persian's belly or face. The Goth was also light on his feet for such a tall man, skipping away from the Immortal's blade when it got too close.

'Their man is getting confused, Dominus, he thought it would be over quickly,' Godda told Theo. 'It will not be long now.'

Theo agreed with that assessment. The Persian's open helm left his face visible and vulnerable to Beremund's spatha thrusts. He was getting redder and redder as the contest played out; beads of sweat were starting to glisten on his forehead.

The Goth warrior sensed the moment and switched the attack. Instead of short thrusts stabbing at the Persian, Beremund launched a blistering combination of cuts and stabs until the man fell backwards to the floor dropping his sword. Beremund held his spatha to the man's face.

'Do you yield?' he asked in Latin.

The Persian understood the meaning, if not the language, and he nodded disconsolately. Beremund turned and raised his spatha in triumph to the assembled audience. Behind him, the beaten immortal, still lying on the floor, grabbed his sword from the floor and tried to stab Beremund in the back.

Theo screamed a warning, as did most of the crowd and the other Romans, and Beremund twisted. The Persian's sword glanced off his mail coat, breaking some rings but not piercing through. Beremund's sword flashed forward and he caught the Immortal in the mouth with the point of his spatha, tipping back his enemy's head as a gush of scarlet blood spilled out over the frozen ground. The crowd went wild at that, they had wanted blood from the start, like an audience in the amphitheatres of old.

'Let us get back to the house,' said Cal to Cosmas. 'I think there will be trouble after that.'

The other Persians had melted away, not even bothering to collect their fallen comrade's body. Beremund took off his helm and checked the Immortal over for jewels, prising a golden ring of the dead man's hand.

'That will do for a prize,' he told Theo.

'Then let us get back.'

The crowds were leaving now that the fight was over. The Romans marched back to the house past the smiling Goturk guards bubbling over with the victory, only to be met with a red-faced and weeping Padma.

'What is it?' asked Theo. 'Is Brother Timothy well?'

'Oh, Theo,' said the girl, rushing into his arms and bursting into tears. 'He has died.'

***

They buried Brother Timothy in the small Nestorian cemetery outside the city. A small grave was scraped in the cold earth by the Goths, and his body was wrapped in linen and covered up with little ceremony. A local priest spoke some words over the rude burial, and promised to record the details in his register. Theo held Padma tight to him as they lowered the body down into the hold and covered it with earth. She had wept all night after the old man slipped away. He had been her and her sister's companion, guide, and mentor for years. The whole mission had been at his instigation, and the two sisters had worked tirelessly with him to bring silk back to the empire.

'Are you well?' he asked her after the service.

She looked up and smiled, eyes shining, and squeezed his hand. 'Yes, because I have you.'

After the funeral, they all went back to their rented house and Padma retired to her chambers. The Goths settled down to games of dice in the stables whilst Theo, Cal and Cosmas sat in the atrium. Cal poured himself and Cosmas a cup of wine and offered one to Theo but the officer declined.

'Well, what now?' said Cosmas.

'We have only just buried our comrade and you are already pestering us.'

'We decide nothing now,' said Theo to Rat. 'So, no complaining. When Padma's sister arrives we will know more. If her part in the mission has been successful, then we merely have to get home.'

'What is her name?' asked Cal.

'Juana, so Padma tells me, she is the older of the two. She and her servant will have come from Serica itself to here.'

'I like it here,' said Cosmas. 'There are lots of opportunities for trade, but we will need to decide our route home eventually.'

Theo waved him away.

'I do not like it here,' said Cal.

Theo and the Rat both looked at him in askance.

'Why?' asked Cosmas. 'You won the race, everybody adores you.'

'Things started going wrong as soon as we got here: The cold is unbearable for my knee, Naghi is here causing trouble, now this duel and Brother Timothy dying...'

'He was very old, Cal. Even older than you.'

Theo cuffed the Rat.

'Nevertheless,' said Cal. 'The sooner this Juana is here and we are away the better. I am starting to think that the stone city is cursed.'

Uba appeared at the doorway before they could respond to Cal. 'Dominus, Prince Tardu is here to see you.'

17

The attack came as they walked through the snow swept streets of Tashkent to the citadel with the Khan's son. Tardu and the Romans had been drinking after the duel, and he had dismissed his guards. Theo and the others had insisted on accompanying him back to the citadel, but only Godda was in his mail coat. It was snowing again, and they chattered excitedly about the duel earlier. The Khan had been overjoyed at Beremund's victory and had given the warrior a heavy golden ring as a prize. Despite his initial reticence, Theo had enjoyed the night too whilst staying sober.

'What is that?' Cosmas half turned.

Six or seven Sogdians came out of the shadows with daggers. The Goturk prince stepped back as three of them went straight for him, pulling his curved sword from its sheath. Godda and Theo both drew their spathas. Theo moved without thinking to Tardu's side, as Godda smashed one of the Sogdians down on the head with his mailed fist. Cosmas crouched back in a doorway away from fighting, but Cal pulled a long dagger from his belt and turned to face one of the assassins.

'I knew I should have stayed in the warmth,' muttered Cal.

'Look out, Charioteer!' Cosmas screamed and Cal ducked.

A blade swept over his head almost trimming his white curls and Cal kicked back with his leg, almost collapsing as his knee ripped in agony. There was a satisfying thud as his sandal caught the attacker in the midriffs. Cal span around, ignoring the pain in his knee, and stabbed at the man in the throat with his dagger.

Theo and Tardu stepped forward in unison with their swords ready. The three Sogdians were quick, but they were farmers facing two men trained in battle from childhood. Theo cut left and right with his spatha killing two assassins outright, whilst the Goturk prince stepped inside one's flailing arm and sliced open his belly with his curved blade, leaving the would be assassin screaming on the floor. They both turned as Godda smashed the last attacker into a wall and cut his throat.

'Where is the Greek slave?' asked Theo.

Tardu was breathing heavily and said something, but the others just looked at him blankly.

'The Greek ran off during the fight,' said Cosmas, emerging from his doorway. 'As soon as the attackers came he took to his heels.'

Tardu gestured to the citadel and muttered some words.

'He wants us to go with him,' said Cosmas. 'At least I think so.'

They followed Tardu to the citadel, blades bloody and still drawn in case another attack came at them. Goturk warriors at the citadel gates took one look at their Khan's son splattered in blood and surrounded them all, shouting at the Romans.

'They are a bit late,' said Cosmas.

'They are bound to try and blame us.'

Almost as if the Goturks had understood the charioteer's words, the steppe warriors started shouting at the Romans, shoving them against the wall and gesturing with their spears. Tardu spoke up at that, and whilst none of the Romans understood his words the tone and manner of speech was obvious. The obsequious change in attitude towards them from the guards was instantaneous.

'That's better,' said Cal, brushing himself down.

'Let us hope it lasts,' said Rat.

They were all ushered into the citadel by the guards as more appeared to hold the gates. The fears were that a wider uprising was underway. It was obvious the attack had been long planned.

'The Greek slave is going to get blamed for this,' said Cosmas.

'He did not make himself look innocent,' said Theo. 'But it does give us a problem.'

'How so?' said Cal. 'We helped, they can hardly blame us.'

'We have none who can speak for us, other than Sogdians, and I rather think they will not be welcomed at the citadel after tonight.'

'There is Uba.'

They were shown into the great hall where a bustle of Goturk warriors was already gathering their weapons. News of an attack on the Khan's son had spread through the citadel like a wildfire. The steppe warriors were angry and set on punishing someone. The Romans stood in silence, unnoticed as the council of chiefs started. The Khan was livid with anger at the threat to his son, shouting at the chiefs.

'What do you think he is saying,' Theo whispered to Rat.

'There is going to be a slaughter,' said Cosmas. 'They will butcher the Sogdians. We are safest here; I would not be in the town.'

Theo nodded and then realised the danger. 'What of the others, what of Padma?'

Now that Brother Timothy was dead, Padma was central to their mission. The Rat's eyes widened when he realised the danger.

'Explain to them our people are in the city.' Theo told him.

'Why me?'

'Because you are the best translator we have.'

'But I don't speak Turkic, Theo,' Cosmas whined. 'I could make a mistake.'

'Just do it.'

Nervously the Rat approached Tardu standing beside his father, and tugged at the prince's tunic. Tardu nodded and smiled at him, and then declared something to his father in a loud voice. Istami looked over at the Romans for the first time and gave them a quick grin. He gestured for Theo to approach with Rat and began speaking. His words dripped of welcome and gratitude even if they could not understand the language.

'What is he saying?'

'I don't understand.'

A Sogdian was brought out by the guards to translate for them. The poor man looked terrified to be in the presence of the Goturk leaders, but he told the Romans of the Khan's welcome. Cosmas could speak enough Sogdian to talk to the local, but it was like Persian whispers translated back to the Khan.

'Explain to him about our people back at the house,' said Theo.

'I am trying.'

The Rat spoke slowly in the Sogdian language. He did not really understand it, but it was similar to other dialects he knew and relied upon that to be understood. After a few minutes of wild gestures and broken sentences, the Sogdian nodded and turned to Tardu and his father and, with his eyes fixed firmly on the floor he relayed the Roman's words. The Goturks understood the danger to the rest of their party in the town, Beremund and the rest of the Goth bucellarii would fight to the death and Padma would burn if they were not warned and protected.

Tardu spoke to his father and a squad was detailed to take Theo back to the house and bring the rest of the party to the citadel where they would be safe. Tashkent was already in chaos as the locals rose up against their Goturk masters.

***

Istami had sent his small garrison into the streets to make an example of the poorly armoured inhabitants for attacking his son. Theo led his small squad through the confusion in the town, back to the building where Padma and the others waited. His bucellarii were all in full armour and on guard at the house when Theo arrived, and the relief on their faces at the sight of their lord was palpable. Beremund told Theo that there had been no attacks on the building, yet, but the screams and smell of burning flesh was getting closer.

'Get the horses,' Godda hissed at them. 'Cover their eyes so they are not spooked by the flames.'

The men rushed to get their kit and horses ready to move out as Padma came to the door of the building. The girl rushed to Theo when she saw him, and he held her close as he ordered everybody to move out.

Sogdian rioters came at the party as they led their horses through the flames and smoke back to the citadel, but the sight of Goturks and Goths in full armour and grim faces soon sent them running back into the shadows. Any who dared come too close were butchered without a second's thought. At the citadel they were allowed to enter and the horses and Goths were stabled. Theo had been given rich chambers recently vacated by some Sogdian official, but the men were happy billeted with their horses.

'One of us should stay with you at all times, Dominus,' Godda told Theo in Latin.

'Why? The Sogdians cannot get at us here.'

'We are in a barbarian citadel during a rebellion.' The gruff warrior raised an eyebrow. 'And you are Rome's representative.'

'Oh, yes, of course.'

The apartments in the palace were rich and well furnished with wide open windows overlooking the city, but Padma closed the curtains to hide the sight of the burning. Cal, and Cosmas settled down on the cushions around a small brazier for warmth, but Theo walked out to the balcony to look over the city closing the curtains behind him to keep the warmth inside.

The screams of the inhabitants reached up to Theo as he watched from the citadel. The Goturk warriors showed no pity in punishing the Sogdians for the attack on Tardu. It was a precarious situation for the Great Khan. Most of Istami's people and warriors were to the north, on the steppe for winter with their herds. Istami only had a couple of thousand men in Tashkent, mostly chiefs and notables and their retinues gathered for the wedding. If the assassination attempt was part of a wider rebellion then the Turks could be in trouble.

Padma came out to him carrying his fur trimmed cloak.

'You will catch your death of cold,' she said.

Theo smiled and took the cloak, buttoning it around his neck and wrapping himself in the soft fur.

'Are we safe?' she asked.

'Safer here than down there.' He pointed to the fires in the city.

She looked worried.

'What is it?'

'My sister will arrive when the snows melt, God willing, she is just over the other side of the mountains in Kashgar.'

'Is it far?'

'Not as far as we have travelled, it is the closest we have been in four years.'

'You are certain that she will be there.'

The girl nodded, but Theo felt that unmistakable twist in his belly. If Padma's sister did not come with the spring melt then the whole journey would have been for naught. They would not be able to return to Rome without the silk. Narses would not forgive their failure. Theo shrugged; they had done their part. Now they just had to wait the winter out and stay alive through

169

a rebellion. A waft of smoke caught him at that point; he could smell the unmistakable odour of burning flesh.

***

For three days the Goturk warriors ravaged Tashkent. Sogdian officials were taken and tortured as the full extent of the plot against Istami and his son was revealed. The Romans, safe from the slaughter in the citadel, had watched from the battlements in horror as the steppe warriors wreaked their brutal vengeance on the locals. Angai and the Utigers that had travelled from Atil for the wedding had happily joined in with the butchery alongside their new Goturk allies. Only Rat had ventured out of their apartments to find out what was happening, Theo sending him each day to speak to any officials who could help. On the afternoon of the third day, Cosmas returned to their rooms where Theo and the others waited nervously for news.

'By the saints it is bitter cold out there,' he said throwing off his cloak. 'It seems to be calming down in the city.'

'Is there anyone left?' asked Theo.

'Not many,' conceded Cosmas. 'The tribesmen have been merciless with the locals.'

'But they have put the revolt down?' said Cal.

'In the city, but there have been attacks on Goturks outside the walls. Messengers have been sent north to bring warriors to Istami, but it will be a couple of weeks before they get here. There is talk of a Hepthalite army gathering to the south. The whole plot was to start with the murder of Tardu.' He nodded to Godda and Theo. 'The two of you put paid to that, but now we are trapped here with hostile natives roaming the countryside and an enemy army approaching.'

'They are not our enemies,' Cal pointed out.

'No, but our mission's success now depends on the Istami and his son,' said Theo. 'Their enemies are our enemies.'

Godda nodded approvingly.

'So what do we do then?' asked Cal. 'Sit around waiting for months.' The slaughter had reminded him of the Nika Riot; it had reminded him of his debt to Narses.

'Wait,' said Cosmas. 'That is all we can do.'

'What of the Persians?' said Theo. 'Were they taken in the killing?'

'No.'

'Damn.'

The Persians had retreated to the merchant compound and stayed there for the last three days. Naghi's immortals had kept any Sogdian rioters off, and the Khan's men had ignored them.

'There are Sassanid Immortal guards with them, as we know,' said Cosmas. 'So the Goturks left them mostly alone. Istami does not want a war with the Sassanid Emperor whilst he is set on destroying the Hepthalites and Sogdians. Naghi and his friends are safe from the Turks for now.'

'How very disappointing,' muttered Cal.

Theo looked out of the window at the dark clouds filled with more snow. 'How long until we can travel?'

'It will be three months before the mountain passes are cleared and my sister can come,' said Padma. She smiled at Theo. 'We are safer here than she is over the mountains.'

'Three months?' said Cal.

'At least.'

'Then we carry on as before,' said Theo. 'There is no need to change our plans. As long as we keep the Goturks onside we can avoid more trouble.'

'What of Naghi and the Persians?'

'What more can they do?'

'The Goturks seek an agreement with the Persians,' said Rat. 'They do not want two wars at the same time. Naghi knows we are up to something, even if he does not know the detail. He has dogged us ever since Chersonesus.'

'He does not know about my sister,' said Petros.

'He is too clever,' insisted Cosmas. 'He must know it is to do with silk; he can see that we are not a caravan or merchants simply looking for goods, and every Persian merchant knows how much gold pours out of Rome to buy the cloth. He may not know the details, but I would wager that he has a good idea what we are up to.'

Theo nodded. 'The Rat is correct, I think. The Persian spy is like a turd that will not flush.'

'Then perhaps we can talk about travelling south to go home when the time is right, if we go back the way we came you can guarantee the Persians will dog us every step of the way home,' said Cosmas, hopefully.

'We shall see,' said Theo.

'That means no,' said Cal to Rat.

'It means we shall see,' said Theo firmly. 'Once we have the silk we can decide.'

'And in the meantime?'

'In the meantime we wait for Padma's sister and keep our heads down.'

The snows came again that night, falling heavy and thick as it settled on the frozen ground. The weather finally ended the slaughter in Tashkent, damping the fires and sending what remained of the population indoors. Any surviving Sogdians were herded into pens to be sold as slaves and the city was emptied of the local population. The foreign merchants in the compound outside the city walls quickly moved into the newly vacated buildings inside the city to shelter from the harsh weather. Outside, the countryside seethed at the massacres. Every day messengers from the south brought word of a large Hepthalite and Sogdian army gathering to expel the Goturks from Tashkent and the Jaxartes river valley. As soon as the blizzards stopped, the Hepthalite host would be moving north to attack the city.

18

Cal and Rat could hear the raised voices from the bedchamber. Theo and the girl were arguing, and the girl was being most vociferous about it. There was a tinkle of glass smashing against a wall.

'She is throwing things,' said Cosmas.

Cal nodded. 'Young love,' he said. 'The making up is just as noisy.'

For three weeks they had waited in the citadel of Tashkent after the massacre. The Romans were feted and welcomed by the Goturks as friends after saving the Khan's son, and safe in the citadel from any Sogdian revenge, but all of them were growing bored and frustrated by the confinement. When word of a Hepthalite army approaching Tashkent had reached the citadel, the Goturks were quick to make ready to march out. Theo had eagerly offered to join them with his bucellarii. Godda and the Goths were only too happy to get involved. Boredom among the men had caused short tempers, and arguments down in the stables had almost come to blows. Without Godda's stern discipline and Beremund's stick, the bucellarii would have turned on each other. The prospect of getting out of the citadel and onto horseback, with a fight at the end of it, had them all enthused. Padma, however, saw things very differently.

'You cannot be serious,' she shrieked at Theo, throwing another clay goblet at him, he ducked to avoid it and it shattered on the wall behind. 'My sister will be here in a few weeks and you want to go off playing at soldiers like little boys?'

'Hardly playing. I am a soldier, my dear.'

'Don't my dear me. You will put the whole mission at risk and for what exactly? What if they lose, what if you get killed, what then?'

'They will not lose,' said Theo firmly. 'I have seen their warriors.'

The Hepthalites have conquered and ruled over most of the Indus valley, further than Alexander ever went. They conquered my people with ease; they have elephants and thousands of men, all the resources of their empire. The Persians fear them, and you fear the Persians.'

'Rome does not fear Persia,' Theo said. 'We just have a healthy respect for them.'

'So healthy you do not bother to send out scouts when you fight them?'

Theo grimaced. 'You've been talking to the Rat, and that was entirely my fault. My officers told me to send out scouts but I dismissed their advice. I do not think Istami and Tardu would make the same mistake.'

'They are outnumbered, that is why they happily accepted seven Goths and a spoiled aristocrat.'

Only a few companies of Goturk warriors had arrived at Tashkent since the slaughter in the city. The snows made it impossible for larger forces to move down from the steppe to help their khan. About three thousand men were available to Istami, but the Hepthalite host was rumoured to be at least twice their numbers.

'What if something happens to you, what then?'

'If something happens to me the Rat and Cal will get you and your sister back to Rome. The mission will still succeed.'

'That is not what I meant!' She looked around for something else to throw at him.

Theo stepped up and took her in his arms and kissed her. That silenced her at least, he thought. She kissed him back for a

175

moment and then broke down to sobbing uncontrollably, sitting on the bed in despair, red-eyed and red-faced. He sat next to her and whispered love into her ears.

'It sounds like they have stopped arguing.'

'As you said, their making up can be as noisy as the quarrel,' said Rat. 'I think I shall take a walk along the battlements.'

'I think I shall join you,' said Cal. 'The grunting and moaning puts me off my breakfast.'

'How is your knee?'

'Better, the poppy helps.'

'In moderation.'

'In moderation,' Cal agreed.

The two of them walked out to the battlements overlooking the broken ruins of the city. Snow had been cleared off the walkways by the few remaining Sogdian slaves in the citadel, leaving them safe to walk along. At the gatehouse, the body of the Greek traitor who had translated for them until the rebellion sat crouched and frozen in a cage dangling over walls. He had been captured and put there to starve to death, but the cold had taken him in only a couple of days leaving the body fresh and unputrified but frozen into place.

'Good morning,' said Rat to the corpse.

'Do you have to?'

'It pays to be polite.'

'To a corpse?'

'He can put a good word in for us with St Peter if this mission goes badly, or the Hepthalites win.'

'These Hepthalites are Huns?'

'White Huns the Persians call them, but they did not go into the west with Attila to face Rome. They went into the south and conquered the Indies. They control most of the spices that trade into Alexandria across the seas from the ports in India.'

'Going south after helping the Goturks beat them does not sound like a wise move then.'

Cosmas had been nagging incessantly about travelling back to Rome by way of the Indies and taking a ship to Egypt. Theo and the Goths were unwilling to leave their animals and had no desire to take an ocean voyage, no matter how much the Rat assured them that it was safe.

'Your knee would be better with the warmth to the south,' said Rat, trying a different tack. 'Travelling back over the steppe in the spring will be hard.'

'Give it up, Cosmas. It is Theo you have to persuade, or the girl, and neither seem disposed to travelling over the mountains.'

'There are passes, and then it is a river journey all the way to the sea.'

'Tell the girl, perhaps she can persuade Theo. Shall we go back?'

'Another circuit, I think.'

The two of them carried on around the citadel battlements, wrapping their cloaks about them, and by the time they returned to their apartments it was quiet in Theo's chamber.

'At least they are not arguing,' said Rat.

'Do not provoke anything,' said Cal. 'I could do with some peace and quiet for a nap.'

Cosmas merely smiled when Theo came out of his bedchamber at their arrival.

'She is sleeping,' he said in a low voice.

'Did you come to some arrangement about the battle?' asked Cosmas innocently.

Cal nudged him sharply in the ribs. 'What did I just say?'

They all sat in silence after that, Theo watching out of the windows at the snow drenched city until Godda arrived with the boy Uba. The goatherd had proved invaluable to the Romans, quickly learning some of their language from Cosmas. He was able to tell them about the local politics, as well as speak to the Turks for them. Uba was one of the few Sogdians allowed into the citadel, and he had become utterly devoted to Theo and the Goths who were in turn just as devoted to him.

'There is word from the south, Dominus. The Hepthalites are only a few days march away. Istami is gathering his host to move against them in the morning. They will be happy to have us along for the fight.'

'Did you have to say it so loudly?' muttered Theo.

Padma came out of Theo's bedchamber at Godda's words and stood at the door with pursed lips.

'So you are all going to play, are you?' She turned on her heels and stalked back into the bedchamber.

'I hope she is worth the trouble at bedtime?' said Godda in Gothic.

'We need to get the men ready,' said Theo, ignoring the question.

'The men are ready and eager to join the Turks; it is you we are waiting for.'

'Are you allowed out to play, Theo?' said Cosmas and Cal cuffed him.

Theo ignored that question as well, going to his chest and taking out his mail armour and undercoat. Uba rushed to help him get it on, tie him into the thick padded coat and pull the mail over his head, then tie him into the armour. Theo took out his spatha and tied it to his belt and put his plumed helmet under his arm.

'I am ready,' he said finally. 'You two look after her, she is vital to the mission's success.'

'I wager she is,' said Rat snidely.

'Without me, she is the only chance you have of getting back to Rome with the silk,' Theo pointed out.

That silenced the Rat. Theo and Godda left with the young boy in tow to join the other Goths and ride south.

'Well what now?' Rat asked Cal.

'Now we wait and pray for victory.'

***

The Hepthalite host numbered in the thousands, but most were poor Sogdian levies with only spears and wicker shields and no armour. There were some horsemen among them, mounted archers like the Goturks and heavy shock cavalry in scale armour, but this was not the full force of the Hepthalite Empire being sent against the Turkic nomads. This was a few minor White Hun nobles wary of losing their power base in Sogdiana, and attempting to drive out the newcomers from the steppe. The Goturks were openly contemptuous of the approaching army. Uba explained all of this to the Romans in his strange mix of Latin, Gothic and Greek that he had picked from Cosmas and the others. The Rat had told Theo that children pick up different languages easily because they are closer to God, but the nobleman was still shocked at how fluent the boy had become in such a short time.

'The Great Khan says that the Hepthalites have forgotten themselves; they are grown fat and lazy living in cities.'

Godda nodded and looked pointedly at Theo. 'When we forget our past we mistake our future,' was all he said.

'Are you a philosopher now?' asked Theo.

'No, Dominus, we are all warriors born; that is rather the point.'

Theo turned back to the boy. 'Where is the Hepthalite army now?'

'They say that it has moved north from Samarkand and is camped around Jizzakh – a town to the south in the hills. Once they move through the pass onto the plains we shall go to meet them.'

179

Theo frowned. 'Why not stop them in the pass?'

'They have spears,' said Godda. 'The Khan would be lose the manoeuvrability his horses give him. Once the Hepthalites are on the plain and marching to Tashkent, it will be a siege without walls.

Theo looked in askance at that, so Godda explained like a pedagogue explaining to his pupil.

'Justinian's armies are different to the Goturks. We would block the pass with our engineers and hold it with our heavy infantry whilst archers and ballista butchered them from range. The Khan has no infantry to speak of, so he allows them to advance and whittles them down from a distance. Think of Crassus at Carrhae.'

Istami had sent men to poison the wells before the Hepthalite advance, fouling the water on the plains with sheep and goat carcasses. The Khan wanted the Hepthalites and their Sogdian allies so thirsty they were forced to eat snow to survive. For three days, the enemy host had waited at a small fort on the edge of the plain for more levies to come in. Once they were finally assembled, the army crawled northwards towards Tashkent. The horsemen in the vanguard were harried constantly by Istami's warriors, with small parties of Turks sweeping around them to raid the column of footmen and baggage. Every time a group of Hepthalite riders was drawn out from the column to drive off the Turks, it would be surrounded by Istami's horse archers and slaughtered. The Hepthalite leaders quickly learned not to retaliate to the Turkic attacks, drawing closer together and slowing the pace of their advance down still further. Theo and the Goths rode with Tardu and the young prince's own bodyguard. Uba had been found a pony and given a padded jacket to ride with them, and the boy was utterly delighted with the gifts. Llew had promised to teach him how to ride and scout, and the twins how to use a bow and sword.

'From goatherd to Goth,' Godda told him, and the boy blushed with pride.

They watched the White Huns from a small rise, half a mile away from the marching column. The Hepthalite host could see them sitting on their horses watching, but made no move to drive them off. The enemy had learned the hard way that any charge would be swiftly butchered by the Goturks. Instead, they were marching directly to Tashkent to besiege the stone city or force a battle. The Hepthalite leaders seemed confident that their weight of numbers would prevail in a fight.

'They have elephants, look,' said Godda.

'We have fought elephants before.'

'Poleanus's ploy,' said Godda with a smile.

'Fire pigs?' asked Theo.

The Goth nodded. 'You still remember something of your learning then.'

'I always felt sorry for the pigs.'

'You are soft.'

The Romans took their idea to Tardu, who grinned with delight once it was explained to him by Uba. The khan's son ruffled the boy's hair and clapped him on the back. Men were sent to find some pigs and flasks of naptha. Twenty or so of the animals were found, and they waited for nightfall to act. The boy, used to the animals, would be vital. Once they had doused the pigs lightly in naphtha, Uba and the Goths drove the animals quietly towards the Hepthalite encampment in the darkness. There were few guards and no scouts sent out by the enemy, the fear of Turkic horsemen keeping them in their tents, and the party went unnoticed as they crept up to the camp. Uba, using a long switch and clicking his tongue, kept the pigs quiet and moving until they were within a bowshot of the enemy camp.

'Now?' said Theo.

'Closer,' said Godda.

When they were about fifty feet away from the tents and campfires, they stopped and spread out into a line with their spears held wide in both hands.

'Once we fire them up, you will need to drive them towards the camp,' Theo told his men in a whisper. 'We will be lit up and visible in the flames, so keep your heads down.'

'Now,' said Godda.

Theo took out a naphtha soaked torch and made ready with flint.

'We only need to fire up a couple of them,' Godda told him, 'and then drive the rest at the camp.'

Theo nodded in the darkness and sparked the flint against his spatha. The torch lit up and he touched it to the tails of three pigs quickly before dousing it in the snow, and the animals exploded into flames from their tails and screamed. They raised up a great noise and started beating the other pigs with their spears and banging their shields. The animals ran towards the Hepthalite camp terrified by the noise and the fires behind them.

'Back,' hissed Godda. 'Back to the horses.'

The Goths all fell back with Theo and Uba, not looking back as they ran. When they reached Tardu and his warriors, the Goturks were laughing hysterically in their saddles and pointing at the scene behind them.

The Hepthalite encampment was in flames. The squealing pigs had run straight to the tents, some catching alight on the campfires, spreading flames and panic through the camp. The elephants could be heard trumpeting in panic at the porcine assault, and the whole encampment was lit up like an ancient Saturnalia feast. Elephants broke free of their handlers and charged through the tents trumpeting in panic, crushing men and equipment until half of them had been spiked, and the other half left free to wander the plain where they were butchered in turn by the Goturks. Tardu ordered his men into arrow range and they all started pouring arrows at any targets revealed in the firelight. For over an hour chaos ruled in the Hepthalite camp. Finally someone managed to get control restored, the fires doused, and the remaining pigs killed off. When dawn broke, the Hepthalite encampment was revealed as a broken smouldering mess. Another group of Goturk warriors arrived to relieve them and Tardu led his men, and Theo's Goths, back towards Tashkent and his father in triumph.

'A good night's work,' said Godda. 'Elephants can be tricky in a battle.'

Tardu and his men, and the Romans, would rest for that day whilst others harried the enemy in the winter sunlight. They would prepare to assault the Hepthalites the following day with the full Goturk host, the young prince informed Theo. His father Istami had been delighted with the destruction of the Hepthalite camp and defeat of the elephants. The steppe warriors, normally so merciless and unthinking of danger, had a distinct fear of the giant creatures and their destruction had raised morale in the Goturk ranks.

'Tomorrow we shall destroy them and send a message to King Ghadfar that these lands now belong to the Goturks,' shouted the Khan.

The assembled men cheered at Istami's words. They were all eager to draw battle with the Hepthalites. Theo and his Goths cheered happily along with them.

19

Istami drew up his army on the plain before Tashkent in three great battalions. The largest, in the centre, was commanded by the Great Khan himself and consisted of his household guards and new troops that had arrived from the north. His son Tardu commanded the left flank, and another Goturk noble was on the right. The whole force was mounted, with no footmen or archers to support the riders. They had bled the Hepthalite army as it advanced towards Tashkent with hit and run attacks in the night as well as the pig attack. Theo doubted that their enemy had slept much in the last week, and the White Huns pace had slowed to a crawl as they advanced on the city. Still, the Goturks were outnumbered; the Hepthalite lords had twice their numbers, but Istami and his son seemed unconcerned at the odds.

Tardu kept the Romans with him on the left as they drew up on the plain. Since the assassination attempt on his life, the Khan's son had become fascinated by the travellers from the west. He asked Cosmas questions constantly about Rome, about Justinian, about the people and their lives at home.

'Will Rome be our friend?'

That was the question that came most often. The power of Justinian's Empire was well known, but the empire was far enough away for the true capricious nature of Justinian's court not to have travelled. Cosmas and Theo both assured the steppe prince that the Emperor would be his greatest ally.

'The Emperor would throw them into a prison as soon as he saw them,' said Godda as they sat on their horses watching the Sogdians and Hepthalites advance. 'If any got close enough.'

'I do not think so,' said Theo. 'The Goturks are too far away from the Empire, even if they come west like the Huns they would only threaten Chersonesus. It would be better for Rome to have an ally ruling the steppe than another Attila. Justinian would happily sacrifice Taurica for that end.

'You are become quite the diplomat.'

'Thank you.'

'It was not a compliment, Dominus.'

'Would you want to fight these horsemen?'

Godda pursed his lips at that and pondered. The old Goth could see that the Turks were excellent horse archers, merciless in battle, well disciplined and devoted to their khan. If they appeared on Rome's borders intent on conquest and plunder, it would be a catastrophe for the Empire.

'We would win,' he said, eventually. 'We always win in the end, but it would cost us Italia, and Greece would be probably devastated again. The country has not recovered from the Huns and Attila and that is a century ago.'

'Or from us Goths before him?'

'Or from us Goths,' Godda agreed, 'but we are Roman now. The Huns are still out there.'

'The Huns are over there,' said Theo pointing to the advancing Hepthalite host.

'They are not real Huns,' said Godda, contemptuously. 'I fear Angai and his Utigers or these Goturks more than those.'

Cal and Rat had remained with Uba in Tashkent. All three were perched on the city walls watching the battle from a distance with the other inhabitants. There were still merchants in the city whose fortunes could be lost in the battle outside, but it was not a big audience. The boy had been miserable at being left behind by Godda and Theo. Cal had kept him from sneaking off after them.

'Can you see anything?' asked the charioteer. 'It is too far away for my old eyes.'

Cosmas and Uba gave each other a glance. The battle was miles away but on the snowscape the different forces could be easily discerned. The charioteer complained about his fading eyesight as they explained what they could see.

'If they get themselves killed, what do we do then?'

'Run away,' said Rat. 'She hasn't come out to watch?'

'Oh no, I would not be in Theo's sandals when he gets back. She reminds me of my granddaughter – stubborn and willful. If he gets back,' Cal added as an afterthought.

'If they get killed we will have to find another way back to Constantinople.'

'Then let us pray they do not get themselves killed.'

The Hepthalites had drawn up to face the Turks with their levy infantry in the centre, armed only with light shields, spears and little metal armour. The Hepthalite heavy cavalry held to the flanks. The enemy horse was the strength of the Hepthalites, encased in metal like Roman Kataphraktoi, but they were far too few in number compared to the Goturk horse. The Hepthalite general would have to rely on the footmen to pin Istami's centre before he could use his cavalry to smash the Goturks. Tardu laughed and pointed at the levy.

'Barbarians,' he said to the two Romans.

Theo grinned at the unintended irony of the steppe warrior's pig-Latin.

The Goturks watched in silence as the Hepthalites advanced to perhaps five hundred metres away, just out of bow range. Theo had expected them to chatter and chirp, but the Goturks were as disciplined as the legions, watching their enemy impassively. Horns blew from the Goturk centre, and Tardu barked orders at his men.

'Stay close to the princeling,' Godda told the Goths.

Tardu led his battle wide on the left flank, with Theo and the others in tow, as the Turk right wing did the same. The Hepthalite horsemen watched them grimly, but kept to their tight formation. There were not enough to charge the Goturks off, and they merely sat on their heavily armoured horses as Tardu ordered his men to move in and unleash arrows at them. Time and time again the Turks swept in and loosed a massive volley of arrows at the Hepthalite host, and then swept back again like waves on a beach. The Hepthalites and their Sogdian levies were helpless to stop them: unable to charge and fixed to their infantry centre. Eventually, instead of watching his army murdered by a thousand cuts, the Hepthalite general ordered the mass of infantry to advance on Istami's centre.

'Now we have him,' called Theo to his men.

As the Sogdian levy advanced, the two Goturk flanks moved wider and wider until they were almost behind the enemy host. The Hepthalite horse on their army's wings finally split from their infantry centre, not willing to be outflanked and attacked from the rear. At that moment, the steppe horns blew again from Istami and the Goturks charged at the enemy from three directions.

Theo held his spear in both hands as he gripped his horse's flanks with his knees in the charge. The Romans had the new stirrups on their saddles, and they revelled in the manoeuvrability it gave them. The bucellarii were tight around Theo, helms closed and spears to hand as they thundered down on the enemy.

They hammered into the Hepthalite flank before the enemy cavalry could get up to a charge. Theo stabbed at the armoured enemy, losing his spear as it twisted into a screaming horse's flank. In one movement, he drew his spatha and cut down at a Sogdian footman who had appeared in front of him with a spear. The crash of metal and animals smashing into each other was just a dull roar inside his helmet. Theo realised that they had charged right through the Hepthalite flank into the back of the Sogdian infantry levy. He pulled on his reins and looked around through the eyeholes in his helm to see that the bucellarii were still with him. There was too much snow and ice thrown up by the pounding horses' hooves for anything else to be visible, but it was clear that the enemy were already running from the battle. He drew the bucellarii around him and then realised that Godda was missing.

'Where is Godda?' he asked one of the metal clad men in Gothic.

'He fell, Dominus.' The voice was muffled but Theo could hear the despair. It was one of the twins.

'Beremund go find him, let us pray he still lives, said Theo. The rest of you follow me, we go for their Magister Militum.'

The few Goths nodded at their lord, and Theo led them straight at the enemy general's standard. There were others charging at the Hepthalite king as well, Goturks from both wings and even some of Istami's best riders who had ridden straight through the enemy centre. The Hepthalite army had been completely enveloped by the Goturk host and collapsed without much fighting. Tardu's wing had crushed the enemy's right flank of horse and smashed into the rear of the footmen just as the other wing had done the same. Istami had led the main body of Goturk warriors in a great wedge that simply ran over the poor Sogdian levy at the centre. The steppe warriors timing of the attack had been perfect, all three battles hitting at the same time, and crushing any resistance despite their lack of numbers.

Around the Hepthalite lords' there was still a grim battle being fought. The enemy bodyguard was filled with well armed and trained men who were as good as anything the Goturks sent at them, and they were prepared to fight to the death. Tardu circled his men around them with bows out and started pounding them with volleys of arrows. More and more Goturks came as the battle elsewhere ended, until a great ring of steppe horse archers rode around the White Hun elite, and slaughtered them from a distance.

What was left of the vast army the Hepthalite satraps had brought north was either dead or streaming back towards Samarkand in terror, throwing away their shields and spears whilst their lords died in a last stand. When the Goturks had thinned the ranks of the remaining enemy troops, Istami ordered a horn blown and the Goturks charged again from all sides. Theo and the Goths charged with them, hell bent on vengeance for their fallen comrade.

'Die! Die! You bastards!'

The young Roman general was exhilarated by the fight, hacking at enemies left and right with his spatha, screaming out his battle cry in Gothic. The cultured urbane Roman aristocrat had been replaced by a wild Gothic warrior like his ancestors. Some of Theo's men watched approvingly through their helms. They may have lost Godda, but Theo had grown up on the quest. He was their Dominus and now he was truly their leader.

The final killing was brutal but short, the last few Hepthalite warriors were cut down without mercy, and their leader was beheaded by Istami himself with one cut of his wide sword. The dark red blood spurted across the churned up field and the headless body toppled to the side as the Goturks made up a great cry of victory. Theo turned as someone tapped him on his helm. It was Beremund; he lifted his visor to speak.

'I have found him, Dominus. He lives but will not last long.'

'Take me to him.'

Beremund led Theo back to the broken bodies and stray horses where Tardu's wing had crushed the Hepthalite flank. Godda was lying on his back, a spear shaft in his side, still conscious but bleeding out. Theo took one glance at the wound and realised it was mortal. There was no saving the gruff old Goth. One of the twins was at his side whispering to him, and Godda held his spatha tightly in his hand. Theo leaped off his horse and cast his helm to the side, kneeling on the floor beside his friend. The old Goth smiled weakly at him.

'One of their footmen caught me as we charged through,' he gasped. 'The humiliation, to be killed by a barbarian peasant.'

'Do not waste your breath, old friend. We shall get you help. Padma understands healing herbs.'

Godda winced. 'I am no fool, nor a Serican maiden to fall for your honey words. I am killed, but the mission must go on. You must return to Rome with the secret of silk, promise me, Theodosius, redeem yourself and your family name.'

'I promise on Saint Anthony,' said Theo.

Godda leaned his head back into Beremund's lap. 'Burn my body, do not bury me in the mud, raise up a pyre like the old days.'

'I promise,' said Theo.

Godda smiled, but Theo could see blood on his teeth.

'You are Theodosius Dagisthaeus, King of the Ostrogoths of Rome. I am proud to have served you, and my ancestors will welcome me in the afterlife.'

I am no king, just a senile senator's grandson, thought Theo, but he merely nodded at Godda's words. The old warrior closed his eyes and his breathing became laboured, ragged, gasping for breath, and then it stopped and his head lolled to the side. There was silence for a moment until Beremund finally spoke.

'He wanted to speak with you before the end, Dominus.'

'You did well Beremund,' said Theo. 'I need an Ourghos to take his place. The rank is yours.'

'I will take it, Dominus, and try and do his memory good service and my duty to you.'

At the start of the journey, Theo had been worried that his men would stake him out on the steppe as punishment for losing Petra. Now he had earned their respect. It was a high price to pay for the men's loyalty. Godda had known him since he was a babe, and had almost always been at his side. The disaster at Petra would have been avoided had Theo listened to the old Goth's advice before setting out. Now, he would have to complete the mission without his mentor. The others were waiting for them when they arrived back at Tashkent, but after a few brief words with Cal and Cosmas, Theo retired to the chamber he now shared with Padma and cried like child.

***

They raised up a pyre for Godda outside the gates of Tashkent. The Great Khan ordered the wood stores to be raided for the Romans, and it was stacked up eight foot high and drenched in expensive naphtha. Beremund stood sentinel at the pyre in full armour as Godda's body was brought out on a litter. Padma and Uba had cleaned the body of blood and then dressed him in a plain white robe. Godda's spatha was placed in his arms and Theo put an emerald jewel at his breast. The tough old warrior looked as if he was sleeping softly as he was brought out and placed atop the tall pyre. Only the Rat complained.

'This is barbarian heresy and soul damning,' he whispered to Cal.

'I have heard you pray to Fortuna, so be silent.'

Cosmas pursed his lips but was wise enough not to pursue the point or start raving in front of the others. Theo and the Goths would never forgive him, and Beremund had a short temper when it came to him at the best of times.

Tardu came out of the citadel to join Theo and the others at the ceremony, some Goturk guards with him, and some of the merchants who had hidden in their compound during the rebellion and the following slaughter and battle came out to pay their respects. Cosmas nudged Cal in the ribs making the charioteer gasp and turn in annoyance at Rat.

'What is your problem?'

'Shhh, look, Naghi.'

Cal followed his glance. The Persian spy had come out to the funeral with some of his attendants and stood watching the Roman party around the burning pyre with a sly smile on his face.

'Damn, I had hoped he was killed in the rioting.'

'Snakes like that always survive,' said Cosmas. 'He is watching us watching him.'

'Ignore him; he can do nothing whilst we have the Khan's favour and his son's interest.'

That was true enough, so Cosmas poked his tongue out at the Persian spy and turned back to the pyre. Padma was dressed in her Nestorian habit, and had brought a local Christian priest with her. The local Nestorian spoke a few words in broken Greek and the girl sang a psalm to honour the dead. The Rat joined in with the singing, his warbling voice off key and thin, but Cal did not have the heart to stop him. Once the priest had finished his prayers, Theo stood before the crowd and spoke out in a clear voice

'This is Godda of Thessaly, son of Dagmar, Doryphoroi of the Illyrian foederatie, chieftain and battle leader. His line stretches back into antiquity, his ancestors claimed descent from the ancient Gods, he never knew defeat and in his death we honour him.'

The bucellarii gave out a great cheer as Theo finished his words. The blonde aristocrat took up a torch and lit it from a brazier, and then he touched it to the base of the pyre at the four corners. The naphtha drenched tinder flickered and flamed up in an instant, and Theo stepped back from the bursting heat tossing the torch into the middle of the flames. Choking black smoke rose up to the sky, and the smell of burning flesh filled their nostrils. Cosmas gagged at the stench but the others ignored him. The Romans all stood with their heads bowed before the fire, but the merchants and other assembled onlookers slowly drifted away leaving Theo and the others alone. Even Tardu, getting bored and cold, retired back to the citadel to get drunk with his men. Uba and the Goths tended to the flames in silence as the flames consumed Godda's corpse.

'It's getting cold,' said Rat.

'We stay until the end.'

Theo and the Nestorians returned to their chambers in the citadel after the funeral, but Uba and a couple of the Goths stayed behind to tend the embers until even the bones were burned down to ashes. The next day, once the embers had burned out, Godda's ashes were gathered together with the jewel and placed in a small amphora to take back to Rome.

'He wanted his ashes taken back the estate and placed in the chapel,' Theo told them. 'I will make sure that happens.'

The weather turned again after the funeral, another snowstorm came down off the mountains covering Tashkent in a thick blanket of snow and making the plains impassable. The Hepthalite lords to the south could not advance on the Goturk city again even if they wanted to. After the destruction of their first army, Theo doubted they would risk another assault until the spring, and by then Istami would have brought more warriors down from the steppe to reinforce his army in Tashkent.

The Romans settled down and marked the short days and long nights as they waited for the spring melt to arrive, and with it Padma's sister and the secret of silk.

20

The thaw had begun, that was obvious to the Romans waiting in Tashkent. Patches of brown grass were visible on the plains from the citadel as the icy snow melted. The Jaxartes River was swollen with melt-water brought down from the mountains, the floods spreading out over the plains and fertilising the farmland. The Sogdian locals, what was left of them, were out making the fields ready for planting, and digging out irrigation ditches for the rice that would soon grow up from the terraces. In Tashkent the Goturks sneered at the mud grubbers and made ready for war. Once the winter snows were gone, Istami planned to destroy the Hepthalite lords who had challenged his rule of the Jaxartes valley. Thousands of warriors were moving down from the steppe to the stone city in answer to the Khan's call. Istami and Tardu would take their bloody revenge for the winter rebellion against them. The Romans waited, impatiently, for the arrival of Padmas's sister and planned their journey home.

'I still think we should travel south,' said Rat. 'The mountain passes will be clear soon and then we can journey by boat and ship almost all the way to Alexandria.'

'We can travel back over the steppe to Atil with ease,' Theo pointed out. 'The Goturks will protect the caravans heading back over the steppe and from Atil. Then it is but a short ride to Chersonesus.'

'But the south is safer. There is war on the steppe, we have all seen that.'

'A war the Turks are winning,' said Cal, 'and Tardu has messages to send to Justinian.'

Cosmas sniffed. 'I hardly think that the emperor is going to be concerned with a barbarian chieftain's missives.'

'Then you do not understand our Emperor or Narses,' said Theo firmly. 'We know the journey home over the plains, we do not know the way back through the Indies.'

'I know the way. I may not have travelled it all before, but others have, it is not so difficult and it could be quicker if we catch the monsoon winds.'

'We shall see what to do when Padma's sister arrives.'

The girl looked over at the Rat and nodded at Theo's words. Her hair had grown, thick and black, shoulder length now not the novice's crop that she had worn when they had started out.

'The monsoon winds would keep us in the Indies until the autumn,' she said pointedly. 'We can get back over the steppe in four or five months to Chersonesus and sail back to Constantinople. It is already February; the monsoon winds will not turn our way for six months.'

'How do you know that?' Cosmas had gone bright red at her words, caught out in his deception.

'It is common knowledge among traders in the east,' she said. 'I am surprised you did not know it.'

'I wager he did,' said Cal cuffing Rat. 'What is the real reason that you want to go to the South?'

'I prefer a boat to a horse,' muttered Cosmas.

'Well, that is not a good enough reason,' said Theo. 'I think I shall take a walk.' He looked over at the Padma. Would you like to join me?'

She smiled and nodded, quickly getting up and following the blonde aristocrat out onto the battlements.

'I wager it is not a walk they are going for,' said Cosmas once they had gone.

'You are a snide,' said Cal.

Theo and Petros walked hand in hand along the battlements saying nothing, just happy to be close to each other. It was a growing romance that Cosmas and the others mocked, but the two had become inseparable during the stay in Tashkent. The Goturk warriors on patrol nodded at them as they passed by. Since saving Tardu during the rebellion and then fighting in the battle, Theo and the Goths were feted by the Steppe tribesmen. Whilst they had kept their mission to themselves, Istami and his son had prepared messages for Theo to take back to Emperor Justinian in Constantinople promising eternal friendship with the empire. Even if they failed in the mission for the secret of silk, an alliance with the greatest power on the steppe would please the Emperor and his secretary. After Attila, and the Goths before him, Rome had looked nervously to the eastern plains. The Huns had almost destroyed the Empire a century before, and only Justinian's reign had seen the western provinces begin to return to the fold. Fritigern found the couple arm in arm looking out over the plains.

'My Dominus.'

The man looked worried and out of breath, as if he had been running.

'What is it Fritigern?'

'It is the boy, Dominus, he has gone missing.'

'When?' Theo frowned.

'He went out this morning and has not returned. Beremund sent him to find a leatherworker in the town.'

'Perhaps he has been delayed with some horseplay,' said Theo. 'It is only a little past noon.'

'It is not like him, Dominus.'

That was true enough. The boy had become the Goths lucky mascot. They dressed him in their clothes, taught him how to ride and use a sword, and Theo had promised him a place in the bucellarii when he was older. The lad had made himself useful, always happy to help and eager to please, and his ability with the local languages and customs had proven invaluable. Godda

196

had thought of him as another son, and Beremund a younger brother. The boy would not go missing without good reason.

'What does Beremund want to do?'

'The twins are going to go into town to talk to the traders,' said the warrior.

'Tell them to stay away from the Persians,' said Theo, 'and do nothing to draw attention. I do not want Naghi causing us any trouble. Not now we are so close to the end. Our contacts will arrive from Serica soon.'

'Yes, Dominus.' The man nodded and turned to leave.

Theo caught Petro's hand in his and kissed it. 'We should return to the others, I think.'

She smiled and followed him back to their apartments where Cosmas and Cal were arguing over a game of latrones.

'The boy has gone missing,' Theo told them. 'Where did you find a latrones board?'

'Llew had one, we borrowed it but the Rat cheats. When did Uba go?'

'This morning.'

Cosmas sniffed. 'He is most probably swilling ale from a shop. The boy becomes more Gothic everyday with his new clothes and hair, and I do not cheat, oh decrepit one. I am simply better at the game than you.'

'It is not like him,' said Cal, ignoring Rat. The charioteer had taken the boy to his heart just like the bucellarii. 'And it is my move.' He smacked Cosmas's hand before the Rat could slyly shift a piece.

'Oh you were young once,' said Rat. 'It may have been a very long time ago, but perhaps some pretty Sogdian maiden caught his eye and he is chasing her skirts.'

'He is little more than a child,' said Theo.

'To Porphyrius the ancient, so are we all,' said Rat.

'I will hurt you,' said Cal through gritted teeth. 'My knee is better now the weather warms, and I can catch you if you run.'

'So you say.' Cosmas shrugged. 'I am certain that the boy will be back before long.'

***

They found Uba's body dumped half naked on a midden. He had been tortured before being killed, that was obvious from the bloody scars on his corpse, and even the rough tough Goth warriors were shocked by the brutality of the murder. All of them were spitting blood in anger and swearing to avenge the lad, Theo included. This was an affront to all of them and there was only one clear suspect.

'He was seen near the Persian compound, Dominus,' Beremund told them. 'That was the last time he was seen alive.'

'Naghi,' said Cosmas. 'It must be him. How much did the boy know?'

'Everything,' said Beremund. 'He was one of us.'

Cosmas winced. 'Then Naghi will know what we are here for as well.'

'All the more reason to kill them all,' said Llew from the corner where he sat with the twins.

'We need to prove it,' said Theo. 'We cannot start a war here without evidence.'

'This is the steppe, Dominus,' said Fritigern. 'We do not need evidence.'

'I think that the Great Khan would strongly disagree,' said Rat. 'He may desire friendship with Rome, but he will not insult the Sassanid Emperor for us. At least, not until he has destroyed the Hepthalites.'

Beremund and Fritigern both frowned at Cosmas's words, international politics was not the lumbering warriors' strong suit, but Llew and the twins nodded sadly. All of them had served long enough to understand that acting without thinking got people killed.

'The Rat is correct,' Theo said. 'We need proof that they did this, and then we shall destroy them. I promise you that.'

Beremund nodded. 'We are pleased to hear that, Dominus. There are some things that cannot go unpunished.'

He left the words hanging in the air and took Fritigern and the other Goths back to the stables. Theo looked at Cal and Rat.

'Well, what now?' he said.

'I will ask about town,' said Cosmas. 'I have made contacts with some of the merchants in the compound.

'Why would they help?'

'Murder is bad for business, and most of them make money from Rome in one way or another. There are enough problems with trade between the empires as is. None of them want more restrictions on their movements. All of them will want to trade with us at some point in the future. It is money that makes the world go around. So...' Cosmas opened his arms and shrugged.

'I thought you said the world was flat?' said Cal with a sly smile.

'It is but a turn of phrase, Charioteer. If we were to go south, I could show you the pillars of the sky and prove to you that the world *is* flat. After seeing the steppe I thought even a dullard as you would understand.'

'Hooked and landed,' said Cal.

'We are not going to go south,' said Theo firmly.

***

They buried Uba in the necropolis of Tashkent, outside the city's northern gate. A pitiful little grave compared to some of the monuments. The bucellarii were all dressed in full armour, polished to a shine, just as they had been for Godda's funeral pyre, and they had wrapped Uba's body in a plain white shift after they had gently washed the blood away. They placed a spatha with a rich jewelled hilt in his hands and a wooden cross at his breast.

'Was he a Christian?' asked Cal.

'Not baptised,' said the Rat. 'There are many Nestorians in the east and on the steppe, but your Goths are all Arian heretics anyway, I am not sure that their beliefs include baptism.'

Beremund gave the Rat a sharp glance and Cal smiled

'They understand far more Greek than you give them credit for.'

One of the twins carried a stone marker that he had carved with Uba's name, and underneath in Latin "A soldier of Rome" as an epitaph. He placed it at the boys head burying the long end deep in the earth so that it would stand the test of time, and then they covered the boy's body with earth as Cosmas warbled out a psalm to the heavens. The Goths had dug the grave in the still frozen earth and tended the corpse. Each of them had cut away a lock of their own hair and cast it into the flames the previous night, swearing to avenge the boy. There was a simmering anger among the bucellarii. They were all hell bent on violence, and only Theo's promise to seek out the killers and punish them for it had stopped them from rampaging through the Persian encampment and slaughtering Naghi and his men. All of them walked back through the melting slush to the citadel in silence, as Theo pondered how to both fulfill both his mission to Narses and his duty to the men and Uba's memory.

'Have you found anything out yet?' he asked Cosmas when they returned to the domos.

'I have not had much time,' protested Rat.

'Get on with it. We need this matter settled before the others arrive from Serica. Once they are here we leave as soon as we can.'

***

Suraj was from the south. An Indian from over the great mountains who traded in spices that he brought from his home in Taxila on the Indus to Kabul and Tashkent. From there, he would buy glassware – most of it coming from Roman factories – and transport it back to his homeland. He was dark, almost as dark skinned as Cal, but his hair was long and straight and held up over his head with golden pins like a Roman matron. The Rat had made his acquaintance not long after their arrival in Tashkent, and the promise of better glassware transported over the sea to Suraj's homeland was the bait that Rat dangled in front of him for information.

'The great Buddha teaches that a man is not called noble who harms living beings. By not harming living beings he is called noble,' The Indian told the Rat.

'You have not met many Romans,' said Cosmas. 'Or Goths for that matter, they live for battle and war.'

'Then why should I trust you? You promise much but you have little to back your words.'

'You know my associates who trade into Barbarikon and they will vouch for me.'

'So you say, but they are far away and what you ask risks my trade here.'

'You want glassware? My dominus can arrange shipments from Rome to Barbarikon over the seas; I have travelled that way before many times.'

The man sighed. 'The Buddha says that those who have no sympathy for life are outcasts.'

'He could be describing Naghi,' said Rat.

Suraj nodded. 'I do not like the Persian, but I do not want to upset trade, and I have no proof of my words only what my servant saw and heard.'

'He can testify in front of the Great Khan for us.'

'No he cannot. You have heard my words and I have spoken the truth, but I cannot ask him to risk himself or our industry. We return south soon, once the spring comes, I do not need the trouble.'

'When do you go south? Will there be Romans in Barbarikon.'

'By the time we get there the fleets will be due,' said Suraj. 'If not already arrived. They come every year as you know, but they are smaller than in our youth.'

'Perhaps we could travel south with you?'

Suraj seemed uncertain at that so Rat did not press the matter, but an inkling of an idea was forming in Cosmas' head. He bade the Indian farewell and returned to the citadel where Theo and the others were eagerly awaiting information.

'Well?' asked Theo when the Rat arrived. 'What did he say?'

'The boy was taken by Naghi's servants in the market, after that he was not seen again, but they heard his screams in the night.'

Cal cursed the Persian but Theo merely nodded.

'How are we going to proceed?' asked Cosmas.

'I will take it to Tardu and hope he can help. The men will take it ill if the boy's death goes unavenged.'

Cal was uncertain that the Goturks would help. They had no friendship for the Persians, but they already had one war with the fading power of the Hepthalites. No wise ruler fights on two fronts, thought the charioteer, except Justinian of course.

'What then?' Cal asked.

'Then we wreak our bloody vengeance on the Persian spy,' said Theo firmly. 'Beremund and the men would not stand for less.'

'Do we really need the bucellarii?' asked Rat. 'Suraj could help us go south to Barbarikon. There will be Roman ships there, traders and imperial officials.'

'Let it go, Rat,' said Cal. 'None of us want to go to the Indies except you.'

The Rat merely grimaced.

21

Spring arrived suddenly. For weeks it had been snow storms and icy slush, but seemingly overnight a cord was pulled and the sun returned. The city was covered in pink and white flowers as the almond and peach orchards exploded in blossom, drenching Tashkent in a haze of sweet honey scent from the fragrant flowers. The few Sogdians left in the city came out of their houses, but their joy at the end of winter was tempered by the arrival of more Goturk warriors from the steppe. Normally there would be a spring festival for the locals and merchants, with people coming from all over the region, but Istami had cancelled the party after the winter rebellion. A great encampment outside the city's stone walls filled with steppe horsemen instead, whilst their vast herds were set to graze on the plain before the stone city.

'It is quite beautiful really,' Cal told Cosmas as he came back from his daily walk around the battlements. 'Now that the snow has gone.'

'When the harvest comes there is a bigger festival,' said Rat. 'It is a most wonderful spectacle by all accounts and traders from all corners travel for the almond oil. I would like to see it. The spring festival is also famed but smaller. I am disappointed at missing it.'

'Stop whining, we shall be long gone by harvest time, I pray.'

Cosmas sniffed. 'I get to do nothing that I want on this trip.'

'We are not here for you, Rat. We are here for Narses. Once the girl's sister arrives we will move on, and the sooner the better. I want to see Calista again, I want to go back to my farm and enjoy my retirement.'

'Sink slowly into dotage, you mean. How many people from Rome had travelled this far? There is so much here beyond silk, I could make a fortune if I had some coin to spend.'

'You think only of profits.'

'It is better than the Goths, they think only of war and vengeance.'

That was true enough; Cal nodded at Rat's words. Since Uba's murder one of the bucellarii had been set to watch the Persians day and night to make sure that they did not slip away before Theo and the others could wreak some havoc. Once the silk arrived, they would put their plans to punish Naghi into action. The Khan's son had been sympathetic to Theo's accusations against the Persians, but unwilling to upset the Sassanids with a Hepthalite war to prosecute.

'The boy's murder requires recompense,' Cal reminded Cosmas.

'Does it really though? I thought our mission was everything. You just made that point, it is why going south is ruled out by all of you, yet we will risk everything for a dead barbarian child.'

'You are just bitter at not getting your own way.'

'I offer solutions to get home with ease and all I ever get back is insults and scorn.'

'Yes, well keep your opinions to yourself around Beremund and the other Goths. They will not take kindly to your words.'

'The dullards do not understand Greek.'

'Theo can explain it to them, and they have all been in the army long enough to pick up some words. They know more than they let on. Godda certainly did.'

'Godda is dead.'

'There is no talking to you when you're being a brat is there?'

Cosmas sniffed and left Cal to take a walk around the battlements and sulk.

Three days later the party from Serica arrived in Tashkent from Kashgar and everything changed. Two Nestorians dressed in white robes, one of them Padma's sister the other a mute Indian servant, were shown to the Roman's chamber in the citadel. The joy on the two girls faces at seeing each other again after their long separation was obvious to all. Broad smiles beamed on both of their faces, and the two women looked so similar it was clear to anyone that they were related. They rushed into each other's arms hugging and laughing and chattering away in their own tongue whilst Theo and the others watched on. Finally Padma turned back to the others.

'Her journey has been a success; she has brought the secret of silk,' said the young woman triumphantly.

Juana's story was as dramatic as the Romans journey to Tashkent. When Brother Timothy and Padma had left the Indies for Rome, Juana and a party of Nestorians had travelled into Serica. After months of travel they had reached the towns where Serican silk was produced and bought the secret from a disgruntled official. She told them that the Serican Empire was divided between north and south and ravaged by civil war, just like Rome in the old days, but once they had managed to get the worm eggs past Serican officials returning to Tashkent had been easy enough if long. They had joined a merchant caravan that had taken them to Kashgar where they waited impatiently all winter. As soon as the snows had begun to melt the pair had left the city and travelled west to Tashkent. The woman was clearly elated at finding her sister again and with the success of the mission.

'So where is it then?' asked Cosmas. 'What is it?'

Juana smiled shyly as Padma explained Cosmas' words to her, and then she took out a walking stick from under her robes. She showed it to them and spoke slowly to her sister.

'The material is woven by worms,' Padma told Cosmas. 'The feed off mulberry bushes and spin the silk like a butterfly's cocoon. Women collect the cocoons and spin them back out into a thread.' Juana put the cane away in a wooden case as her sister continued. 'The worm eggs are packed in the cane and dormant for now. Once we reach Rome, they can be hatched on the mulberry bushes and the silk trade becomes Roman.'

'So not giant spiders then?' said Cosmas. He sounded disappointed.

Cal slapped his forehead at Padma's words. 'That is why the Emperor has started planting mulberry bushes all over Greece. He paid ten solidus for every bush that flowered. Estates all over Attica have been digging up vines and planting these useless trees for him. The gossips all thought it was something to do with the late empress's perversions but now I understand.'

'The emperor has been planning this for a long time,' said Theo. 'That is clear; it is also clear how important this mission is to Narses now. Our fortunes will be made when we return.'

'It is going to break the fortunes of many merchants both Roman and Persian,' said Cosmas with a frown.

'But not of those who are in on it at the start,' said Theo to him. 'People like you, Cosmas, will become grotesquely rich.'

'That is true,' said Rat with a smile. 'But it means every trader on the road home will want to stop us. Naghi is not our only problem now.'

'Only if word gets out.'

'We do not know what the boy told the Persians. What if he…'

'Uba will have said nothing,' said Theo. 'He was loyal and one of us.'

Cosmas sniffed at that, but stayed silent with Beremund glowering at him. The Rat was unconvinced that the youth could have withstood Naghi's torturers.

'Perhaps you judge the boy by your own standards,' Cal whispered to him.

'It does lead us to our final problem before we leave for home,' said Theo. 'We must deal with Naghi and the Persians. Such an affront to us is an affront to Rome itself. It is time to take our revenge.'

Beremund nodded grimly at Theo's words. The bucellarii were still hell bent on avenging Uba before they left, and nothing Rat could do or say would dissuade them. Cosmas understood that well enough and left to walk along the battlements as the others discussed the plan of action. He wanted as little to do with their blood oath as possible.

'They will poke the hornet's nest and then wonder why everything becomes a disaster,' said Rat. 'I am glad I am not an honourable man, a surfeit of honour causes trouble.'

He stared out over the stone city, sparkling in the spring sunshine, and sighed.

***

The discussion had been going on for almost an hour with no conclusion. Whilst all of them, except Cosmas, were eager for revenge on the Persians, the means to achieve it were seemingly beyond them. Every idea was met with objections or problems.

'Why can we not just go down with our swords and deal with it the usual way?' said Beremund angrily, frustrated at the long conversation. 'We chop them up into bits with our spathas. That is what Godda would have done.'

'The Great Khan would not be happy with us murdering the Sassanid Emperor's ambassador openly,' said Theo. 'Our denials must be believable, if he is to ignore it.'

'Perhaps we bar the doors of their domos and burn it down.'

'The buildings are made of stone with a flat roof that has guards,' said Beremund. 'They will not just catch fire, we would need naphtha.'

'We cannot start a fire in the city either,' said Cal. 'It could spread through the neighbourhood and kill innocents.'

'This is not Constantinople,' said Theo. 'The buildings will not catch like dry tinder and spread, but Beremund is correct that we would need naphtha and that makes it too expensive a solution.'

'Still, it is not right.'

Cal had lived in the capital for years, but Tashkent did not have the poorly built tenements that plagued the Roman cities. However, the objection was the same: how would the Great Khan react if they started fires and it spread?

'We cannot burn them out, cannot openly kill them, we cannot provoke a battle with them. This is the most difficult revenge imaginable,' said Theo.

'What about the girls?' asked Cal. 'What do they think?'

Theo grimaced. 'They think all men are fools, especially us, at least that's what Padma told me.'

The two women, like the Rat, were not party to the discussion. Padma had been scathing about the Roman desire for vengeance and her sister was still shyly unsure of herself around the tall Goths. They had both retired to the chambers that Padma shared with Theo. The smitten boy was increasingly in thrall to Padma – Beremund and the bucellarii were worried that he was becoming 'cock happy' as they told Cal. Theo's insistence that Uba's death could not go unavenged had stopped them from outright defiance. Beremund had cracked the grumblers' heads together and they all adored Padma, but the long confinement over the winter had made everyone's tempers short.

Cosmas finally came back into the room holding his small bible and mumbling the words aloud whilst the other three had argued how to kill Naghi and the others. He sighed when he realised that they still had no solution to their Persian problem.

'I can get poison,' said Rat. 'And tainting their foodstuffs would be easy enough compared to burning or battling, and less easy for the Goturks or Persians to point the finger of blame at us afterwards.'

'Poison!' Cal was even more disgusted by that idea than burning the Persians out. 'It is a vile way to deal with a problem.'

'Grow up, Charioteer. Dead is dead, what matters the manner of murder?'

The Rat had none of the others' notions of honour. It was the reason he had no desire for revenge. It was not a lack of concern for Uba, Cosmas had liked the boy as much as the rest of them. It was simply that the whole plot seemed pointless to the little merchant. There was no profit in it, and too much to lose if they were caught. The Rat was surprised that Theo would risk everything for some Sogdian boy, particularly now that they had the silkworms. For Cosmas, getting back to Constantinople and delivering the worms to Narses was now paramount. If they could take the southern route home, then the better for Rat. That way, he might at least be able to turn some profit on the journey as well as the information he had already gleaned on the outward leg. Such an opinion did not endear him to Cal, or Beremund and the other Goths. Theo, on the other hand, was schooled in the machinations of the Roman court in Constantinople and had no such squeamishness when it came to assassination. Poison was just another political weapon to the aristocrat.

'Where would you find such here?'

'I have spent the winter talking to merchants, making contacts for future trade,' said Cosmas. 'There is one from the Indies who can procure it for me. He will keep silent about it.'

'How can you trust someone who sells poison?'

'Nobody likes to be complicit in murder, Theo, and people who deal in such potions tend to be discrete.'

'It is not murder,' said Beremund haltingly in Greek. 'It is justice.'

'Yes, well I am certain that the Khan's officials will not see it that way, so let us call it what it is and not dress it up in fine words – even when poorly spoken.'

The tall Goth glared at Rat.

'It is little wonder that you have so few friends,' said Cal.

'I will always have you as my friend, Charioteer.'

'You are incorrigible. How would we taint their foodstuffs, if we are to commit such a sinful act?'

'They get deliveries of food from the market,' said Beremund in Latin. 'Every other day some is taken from the market in the square to their house by Persian guards. They use the same merchant. We have been watching them.'

'So, we spoil their grain, or taint the wine, or both,' said Cosmas. 'You are resourceful men, I am sure you can come up with the means to do that?'

Theo paused whilst he considered the plan. It was his decision. He understood that this was a risk to their mission, an unwanted risk, but also he did not want his bucellarii sullen and rebellious all the way home with no Godda to keep them in check. That is as much a risk to the mission itself as killing the Persians, he decided. The reality was that he was as bloodthirsty as his men and there was enough of the pagan Goth from his upbringing to desire restitution for the boy. Perhaps I am learning some responsibility, he thought. Finally he nodded and looked over to Rat.

'See your contact and get the poison,' he said. 'Make sure that he understands that this is a secret.'

'As I told you, anyone who deals in poisons and potions is well aware of the need for discretion,' said Rat. 'We can trust the Indian.'

***

Suraj of Taxila was surprised by the Rat's request, but easily able to find a concoction that would work for their design. He was, however, determined to make it a profitable transaction for himself. Suraj did not wish to be dragged into the feud between the Romans and Persians in Tashkent, but there was no sin in making coin from their conflict. He rubbed his hands together and smiled at Cosmas.

'It will be very expensive.'

'Yes, I thought you would say that, but it is not my coin so that is not my concern. Try not to make the price too extortionate else even our young dominus might balk.'

'I am certain we can come to some accommodation, but I do expect discretion.'

'Absolute discretion should give a discount,' said Cosmas leaning forward with sly smirk.

'Are you really going to haggle over a murderer's tools?'

'You started it,' said Cosmas. 'I would have happily paid an expensively reasonable price.'

The two of them sat for nearly fifteen minutes bargaining over the potion. They finally agreed on the amount and Suraj reached into a large trunk and pulled out a small glass vial.

'Arsenic,' he told Cosmas. 'The king of poisons. There is enough here to wipe out an army.'

'Arsenic in the wine improves the flavour, so I am told,' said Cosmas. 'I would not like to test the theory.'

Suraj laughed and Cosmas pulled out the small bag of coins that Theo had given him, taking out some gold solidus and counting them for the Kushan merchant. Suraj bit down on each coin to check it.

'Do you not trust me?'

'No more than you trust me.'

'It is a sad indictment of the world when two travellers cannot trust each other.'

'We are not travellers, friend Cosmas. We are traders, and profit is everything to us. We are different from normal men,' said Suraj. 'You know that.'

Once the potion had been paid for, Cosmas begged his leave of the merchant. He tucked the glass vial into his robes and returned to the citadel where the others were waiting. The Goturk guards nodded to him as he passed through the gatehouse and he hurried up the steps to the Roman chambers.

It has been a worthwhile exercise, he thought. If we can get home safely, the contacts I have made this winter could prove very profitable indeed. We just need to get home.

Theo and Cal were still awake and waiting for the Rat. They both looked up when Cosmas entered.

'Well?' asked Theo.

'I have the poison,' said Rat.

'Well, now we just have to get it into their wine without being caught,' said Cal. 'Do you have any plans for that.'

Theo grimaced. 'I have been thinking about ways but...'

'I can do it,' said Cosmas.

The other two both looked at him in surprise.

'What are you up to Rat?' asked Cal. 'First you want no part of the plan, now you procure the means and propose the deployment.'

'Our best chance of getting home is if we succeed, the last thing I want is for one of you blundering oafs to get caught and us to be hanged, or tortured, or whatever these barbarians do to execute people.'

'I believe they tie your arms and legs to different horses and whip them to rip you apart,' said Theo glibly.

The Rat blanched at his words.

'Well then, I am best suited to success. I can get it into the wine before it is delivered to Naghi and the others, but we will need to leave directly afterwards. It will be clear what we have done to anyone, after the event.'

22

Cal was the first to awake the next day. Theo was ensconced in his chambers with Padma, whilst her sister had slept in the common room. She smiled shyly at the old charioteer as he clumped into the room wincing at his knee.

'I suppose you had to escape their amorous adventures,' he told the girl, as he poured some poppy juice for his knee into a cup of wine and watered it down. 'It must be difficult for you, waiting so long to see your sister again to find she's enraptured by a foolish aristocrat.'

The woman Juana nodded uncomprehending at his words, and then pointed to the poppy juice.

'Opium,' she said.

'I do not understand?'

She pointed at the bottle he had tipped into the wine

'Opium.'

'Ah, it is for my knee you see, He rolled down his long stockings to show his swollen arthritic knee.

She slapped her hand to her mouth at the sight of his red skin and pointed at the poppy juice, shaking her head. She frowned searching for a word in Greek.

'Bad, 'she said finally.

'Oh, I know it is bad for me, but what choice do I have. It is pain or poppy.'

Padma came out of her chamber, dressed in a thin robe, and her sister spoke to her sharply, pointing at Cal.

'What does she say?' he asked Padma.

'Juana says that the poppy is bad for you,' said Padma. 'It will cause a dependence and damage your aatma.'

'What is my aatma?' said Cal.

Padma paused as she thought about the correct word for the old man. 'Your essence,' she said finally. 'It is the best translation.'

'Well, I don't want to lose my essence.'

Her sister started jabbering away again at Cal and he looked back to Padma.

'She knows of a powder that will ease the pain over time and bring the inflammation down. You will have to add it to your food, every meal, and it will not be as effective in the short term, but it will be better for you in the long run. She says you are too old to be indulging in the poppy. If you will take her to the market she can find the spice easily enough.'

'I will happily accompany her,' said Cal. 'Anything to fix my knee and the poppy juice is bitter even in wine.'

The spice was easy enough to locate in the market, one stall had great clay pots piled high with a yellow powder. She spoke to the merchant and ordered him to fill a large pot with the stuff. Cal sniffed at it.

'Why it is Indian Saffron. That is expensive, almost as expensive as the poppy.'

'Turmeric,' said the girl

The vendor only wanted half a solidus to fill an ampohora of the turmeric. This far east the spice was common and cheap. Back home in the Empire it was far more expensive and difficult to get hold of, but there was enough in the amphorae to feed a family for a year and Cal for a lifetime. Once the powder was paid for, the two of them turned to walk back to the citadel and the girl linked her arm with the old charioteer as they walked along.

'I should get a cane,' said Cal, 'but the Rat would tease me mercilessly.'

She just smiled uncomprehending at his words and he smiled back.

She will have to learn our language soon enough, thought Cal. It had taken the whole outward journey for their diverse group to manage a reasonable level of communication.

There was a sudden jolt as if they had both been grabbed and pulled to the side, and the earth beneath them shook. Both of them fell to the floor as a loud roaring filled their ears. The pot of turmeric cracked as it hit the cobbles, spilling the yellow powder and sending up a pungent cloud. There were people screaming and animals baying all over Tashkent. Cracks appeared in the road, ripping through the masonry; buildings collapsed in an instant, crumbling into heaps of rubble and dust with the occupants buried alive. The brick and stone buildings of Tashkent were shaken to their foundations, breaking up and shattering as the earth trembled. The shaking went on and on and Cal pulled the girl to him to keep her safe from falling blocks of stone.

In the citadel the Romans were thrown to the floor of their chambers, their possessions crashing about them, pots shattering and amphorae cracking and spilling the wine all over the floor. Theo leaped out of his bed and reached for his sword and then fell over with the shaking; he just lay there terrified as the citadel shook. It must have gone on for a few minutes until the thunder in their ears stopped and the earth was still. There was silence for a moment, then the screams and cries started up from outside.

'What in the name of all the saints was that?'

He could hear more cries coming up from the city, and shouts of alarm in the citadel.

'Earthquake,' said Cosmas as he entered the chambers to check on Theo. 'Cal and your sister-in-law have gone shopping.'

'She is not my sister-in-law,'

'Yet,' said Rat.

'Why is God angry with us to send such a message?'

'People think the world is round,' said Cosmas glibly. 'When it is clearly flat as unleavened bread. That would be enough to upset even a merciful deity.'

Theo narrowed his eyes at Rat's words.

'What of Cal and Juana, why have they gone into the town?'

'They went to get some medicine for his knee.'

Once the shaking had finally stopped, Cal scooped up what was left of his turmeric into the broken remains of the pot. The girl stood up and brushed herself down, said something to Cal and pointed to the citadel. The charioteer's mouth dropped open when he followed her gesture. The Great stone gatehouse had a wide crack right through the middle, breaking the gateposts and lintel. There was rubble and dead bodies there – people killed by falling masonry as the walls had crumbled about them.

'My God, what have you done,' said Cal.

The girl tugged at his coat, pulling him along, back to the citadel where they had left the others. The worry on her face was palpable, but Cal thanked the Lord God that they were both unharmed and prayed that the others were safe. There were no living guards at the gates, just bodies, and they crawled through rubble to get back inside the citadel. Goturk warriors saw them, but looked utterly stunned by their experience as the pair emerged from the broken gatehouse. Most of Istami's people were outside the city walls in a vast encampment, much safer in their tents than within Tashkent's walls. Juana grabbed Cal and pointed again, muttering something in her Indian language at him. There was a great crack in the wall; a large v that had crumbled away the battlements where her sister and Theo walked every day.

'I am sure they will be fine,' he said reassuringly to the uncomprehending girl.

Then he saw where the bucellarii had been sleeping down by the stables. Great stone blocks had crashed down from the walls onto the Goth quarters below. Beremund emerged from the rubble and Cal rushed over ignoring the pain in his knee. There were two others still alive – Llew the Briton and Fritigern - but the other bucellarii had been struck by falling stones. There was no saving them.

'The twins died together,' said Beremund in his pig-Latin. 'Killed by the same stone. What of our Dominus, is he safe?' The grief at the loss of his comrades and fear for Theo was palpable on the warrior's face.

'I know not,' said Cal. 'But I will find out.'

Beremund nodded and turned back to his men and their broken bodies as Cal and Juana climbed broken steps back up to the chambers that the Romans all shared. Theo almost crashed into them as he came down in the opposite direction. The relief on his face was palpable at the sight of them.

'Your men,' said Cal. 'They…' He shook his head sadly. 'Three of them have been killed. The others seem unharmed but we have lost horses too.'

Theo blanched and then nodded. 'I will go to them. Get yourself back to our chambers Padma will be relieved. We will not be staying here long, get your possessions together, I want to be outside the city walls tonight. My grandfather says the shakes always come in threes.'

Cal nodded and started climbing the stairs again with the girl in tow as Theo rushed down to his remaining Gothic warriors.

The two women were relieved at seeing each other, rushing into each other's arms, but there was no time to waste. The Rat had already thrown his few belongings into a sack and was waiting whilst the girls and Cal took only a few minutes to be ready. All of them had been travelling lightly except Theo with his trunk and armour. Cal and the Rat dragged the young aristocrat's belongings down to the courtyard out of the building.

'He thinks we are his servants,' moaned Cosmas.

'Stop whining.'

There were more steppe warriors now, coming in from the camp outside the city and searching through the rubble for any survivors.

'There they are,' said Cosmas, spying Theo and the others. 'Most of the horses seem fine.

They placed the bodies of the twins and Ademar onto horses and led them out of the city to the plain, away from the threat of collapsing buildings and into the open. Outside, if the earth shook, they would fall down but not be crushed by crumbling houses.

'So much for our luxury,' said Cosmas sadly.

'Three of our own are dead,' snapped Cal. 'And you still think only of your own pleasures.'

'Dead is dead, they are with God now. I would suggest that the Kingdom of Heaven is a better place than here.'

'I would suggest that you keep your mouth shut.'

Rat made a face at Cal but said no more as the moved through the chaotic streets.

Outside the city walls the destruction was even more shocking. Once grand buildings were now little more than piles of rubble, and the great walls that protected the city had been broken and cracked in numerous places. It would take years to rebuild. The only saving grace – from a moral standpoint – was that most of the Sogdian locals were away after the winter rebellion had failed. It had been the merchants and traders who had made the place their home and who had been worst hit. Two more shocks came in the hours after the earthquake had first struck, but each was weaker than the one before. Tashkent was left in ruins as night fell.

'Do you think that the Persians were crushed?' said the charioteer to Cosmas.

'We can only pray so,' replied the Rat. 'It would at least solve one of our problems.'

Those hopes were quickly dashed. The Persian party emerged from the ruins of Tashkent seemingly unharmed by the ordeal. Naghi the Snake was among them safe and sound. He smiled and waved at the Romans, and then sent a servant over to enquire as to their wellbeing and offer his assistance. Theo politely declined before his furious Goths cut the man down.

'Get the tents up,' he told them with as much authority as he could muster, and Beremund barked at them to move. They laid their comrades bodies on a linen sheet on the ground.

'We will bury them with Uba and Brother Timothy,' said Theo. 'Then we will act. I think it is way past time for us to move on.'

The men nodded, they had not forgotten their revenge and whilst Naghi could not be blamed for the earthquake, the disaster had made the bucellarii hatred of the Persian spy more furious.

Once the tents were set up and a semblance of a camp organised, Theo held a council of war with the others. Beremund sat in Godda's place with his Dominus's approval. The Bearlike warrior was proving a good subordinate, although Theo missed the wry wit of his old teacher. The two sisters and their mute Serican servant along with Cal and the Rat all gathered in Theo's command tent. Fritigern stood sentinel against intruders whilst Llew prepared their comrades bodies for burial. All across Tashkent bodies were being pulled out of the broken rubble and made ready for the afterlife: Christian, Zoroastrian, Buddhist, all had their cemeteries and necropolis' around the town. It was going to be a busy few days digging at the cold earth for the remaining Sogdian slaves.

'Well,' said Cosmas. 'That was unexpected, what do we do now?'

'I think our plans have to change,' said Theo.

The Rat raised a quizzical eyebrow.

'How so?' said Cal. 'We still need to get back to Rome and the sooner the better. That is still our priority.'

Padma whispered to her sister and the two women nodded at Cal. Juana smiled at the old man's words.

'We shall go south over the mountains to the sea and take a ship back to Rome,' said Theo.

Cal looked at Beremund who nodded approvingly. Theo had clearly discussed his plan beforehand with the warrior.

'Why the change of heart?' asked the Rat.

'I thought you wanted to go over the mountains to the south?' said Cal.

'I do, I think it is the best way to return home, if a tad longer, but I would still like to know why.'

'Because there is war on the steppe, and less of us to travel that path now, and well, we still need to deal with Naghi and then escape,' said Theo.

Cosmas winced at those last words, but Theo outlined his plan and the grin grew wider on his face. The poison so expensively procured would still be used to taint the Persians foodstuffs and then they would leave in two parties. Beremund, Llew the Briton, and Fritigern would travel west back the way they had come to draw off any Persian pursuit. Theo, the women, Cal, Cosmas and the mute Indian servant would go over the mountains into the Indies and to the coast where there would be Roman ships.

'It all sounds so simple,' said Cal. 'Why then do I worry we jump from the cooking pot into the fire?'

'Because you are a grumpy old pessimist,' said the Rat. 'The passes are clear now and we can get to the Indus in less than a month. After that it is, to coin a phrase, plain sailing to the sea, we change boats and go all the way back to Miles Hormuz, and then it is a short ride to the Nile, Alexandria and home. We will be back before the winter solstice.'

'We would be home by Saturnalia,' said Theo with a smile. 'It is still always celebrated at the estate.'

'A pagan tradition that should be stamped out,' said the Rat.

'I wish we could stamp you out,' said Cal, and tweaked Rat's pointed nose in jest.

'You are in a good mood, of a sudden.'

'I have just survived a disaster, I mourn our lost friends but I cannot deny I am giddy with life.'

'Have you been taking the poppy?'

'No more poppy for me,' said Cal. 'It was dulling my senses and making me morose. I have the Indian Saffron now.'

'Turmeric,' said Juana and smiled at the old charioteer.

23

The Romans left Tashkent a week later after the funerals in one big party, conspicuously and heading north towards the steppe but leaving Cosmas behind with his Kushan contact. They travelled towards the Jaxartes River for a day, before camping down in a narrow ravine hidden from prying eyes. The next morning, Theo, Cal and the girls bade the Goths farewell and turned their horses towards the mountain passes.

'Stay out of trouble,' Theo told Beremund and the others as they made ready to leave. 'Get to Atil as quickly as possible and you will find help to get to Chersonesus. Be conspicuous; remember you are to draw away any pursuit from us.'

'Yes, Dominus.'

The Goths were pleased to finally leave Tashkent even if it was as bait for the Persians. The city had been a bitter experience for all of them. Godda killed in battle, the others killed in the earthquake and Uba's foul murder by Naghi. All of them wanted to get home as quickly as possible and away from the stone city. They believed that the place was cursed.

'Once you are in Chersonesus have messages sent back on our path to the Indies. If all goes well we shall be back home by winter.'

'Yes, Dominus, and your mother?'

'Do not tell her anything of worth, she will only worry. Just reassure her. You can tell my grandfather everything, and tell him to plant the mulberry bushes instead of vines in the south orchard.'

'Yes, Dominus.'

The bucellarii should cross the steppe before Theo could sail across the oceans into Miles Hormuz and onto Alexandria. They watched the Goths in silence as they rode away to the north and disappeared from view.

'I half wish I was going with them,' said Cal. 'I would like to get home sooner.'

Theo clapped him on the back. 'We shall get home before the end of the year, my friend, you will save your farm and your granddaughter's debts will be repaid. You can trust me on that.'

'I trust you. It is the Rat I have concerns about.'

Cosmas had been left behind in Tashkent to deliver their parting gift to the Persians. He would meet up with them in two days at an oasis to the south of the city. It would be clear of any local Sogdians after the Goturk raids and patrols. Since the battle before Tashkent in the winter, there had been a growing Goturk presence as more and more of the steppe warriors poured into the fertile river plain. The Great Khan and his son had given messages for Justinian written in Greek on clay tablets declaring their eternal friendship with Rome for Theo to carry back to Constantinople, and the Roman aristocrat understood that this diplomatic success was almost as important for Rome as the secret of silk. Once Cosmas had rejoined them, after he had poisoned the Persians, they would travel as quickly as possible home through the great mountains and then the Indus River – as long as Rat was successful that was. Even Theo had to admit that the little merchant had become vital to their success in getting home.

Theo smiled at Cal. 'The Rat wants to get home as much as we do. He told me he plans to write a book of his travels that will prove to all, including the Patriarch in Constantinople, that the world is flat.'

Cal burst out laughing, the first genuine guffaw of mirth since the earthquake.

'What is so funny?'

'That our lives and future wealth, and my granddaughter's freedom, are dependent upon a man who thinks the world is flat and irritates everyone that he encounters.'

Theo could see the ridiculous situation for what it was and joined the old charioteer in his mirth. The two women both looked at them as if they had both gone mad. Juana had obvious concern on her face at the strange Roman behaviour. Padma assured her sister that they were loyal and brave, if infuriatingly stubborn about some things and clearly uncivilized compared the cities along the Indus or Ganges rivers.

'Barbarians,' Padma told her sister.

'Come along,' said Theo wiping the tears of laughter from his face. 'Let us find this oasis and wait for Rat to arrive.'

They rode through the morning, mostly in silence apart from the odd question to the two women from Theo as to the direction they should take. Juana had travelled this way to meet with them, and knew the route as far as Kashgar. Normally the road would be full of traders, even in this early season, but the war in Sogdiana meant that most now avoided the region. The rise of the Goturks was unsettling trade on the caravan routes but it would only be temporary. The Great Khan had assured the merchants in Tashkent of that, and his older brother in the East had already secured the roads beyond the mountains as far as Serica. Soon the movement of goods from east to west would be uninterrupted and the roads would be filled with people again.

'There, down there,' called Theo. 'That is where we are to wait for the Rat.'

The stone built way station at the small oasis was empty but dry, and Cal was able to start a fire with some wood and kindling left for others to use by the last occupants in the autumn. Nobody had been through there since then, and the local Sogdians had fled after the Battle of Tashkent. The five of them huddled around the flickering firelight and waited for Cosmas to arrive. Juana'a servant made up a tisane to drink which the Romans both declined, but Padma and Juana sat back and sipped the hot liquid gratefully.

'We came this way from Serica,' Juana told them through Padma's translation. 'There will be other travellers on the road soon from the east.'

'Are you worried about Serican agents?' asked Theo.

She shook her head. 'There is war in the east occupying them, and none knew of our mission.' She smiled at her mute servant and the big man smiled back. 'We were most discrete,' she said pointedly to Theo. 'If there is to be trouble, I think it will come from your Persian enemy.'

'How long are we to wait for Cosmas?' asked Cal.

'Two days,' said Theo. 'If he has not come by the third morning we are to leave without him.'

***

Cosmas waited until it was dark before sneaking through the streets of Tashkent to the food merchant. The Persians took delivery of basic foodstuffs every three days: fresh bread, root vegetables, and sacks of beans, were piled up by the Sogdian slaves, loaded up on a cart and hauled over to the small compound outside the city that Naghi had made his base of operations. Cosmas knew that there was no way to slip the poison in the wine once it had been delivered to the Persian camp, even if he could somehow gain entry. Instead, he had bribed one of the slaves, with Suraj's connivance, to let him into the warehouse the night before. The Sogdians had left the untethered cart inside the gates, unguarded, and loaded high with foodstuffs to deliver to the Persian camp in the morning.

'They had better be waiting for me when I get out of this town,' thought Rat.

He rapped three times on a side door to the warehouse, just as Suraj had instructed, and waited for the response.

For a moment he worried that the Kushan trader had sold him out, but then a hatch in the door shot back and a brown Sogdian face peered out. Once the man inside saw that Cosmas was alone, the door opened to reveal a quiet warehouse. There was no trap and Cosmas was almost exultant at his plan's success, offering up a prayer of thanks for God's benevolence.

'It is clearly a good thing that I do,' said Rat to the uncomprehending Sogdian slave. 'Else the good Lord God would have put a stop to it.'

Pleased with his moral and theological sophistry, he located the cart and found the amphorae of wine sealed and loaded up. Taking a candle out of his satchel and lighting it from a lamp, Cosmas started heating the wax seal around the cork of each amphora with the small flame. Once the first seal was warm and pliable, he took out his knife and peeled it back, taking care not to crack the wax. Then he slowly jimmied the wooden stopper out of the amphora until it came loose with a pop, flying up into the air as Cosmas juggled to catch it. Finally, he drew out the small vial of arsenic that Suraj had sold him, tipped some into the amphora and shook the clay pot around to swill the poison into the wine. Then he reversed the process with the cork and carefully used his lit candle and a flat blade to reseal the container.

Rat repeated the process five more times until all of the wine was tainted. Once he was satisfied that the Persians would not notice that the amphorae had been tampered with, he left the warehouse and returned to a small house that Suraj kept just off the market square. The Kushan's help had been expensive, but Cosmas was happy enough with the evening's work. He had dreaded the thought of travelling back over the steppes with the bucellarii to Chersonesus. Poisoning Naghi was his bargain to go south into the Indies; it was merely a bonus that he despised the Persian spy.

'Is it done?' asked Suraj when he arrived.

'Yes.'

'Then we leave now.'

'In the darkness.'

'By the time we awake the Persians will be dead. I would rather not be around for the investigations.'

'Do you think the Khan will take it badly?'

'Not so much, he can deny all responsibility and we will be gone. Istami is more concerned about his war with the Hepthalites, but it is still best that we are on our way.'

Rat agreed with that, he wanted out of the city as quickly as possible.

Suraj led him through the dark deserted streets of Tashkent to a small house tucked up against the great encircling walls. The building, like so many others in the ravaged city, had been abandoned by the Sogdian occupants during the winter. A stout door with an untampered and expensive lock showed that the place had been left alone during the riots and subsequent massacres. Suraj took out a heavy brass key and wiggled it in the lock until the mechanism clicked and he pushed the door open. A dusty musty smell lingered inside, and the Indian pulled Cosmas in with him and closed the door, quickly locking it behind them. In the darkness, the Kushan found an oil lamp and sparked it into light.

'What is this place?' asked Cosmas.

'Our means of leaving the city.'

Suraj counted flagstones on the floor.

'Three from the left corner and two down,' he muttered.

Once he had located the stone that he wanted, he pulled out a small knife and slid it down between the flagstones. After a few moments fiddling with the knife he hooked up two silken cords concealed in the cracks.

'Give me a hand,' he said, nodding to one cord.

Cosmas grabbed one of the cords and Suraj the other and they both tugged at the flagstone. It creaked and groaned for a moment and then came free with a big pop, like a boot stuck in deep mud, to reveal a dark shaft descending into the bowels of the earth. The hatch that they had hooked up was mostly made of wood with only a thin veneer of stone to conceal the entrance

'A tunnel?'

'Really, Cosmas, you do have an irritating habit of stating the obvious. Come along, we want to be away from the city before the sunrise.'

Suraj held the oil lamp above the shaft, casting light down into the darkness. Cosmas could make out small footholds cut into the stone for a man to climb down.

'Get in then,' said Suraj.

'You first,' said Rat, eyeing the dark hole warily.

'I need to pull everything down behind me, get down a few metres and I will follow with the light.'

Cosmas gulped but slid himself into the tunnel shaft, placing his feet carefully in the holes and slowly started down into the darkness. All the while he was praying that the Kushan was not about to entomb him in the bowels of the earth. Suraj waited for Rat to descend and then followed him down, pulling the trapdoor down behind them and making sure that the silken cords were laid for the next person to use. Once they were both perched in the shaft, they slowly climbed down a step at a time. The small oil lamp placed in niches on the opposite wall and moved as they descended. After a minute or so, Cosmas could see an empty blackness below him and could not feel any more walls.

'There is a chamber,' he said to Suraj above him. 'How do I get down?'

'Climb as low as you can and then drop.'

'Drop into the darkness?'

'It is not far.'

'That is very easy for you to say.'

'I have done it before, Cosmas I assure you it is only a couple of gaz drop.'

Rat sighed – he had no idea what a gaz was - and let go of his handhold, falling down into the darkness and hitting the floor with a grunt and a moan.

'Remember to bend your knees when you land.'

There was a pause. 'A little late to mention that now.'

'Here take the lamp.'

Suraj passed the oil lamp down for Cosmas to take, revealing a small chamber cut into the stone and another tunnel sloping down but tall enough for them both to walk.

'This leads under the walls and then takes us to caves under the city.'

'The Goturks?'

'They do not know of this, it is a secret of the merchants of Tashkent.'

Cosmas did not question that, such a means of entry and exit to the city would be worth a fortune in normal times. Merchants would be able to avoid the prying eyes of customs officials and their taxes. It was another useful piece of information for Rat to exploit in the future.

'Come along.'

Suraj led the Rat through the tunnel, holding the lamp up so they could see their way in the gloom for perhaps one hundred paces. He paused at one point where the tunnel narrowed and they both had to crawl through a small opening.

'We are under the walls here.'

Cosmas nodded and followed the Kushan through until they came into another small chamber.

'These caves are close to the city. We are nearly there now.'

It was easier once they had passed under the walls. The cave complex was not deep or extensive, merely a fissure in the stone that led to the surface. Cosmas could smell the outside, a whisper of fresh air in the musty tunnel.

'Well that is a relief,' said Suraj as they climbed into the moonlight.

'What?'

'I was a little concerned that the earthquake might have damaged the tunnels or brought the roof down.'

'What would we have done then?'

'I would have abandoned you in the tunnels and returned to the city.'

'That's comforting to know.'

'Ah, Cosmas, it did not come to that.'

They had emerged from their subterranean travels onto the plain outside the city walls. Suraj's Sogdian servant was waiting for them with two horses, saddled and ready to ride.

'We need to get away from the city and to the others at the oasis south of here,' said the Kushan merchant. 'It will not be long before the Persians take their delivery of wine and the alarm is raised. We need to be gone from here by then.'

The two of them rode off at a trot into the night looking for the oasis and Theo, Cal and the women, whilst Suraj's servant returned to the city.

'Can that one be trusted?' asked Rat.

'Yes,' came the reply.

24

They woke at dawn and made ready for the journey ahead, whether Rat arrived or not. It was warm in the spring sunshine but the last vestiges of the winter remained in the shadows and they all kept their cloaks wrapped around to stop the chills. The two women were packed and ready whilst Theo and Cal saw to the horses.

'He should be here by now.'

Theo smiled at the old charioteer. For all his gruffness Cal had proven useful on the trip, and he seemed to be the only person who could keep Cosmas in line. Perhaps Narses had understood that about the African all along.

'I do not think he will tarry long, the sun is barely up.'

'Still, he should be here.'

'Do you think that he would betray us?'

Cal shook his head. 'He wants to go home as much as you or I, but he wants to profit from it as well.'

'Narses will reward us when we return.'

The old charioteer smiled back at the nobleman. 'He will reward you perhaps, but you have contacts and can cause some trouble at court. The Rat and I are more expendable and Narses is an arsehole.'

Theo clapped him on the back and laughed. 'I will see to it that we are all well rewarded for two years of our life.'

'You think it will be that long?' Rat said it is just over the mountains.

'Padma says that "just over the mountains" is almost a thousand miles, and then we have a river journey that could take weeks before we reach the coast.'

'There had better be Roman ships there when we arrive at the sea; else I will wring Cosmas's scrawny neck.'

'You keep saying that, but if you always fail to carry out the threat why should he believe you?'

Cal gave him a hard stare.

'Oh do not take offence; it is something Godda tried to drill into me. As an officer you must be prepared to carry out your threats else the men will lose respect for you.' He shook his head regretfully. 'I should have listened to him more.'

'Fortunately I am not an officer and the Rat is not a soldier, else I would have had him cleaning shithouses for the rest of his life, but he knows me well enough not to take things too far.'

Padma called over to Theo. 'There is someone coming.'

'There you go,' said Theo to Cal. 'The Rat has arrived.'

Even so, Cal noted that the blonde aristocrat had his hand on his spatha hilt as he climbed up to the roof of the way station to see who was approaching.

The two horsemen rode up to the oasis wrapped in cloaks and scarves. Theo and the others watched warily as the men looked around, and then Cosmas drew back his veil and smiled.

'No welcome for Cosmas the Brave?'

They all smiled in relief and gathered around Rat before he could dismount, pestering him with questions.

'All of that can wait until I have rested a while,' said Cosmas.

'No actually it cannot,' said Rat's companion. 'We need to move on today.'

'But we have been riding all night, Suraj,' Rat protested.

'You will sleep better tonight, then,' said Suraj. 'But we need to put distance between ourselves and Tashkent.'

Theo and Cal and the girls all agreed with that sentiment once it was translated, as they had been waiting for two days, but Cosmas still whined as they all mounted up and made ready to leave.

'Not even a moment's rest to take some tisane or breakfast?'

'You don't like tisane,' said Cal. 'You told me it was too bitter and foul tasting.'

'Traitor,' hissed Cosmas at the charioteer.

'There is a small village where we camp tonight,' said Suraj. 'They will have tisane for you.'

The Rat sighed and grumbled some more, but the others were firm in their insistence that they got moving. Once the Persians had been poisoned, or discovered the poison in the wine, there would be trouble. Theo and the others were counting on it only affecting Naghi and his company, and that the Great Khan would consider it beneath him to punish the transgression – particularly if the culprits had already left his realm and he hoped for good contacts with Rome in the future. There were, however, no certainties. They had learned in Tashkent that the steppe khan was as fickle and as capricious as any Roman emperor.

Suraj led them east from the oasis, the sun shining in their eyes as they rode for almost three hours in silence. Theo would glance across at Padma now and again, just to check that the girls were coping with the journey, and she would smile back at him.

They cope well enough, thought Cal. These two women seem far more used to travel than the rest of us.

'How did you get out of Tashkent?' he asked the Rat riding alongside.

'Oh it was quite spectacular, Cal. We crawled through tunnels under the walls. Did you know that there are caves beneath the city? Only small ones but big enough for men to use.'

'And the wine was tainted?'

'Yes, they will have picked it up by now and be supping all the way to the necropolis.'

The next village was deserted and burned out from the winter raids. It was only a small place with five or six houses and an old stone way station for merchants to use on the road. The Goturks had destroyed it during the winter, driving the Sogdian locals to the south, killing their animals and spoiling their fields. Suraj was taken aback by the destruction.

'I did not expect this.'

'The Khan sent men out after the uprising,' said Theo, once Padma translated the Kushan's words. 'I expect that there will be other places burned out as well.'

'It is just as well that we are heading eastwards then,' said the Kushan merchant. 'I do not think that you would be welcomed to the south.'

They camped down for the night, much to Cosmas's relief, and Suraj explained the journey ahead to answer the Romans' questions.

'It is perhaps a week to get to Osh, Buddha willing,' said Suraj. 'Then we will turn south and cross the mountains. We will have to buy clothes and equipment in the town for the passes at this time of year.'

'And the mountains?'

'The mountains are treacherous. Normally I would go to the south across the plains to the city of Kabul and then take the easy passage over them. This way is more arduous and there are bandits. We will need to find a caravan to travel with for safety.'

'Why did we not take the southern route if it is easier?' asked Rat.

'Because the Sogdians and Hepthalites will have closed the trade routes down with a war coming. This way we avoid them and hopefully throw off any pursuit from Tashkent, and it is away from Persia. I will know more when we get to Osh.'

They all settled down for sleep in the ruins. Theo made sure that one of them was awake at all times on watch, just like an army would be, and he would not listen to Rat's complaints.

'You are on first watch,' he told Cosmas firmly. 'Then you can sleep the night away. There are no bucellarii to look after us now, so we must be as disciplined as the legions if we are to survive.'

'You spent too much time with Godda,' said Rat sniffily, but settled down for his watch as the others fell asleep.

'Well, Cosmas, my old friend,' said Rat. 'This could be our most profitable venture yet. Not only do I make new contacts for trade that will pay out over time, I also get to show these unbelievers the Pillars of the Sky.' He smiled and closed his eyes, just to doze, and the next thing he knew was Cal shaking him awake.

'If we were really in a legion it would be the fustuarium for you for sleeping on watch. I should tell Theo and he would beat you himself.'

'I was just resting my eyes,' said Cosmas.

'Resting your eyes? You were snoring like a pig. Go and get some more sleep and be thankful that our young dominus did not catch you.'

'He is not my dominus.'

'He is until we get back to Constantinople, then Narses can have you, and the sooner the better.'

'Do not worry old man, I will look after your granddaughter should your aging limbs fail you.'

Rat scarpered with those parting barbs before Cal could grab him, and went inside the building to sleep. The charioteer climbed up to the roof and watched for attackers in the darkness.

***

It took ten days for them to reach the town of Osh to the east of Tashkent. A small place with only low walls nestled at the eastern end of a fertile valley and surrounded by brown mountains. There were caravans there waiting for the weather to get better before moving on to Kashgar and Serica in the east, or Tashkent and Kabul in the West. There would be a few caravans that went south over the mountains into the Indies, but they would be smaller. Few merchants risked crossing the mountains even in the summer.

'We will have to sell the horses before crossing the mountains.'

'They do not look so tall,' said Cal. 'The Alps are bigger and Hannibal got elephants over them.'

Suraj gave Cosmas a knowing smile.

'These are not even the foothills of the foothills, Charioteer,' said Cosmas in explanation.

They settled down in the merchants' compound of Osh, put up their tents and hobbled their horses in a coral. The two women were the most concerned about the journey southwards. Juana had spent the winter in Kashgar avoiding Serican agents, and there were Goturks warriors there as well. Istami's elder brother Bumin Khan ruled the city like his brother ruled in Tashkent, but there were still Serican traders in the town, and the girl had spent most of the winter in hiding with her solitary guard. The two of them had travelled to Osh and Tashkent as quickly as they could to get away, and the thought of returning that way had them both worried. Juana's mute servant could communicate with both girls, having known them since childhood, but the others had to rely on gestures with him.

'Fear not,' said Cosmas to Padma. 'We do not intend going back to Kashgar, we shall go south from here and meet the road that will take us up into the mountain passes.'

Neither of the girls had travelled over the great mountains on their journey, of all of them only Suraj the Kushan had any experience of the route, and he did not paint a pretty picture of the road ahead.

'We will travel on foot once we reach the foothills. There is no choice in that matter,' he said to Theo before the nobleman raised an objection. 'The horses will not get over the passes. Traders normally stop and transfer goods at Varshadeh from porters to camels. I will see if there is anyone travelling through the mountains to Hunza from here, but if not we shall find someone in Varshadeh.'

'Why travel with others? We do not have much baggage; can we not sell the horses and hire some porters?'

'There is safety in numbers, princeling, and word of you and your gold coins would spread through the mountain region like an avalanche in springtime. There would be bandits and thieves every step of the way. If we go with a caravan we will be safer.'

'You have travelled this way before?'

'Oh no, and I expect you and Cosmas to keep your word. I want the gold and the glassware shipments when we get to Taxila.'

Taxila was Suraj's home on the Indus. From there they could take a riverboat all the way to Barbarikon and the coast. The Kushan left to find his contacts in Osh who would have news for him.

'Can we trust him?' said Cal, stating the obvious.

'He will keep his word,' said Rat. 'We have dangled a fortune in front of him that only the Emperor of Rome can grant. His greed will keep him loyal.'

Suraj's price had been high. He had sold them the poison, given them the means to get it to Naghi and the Persians, and would guide them over the mountains to the Indian coastline where there were Roman ships. In return, he wanted all the remaining gold that Theo carried and contracts with Imperial approval for the glassware that was shipped at such high cost from ports on the Red Sea to the Indies. Theo had agreed to the Kushan's demands because he had no choice, but he realised that the silk worm eggs lying dormant in Juana's cane were worth ten thousand shiploads of glassware. Narses would complain about the price but he would pay up.

'You will have to walk you realise, old man,' said Cosmas pointedly to Cal. 'Do you think the knee can stand up to the punishment.'

'Of course it will and less of the old.'

In truth, Cal was concerned about the journey, but the potion of cumin and bhang that Juana made for his knee seemed to be having an effect. Certainly the swelling was going down and it was less sore and red. He still had the small gourd of poppy juice in his baggage, but had not reached for it in the weeks since taking the new potion. The poppy dulled the pain but it did not take it away, the Indian potion did both after a while but it did not fog the brain.

'Stop baiting him, Cosmas,' said Theo. 'It is your watch.'

'But it is still early.'

'Best to get your turn done sooner,' said Cal. 'You do not want to be falling asleep.' The last he added with a sly wink at the Rat who spluttered and picked up his cloak.

'We are in a caravan park, who will attack us here?'

'Then it should be a quiet watch,' said Theo.

Rat went and sat outside the tents and watched the horses, taking note of the other traders setting up their fires for the evening. There was a market in Osh, and there was coarse silk being made here too, not the finest quality but good enough for the markets of Rome. The sun was setting when he saw Suraj returning from the town, picking his way through the tents. The man was in a hurry, holding his cloak around him from the fresh wind but clearly troubled with a furrowed brow.

'What is it?' he asked.

'Come inside,' he said. 'You will need to hear.'

The others all looked up when then entered Theo's pavilion. The concern on Suraj's face was clear in the flickering lamplight.

'What is it?' said Theo.

'The Persians are coming. We will need to leave tomorrow at first light.'

He explained what he had found out with his contacts in Osh. The poisoned wine had been remarkably effective, killing six of the Persian merchants who had supped it, but Naghi had somehow survived and the spy was on their trail.

'He did not go north after Beremund and the others?'

'He is spending gold, he will find out which way we travelled soon enough.'

'How do you know this? We have travelled directly from Tashkent, seen nobody, how has the news reached here before us?'

'The birds told me,' said Suraj cryptically.

'Pigeons,' said Cosmas in explanation. 'The traders on the road use pigeons for important messages.'

'Then we break camp at first light and ride to the south. He will assume that we are going to Kashgar. He does not know of Juana or where we go now.'

'Let us pray so,' said Cosmas.

25

They left the town of Osh in the gloom before dawn, picking their way through the merchant encampment and riding at a brisk trot to the south. Suraj was constantly urging them to go faster and faster as the sun rose until Theo finally called him to order.

'We cannot gallop all the day,' the aristocrat told the merchant via Cosmas. 'The horses will break down by mid-morning.'

The Kushan merchant nodded sadly. 'We must get ahead of them.'

'They are days behind us,' said Cosmas.

'As I pointed out last night, we were too leisurely on our journey from Tashkent. We could, and should, have done it in half the time. Once the Persians realise your other party is a ruse they will be on our trail again. We must get to the mountains before them if we are to escape.'

'We will be safe in the mountains?' asked Cosmas

'From the Persians, yes, but then we have the mountains to deal with.'

'Out of the pot and into the fire, then,' said Cal. 'That about sums up our whole journey so far.'

They travelled in silence after that. The two women proving themselves to be as good as the men on horseback, both riding like Goth women with their skirts hitched up showing off bare legs. They directed the animals like warrior maidens, and Theo kept casting appreciative glances over at Padma until he almost collided with the Rat's horse. Her transformation into an Amazon was distracting for the aristocrat.

'Will you keep your eyes on the road ahead not your bed tonight,' snapped Cosmas.

'It is time to break our fast, anyway,' said Theo, going red in the face at Rat's jibe.

There was not much for food that night, and the lack of supplies was a nagging problem for Theo. Godda had drummed good supply lines into him, and even on the disastrous Petra campaign the aristocrat had made sure the men always had enough to eat. There were wells on the trail that they could fill their skins and quench their thirst, but only some hard cheese and a sack of millet on their pack animals for food.

'We need to buy some victuals before we get to the mountains,' he told Suraj. 'We have perhaps two day's food and none of it is appealing.'

Suraj shook his head. 'There are few villages along this road; the winter has been hard and stores will be empty. I doubt there will be much spare for passing travellers. When we get to Tashkurgan we can get supplies.'

'How far?' asked Cal.

'Four more days.'

'We will have to go to half-rations,' said Theo. 'So we at least have some warm food inside us each day.'

None of them were enthused by that prospect. They settled down that night with their paltry supper and then pulled their blankets over themselves to sleep.

'You take first watch,' said Theo to Cosmas.

'Why does the Kushan not get a turn instead?'

'Because I trust him less than I trust you, and that is saying something.'

'That is hardly fair,' protested Cosmas. 'I have served you well on this journey.'

'Just make sure you do not fall asleep this time.'

'Cal told you.'

Theo grinned. 'No, but you just did, and I will beat if you fall asleep again.'

'What would you do without me?'

Theo looked over to the Kushan and Juana and her mute servant. 'These three seem accommodating and knowledgeable. I am certain we could make it across the mountains and to the sea without you.'

'You just said you trusted me more than the Indian.'

'Ah,' said Theo tapping his nose and pointing at the Rat. 'But I like him more than I like you.'

Cosmas pursed his lips at those words but said no more, leaving their secluded campfire and climbing to rocks above to keep a watch on the road. Every now and again he would peer back down at the camp, but everyone had quickly settled down for sleep. Rat muttered bitterly about the lack of appreciation for his services. He was still complaining when Cal came to relieve him.

'Just go to bed will you,' said Cal. 'We have enough to worry about without your whining on top. What do you care for Theo's appreciation? It is Narses's appreciation we need to worry about.'

'The boy is cock-happy,' said Cosmas. 'He only cares about the girl.'

'Are you jealous?'

'Of course not, she is half my age.'

In truth Cosmas was somewhat jealous. Not of Theo and Padma's romance. He found that nauseatingly amusing, but when they had started out on this adventure the girl and her monkish mentor had been Cosmas's charge and Rat had enjoyed talking to them. After Brother Timothy had died in Tashkent the girl and Theo had quickly become inseparable and Cosmas felt left out.

'You are like a jealous child in school,' Cal told him.

'And you are a grumpy old man with a bad knee.'

'Stating an obvious truth is hardly a well crafted insult, Rat. You are losing your grip. Go to bed and get some sleep. We will move on early in the morning.'

'We always do.'

Cosmas climbed back down to the camp and found his blankets, and settled down for a broken night's sleep on the cold earth. He awoke to the smell of frying meat in a pan.

'I caught a hare in the night,' said Theo, proud of his triumph. 'It is not fat, and not much meat, but enough for a hearty breakfast before we set out.'

Cosmas sat up in an instant at the thought of some fresh meat, although Suraj declined the offer.

'I follow the teachings of the Buddha,' said Suraj. 'I do not eat animal flesh.'

'That must be a boring diet,' said Cosmas, gobbling his fried rabbit and porridge up as soon as Theo scooped some into his bowl.

'I get by,' said the Kushan.

Once everyone had broken their fast, they packed up the horses and set off again at a brisk pace. Suraj took care to avoid settlements and give no word of their passing to any Persian pursuit, until they settled down in the wilds that night to camp. Despite the cold nights and the poor food the party was generally in good spirits.

***

It was cool and dark in the cave – a man-made hiding place carved out of a fissure in the yellow rock. Their horses were corralled outside the entrance but concealed from prying eyes by a steep sided gorge. Suraj had led them off the road before nightfall to camp here.

'What is this place?' asked Theo.

'It was a temple once,' said the Indian, 'before the Huns came. Now it is a stopping place for those on the road for those that know about it.' He smiled. 'Fortunately few do.'

'A temple to whom?' asked Rat, looking around.

'Does it matter?' said Cal.

'It depends on who it was?'

'Worshippers of the Buddha on the road would come here,' said Suraj. 'There were monks living in the cave who would provide rest and food for the weary.'

'This Buddha is a pagan god? Like Jupiter or Minerva?' said Theo, once Cosmas had translated.

The Rat snorted derisively at the ancient gods names.

'No,' said Suraj. 'The Buddha was a man, like Zoroaster or your Jesus.'

'Jesus is the son of the one true God,' Cosmas pointed out.

'So you say,' said Suraj with a flicker of a smile. 'Buddha's father was merely a king, not a god, but he spent his life as a teacher and student.'

'And the Huns destroyed this place?' said Theo, anxious to avoid a theological debate. 'Under Attila?'

'The Hepthalites not Attila,' said Suraj. 'White Huns. They slaughtered everybody and torched the buildings because they did not understand them. That is often the way.'

'Attila did the same in the west,' said Theo. 'It has taken nearly a hundred years to recover what was lost when the Huns came. There are still provinces for Rome to restore lost since the west was shattered.'

'It is the same all along the Indus, devastated cities and overgrown farmland. Will the Goturks be the new Huns?' said Suraj. 'That is the question that bothers many along the river now. Our memories are long; the people from the steppe bring only fire and death when they arrive.'

The next morning they reached Osh. A small town on the edge of a great cold desert and in sight of the foothills of the Pillars of the Sky, as Cosmas insisted on calling them. It was a huge mountain range that divided the lands of the Indus from the steppes and deserts to the north. The peaks were snowcapped all year round, with great ice glaciers and mountain paths where only a single person could walk. Their animals could not travel with them. Suraj and Cosmas went to the market to find a caravan that would take them over the mountains and a trader who would take their horses. Much of the gear that they had brought with them from Rome would be pointless in the mountains. Theo looked sadly at his mail coat and gleaming helmet that had been sitting on the packhorses backs since Tashkent. They were both worth a fortune, but the weight was too much to carry and it was too heavy to walk in for days on end.

'You will have to leave it,' said Cal. 'It is one of the advantages I have in travelling lightly. I have less to jettison.'

'My grandfather gave me the coat when I was given the Petra command,' said Theo. 'But I think he would understand me selling it now. We can get some furs and food for the journey.'

'Ever the stoic Roman pragmatist?'

'I would have refused to leave it behind once,' said Theo wryly. 'Perhaps I have grown up some on this trip. Losing Godda...' Theo could feel himself welling up. 'It was a shock. He has been with me since I was a boy. It's enough to make a man want to drink again.'

'You won't though.'

'No,' said Theo. 'It is better to water the wine. I have learned that lesson.'

Since the budding romance with Padma had flourished, Theo had avoided drinking and certainly not to excess. Cal had known pilots in the hippodrome addicted to the vine; he

247

understood how difficult it was for this blonde Roman to resist the easy temptation. Few of the men he had known had managed Theo's level of abstinence. Cal was almost proud of the boy.

'The love of a good woman brings even the wildest man to heel,' said Cal with a wide smile.

Theo looked at him suspiciously, expecting a barb, but realised that the old charioteer was being genuine in his praise and the aristocrat blushed.

'I am not sure my mother will be so impressed when I return with her. I can imagine her horror.'

'Why?'

'She has always planned a match at court for me, some vapid daughter of another aristocratic family who has never been outside her own domos. I think I would be bored.' He dropped his voice to a low whisper. 'We may marry before we leave the Indies. Then she cannot argue, Cosmas can carry out the ceremony. He is, technically, ordained.'

Cal could quite imagine what a rich Roman matron would say if her son arrived with a strange foreign bride in tow. A Nestorian marriage would be tested in court, particularly one carried out by Cosmas the Rat, and the family's money would buy the judgement in their favour. He did not tell Theo that. He merely clapped the boy's back.

'I will stand as witness for you,' he said.

Theo smiled at that, but tapped his nose. 'Do not tell Rat yet,' he said. 'You know what he is like, he would tease us mercilessly and Padma does not understand his humour.'

'I do not think that many people understand his humour.'

The Rat and Suraj arrived back from the market at that point, all in a rush and a bustle. They had found a caravan that was going over the mountains, and porters that could be hired and the horses sold.

'I will not need to leave behind my mail coat?' said Theo.

'No,' Cosmas told him. 'We can ride our horses to the last way station before the high valleys. And then they will bring them back to Osh. The horses will pay for our passage and the porters to carry our equipment. We had to offer more gold for furs. So you will still have to open your purse.'

'There is not so much left in it now,' said Theo going to the small chest where he kept the gold coins Narses had given him so many months ago. Cosmas peered over his shoulder.

'There is more than enough there,' he said.

'And once we are over the mountains what then? We have to pay Suraj. How do we pay for passage home?'

'Once we get to the coast you can flash your rank and credentials,' said Cosmas. 'There will be Roman ships there making ready to return home. We are doing the Emperor's business so they will have to help.'

Theo grunted but handed over the gold to Cosmas and Suraj to pay the merchant. Getting over the mountains was their main concern now. Once they reached the Indus River they could worry about home.

**

It was a wizened little man who took their horses away at the way station; grey haired, with sunken eyes barely visible in the wrinkled folds of his face. Theo and the others could not shake off the feeling that he was laughing at them as he led the beasts away. Their baggage had already been taken by the porters who would carry it over the mountain passes. Nearly five hundred men, short in stature compared to the Romans, all dark haired and wiry with wispy beards, would creep along the narrow trails, over ice and snow, rock and rubble, all the way to the Indus Valley. Cal noted that the porters were fleet footed, skipping along even with tall packs tied to their back.

'What it is to be young,' he said sourly.

The charioteer was worried about the march over the roof of the world. The cumin potion that the Nestorian women had made for his knee had reduced the pain to a dull ache, but he faced at least six weeks of gruelling trek through rough ground. The fear that he would not make it and they would have to leave him on some cold mountain path gnawed at Cal. He had cut a stave from a willow tree to use for walking, and then endured Cosmas's barbs about his age and decrepitude for two days as they rode to the meeting point. He tested the staff after the horses were led away. It was strong enough, he decided, and he could always use it as a cudgel to batter the Rat.

Food was dished out of a giant pot by the caravan master once they camped at nightfall. A spiced hot stew with unidentifiable globules of fatty meat was ladled onto a bowl of coarse rice and a loaf of warm unleavened bread. All of them gobbled it up, grateful for some variation to the millet gruel that they had been subsisting on since Tashkent. Suraj declined the meat sauce but took the rice and added some dried fruit from his own pack.

The next morning they started the long trek over the great mountains. Cosmas alone was excited at the prospect, the others were merely resigned at the long march ahead, but the Rat was overwhelmed at finally walking through the pillars of the sky.

'I do not see how this is evidence that the world is flat not a globe,' said Theo. 'These are tall mountains, perhaps the tallest in the world...'

'The tallest you have ever seen.'

'I will happily concede that,' said Theo, 'but the point remains that it is not evidence of a flat earth whilst there is considerable proof of the opposite.'

'Of course it is evidence, these are the very pillars that God constructed to hold the firmament above us.'

'There is no logic to that statement.'

'It is not about logic it is about theology.'

'Why are you arguing with him?' said Cal. 'You know what he is like. Nothing you say or prove with evidence will sway him from his foolishness.'

'Some foolishness, if it was not for me we would not be going home.'

'We are in unknown mountains with no horses, going to lands none of us know, with only the promise of Roman ships at the end of the journey,' said Cal. 'I think it is a little early to be counting your chickens in the going home regard.'

The trail they followed was well worn, winding along the side of a tall valley with a peak that seemed to get further away as they climbed. It was already cold in the wind, the spring sunshine too weak to warm them as they walked. Whilst the Romans shivered, the porters strolled half-naked; chattering away in their strange tongue and smiling and laughing. Suraj had told them that the porters were not slaves but freemen from the mountain tribes. The Huns, the Hepthalites, the kings of the Indus Valley, the Goturks not even Alexander had tried to conquer the peoples in this mountain range.

'It would be suicide,' Theo said, after Suraj had finished his explanation and Cosmas had translated. 'No army could fight in these lands.'

'The mountain kingdoms are independent in spirit,' said Suraj. 'But the kings are not fools. They fight amongst themselves all the time, but rarely bother trade caravans; they know there is more profit letting trade move freely. There are bandits though, and the snow and ice is as much a danger as any man.'

'How long?' said Cal, asking the question that was on everyone's tongue.

'Six or seven weeks if we are fortunate, it could be as much as three months if the going is difficult.'

Even Suraj had not made this journey before. Normally, he would have gone south from Tashkent over the plains through Bactria and Hepthalite lands before taking one of the lower passes that were open all year into the Indus valley.

'There are still Hepthalites there?' said Cal.

'Some, but they grow fat in their palaces and do not disturb our trade. Once we are over the mountains we can find passage on the river to Taxila. My family is there and can arrange transport onwards to the coast. When we meet your countrymen in Barbarikon I will expect my payment.'

The Indian's payment was a lucrative contract for Egyptian glassware shipped from factories on the Red Sea across the ocean. The trade was common enough according to Cosmas who had travelled the route himself. Suraj carried a small wooden tablet that Theo had affixed his seal to confirming all the details in his only luggage: a well bound chest. Most of the man's trade seemed to be done on promissory notes, from what the Romans had discerned. Wooden contracts that would be passed around until someone fulfilled them and someone else made payment. It was a confusing system to outsiders, even Rat confessed himself baffled by it all, but to the traders in the east it was their lifeblood. Suraj's wooden tablets were his fortune, and the one bearing Theo's seal his most lucrative promise.

26

The giant scale of the mountains had the Romans taken aback. For once Cosmas had not been exaggerating when he called them the pillars of the sky. From a distance, the snow capped peaks could have been the Alps in the north of Italia. It was only as you got closer and realised that these mountains towered over anything they had seen before. Even Cal, who had grown up in the shadows of the Atlas Mountains in the west, was dumbstruck by the majestic peaks. Every morning they would break their fast with porridge of barley flour mixed with rancid yak butter, and tea that tasted foul but was warm and filling. The Romans all declined the local butter chai tea after one try, but the two sisters and their servant happily drank it.

'The taste on her tongue will be of rancid yaks,' whispered Cosmas to Theo as the girls supped their tea.

Theo cuffed him without saying a word.

'My, that is overly familiar,' protested Rat.

'With you, familiarity truly breeds contempt.'

They pulled on their furs and made ready to march on. Cal shielded his eyes from the morning sun and gazed up the valley at the snow capped peaks beyond.

'And we are supposed to cross over them?' said the charioteer.

'Pass through them,' Cosmas informed him. 'The peaks are so high that no man has scaled them, only the angels go there, but in the valleys there are people.'

The people in the valleys were herdsmen and farmers grubbing subsistence out of the meagre soil of the mountains. Small villages with squat, flat-roofed, wooden houses clung to the sides of the valley. Their yaks were a type of heavy shaggy long horned cattle that herded together in the lowland pastures and provided meat and milk. Cal and Theo both eyed the animals with interest for their farm and estate respectively, but both quickly concluded that the beasts were far more trouble than the docile stock back at home. The dark haired herders would bark and bellow at them using big dogs to herd them along the valley floor.

'Look at those hounds,' said Theo.

The herd dogs were the size of a wolfhound and covered in a thick shaggy brown fur. All of them had a smiling face with lolling tongues and intelligent amber eyes. One of them came over to the aristocrat, sniffed at him and licked his hands before returning to his master's call.

'I wonder how much a puppy would cost?' Theo was enthralled by the beast.

'Do we really need a puppy when we have a Rat?'

'I am going to ask Suraj when we stop.'

'You will return home with a dog and a wife, and your career restored. It has been a good journey for you.' Cal smiled at the blonde aristocrat.

'And for you, Charioteer. We would not have made it this far without your help. I will make sure that Narses understands that.'

Theo knew that Cal had not wanted this task, and had been longing for home almost as soon as they set out on the steppe, but he spoke the truth. Cal's skill as a charioteer had won them friends on the steppe in Atil and then with the Great Khan in Tashkent.

'I trust Narses not at all, but it is true he keeps his promises.' Cal shrugged. 'Yet, I am certain that he will have some sting in the tail even if he does pay up.'

'Even Narses cannot complain about our success, if we make it back. We have the secret of silk.'

That evening Theo asked Suraj about the dogs, if there was a trader who could find him a puppy or young hound to take. It would be easy enough, according to the Indian merchant, especially as Theo was offering a gold coin for the animal. He spoke to the caravan owner, and the next morning an old man turned up at the Romans' campfire carrying a bundle of brown fur with a wagging tail and lolling tongue. The girls quickly fell to cooing over the puppy, as Cal and Theo checked the hound for fleas or signs of weakness.

'He looks every bit like a little bear,' said Padma.

'Then that is what we shall call him,' said Theo. 'Ursa.'

The dog looked up at Theo's voice.

'He knows his name already,' said Cal.

'It had better not slow us down,' said Cosmas sniffing.

'Worried that the hound is a ratter?'

'Worried about any distractions from our mission, Charioteer,' said Rat. 'We have been travelling through friendly lands up until now. After today we will be in less hospitable territory. Suraj says there are bandits ahead.' He nodded at the Indian.

'That is true,' said Suraj as Cosmas translated. 'We are a big enough party to see off most threats but the next few weeks travel will still be dangerous.'

The locals watched the caravan pass in silence that day, winding its way south along the vast valley, up, up, up, ever upwards towards the high pass. At the top they paused, all of them finding it harder to breath in the thin mountain air, before descending into the next long glacial valley. The porters seemed unaffected by the altitude, skipping along happily and making Cal curse their smiles. The caravan was high enough now that the few trees were stunted and the winter's snow was not fully cleared away, but they were still climbing. Each valley they traversed, every ravine they followed, was higher than the one before. Every pass was more difficult to reach than the previous one, and every day brought more difficult terrain to traverse. That night they camped away from a village nestled in the slopes on the other side of the valley. They could see the lights flickering in the blackness in the distance, and a double guard was put around their baggage by the caravan owner. Theo, Cal and Cosmas still kept to their own watch rota to look over the small Roman party, with Theo and Ursa the hound always taking the last watch together. Everybody was on edge that night, but nothing untoward happened and they moved on again the next morning.

'Are the villagers over there trouble?' Theo asked Suraj through Cosmas.

'Sometimes,' he replied. 'There have been incidents in the past so the caravan avoids it now. Mostly it is petty theft but it leads to arguments with the locals. Further on there are bandits who will attack small caravans or the unwary. War between the Goturks and Hepthalites will mean more travellers try this road to avoid the fighting.'

***

Theo quite enjoyed his turn on watch each night. The camp was quiet, Cal's snoring the only sound, and he could ponder their plans to get home without Rat's interruptions and irritations. The mountains were the last great obstacle to their success, he concluded, once they were over the other side Suraj assured them that travelling along the Indus to the sea was easy enough. The expense still bothered him. By the time they reached the ocean, and hopefully the Roman ships that would be there, Theo would have spent almost all the coin that Narses had given him for the journey. He hoped that the merchants at Barbarikon would prove amenable to giving them homeward passage.

'Six of us and a dog,' he said, scratching the puppy under its chin. 'We will have travelled even further than Alexander.'

Suraj had told him of his home Taxila on the banks of the Indus that had been founded by the great conqueror a thousand years before. Now Theo had emulated Alexander and travelled as far east as the Indus. It would be something to talk about at court, but he had learned not to take anything for granted on the journey. They would be travelling through lands ravaged by the Hepthalites and ruled by their petty vassals. In Taxila they could find a boat for the coast. He prayed that it would not be an arduous journey. They had escaped Naghi and the Persians after going up into the mountains, but the elements could still bring everything to disaster.

'We may have cut out the war between Goturk and Hepthalite and avoided the Persians by coming this way, but it will not be easy to cross these mountains,' he said to the dog.

Ursa rolled onto his back for Theo to tickle his belly in response and the aristocrat obliged.

'I wonder if Beremund and the others have managed to get away?'

If everything had gone as planned, Beremund, Llew and Fritigern would have made it to the steppe by now and be travelling to Atil. He prayed to Saint Anthony for them to find their way home.

'That is the one advantage we have,' he told the dog. 'We have escaped the Persian pursuit. Naghi will not follow us into these mountains, even if he realises that we have come this way.'

He had stopped tickling the animal's stomach and Ursa looked up, tongue lolling and hooked his paw onto Theo's arm to drag it back down to tickling the belly. He smiled and resumed the canine massage.

Once they reached the Indus, Suraj had assured them, they could find boats to take them south. They would have to port over falls and white water, but out of the mountains the river would take them south as fast as a man could ride a horse. He looked up. There were shouts and conversations starting among the porters. It would be dawn soon.

'You are supposed to be on watch, but I crept up on you.'

Theo turned at her words; a wide grin on his face.

'Good morning, my queen.'

Padma smiled back. 'Flatterer. I could not sleep, not with Cal's snoring and the Rat's farting.'

They had all taken to sleeping in Theo's pavilion tent since coming into the mountains, it was roomy enough for all of them to huddle down and separate tents seemed pointless with their diminished party. Only Suraj kept to his own tent, keeping apart from the Romans. The new sleeping arrangements did, however, curtail Theo and Padma's romance somewhat – that and the arrival of Padma's older sister who was not as impressed by the blonde nobleman as her younger sibling. Their mute servant was big, even Cal was wary of him, but the man simply tended to the two women and ignored the Romans.

'Have you let the fire die down?'

Theo had forgotten about keeping the flames fed in the night, and Padma knelt on the frozen ground to blow the embers back into life. The dog rolled onto its paws and plodded over to see what she was doing, sniffing at her.

'You are as bad as your master,' she said patting him away.

Ursa sat on his haunches and cocked his head as the fire sparked into life and Padma turned back to Theo.

'I want some butter tea and a kiss before the others wake up.'

'Best you kiss me first, then,' said Theo.

She came into his arms and they kissed, only breaking off the embrace when Rat's distinctive whine came at them from the tent.

'I hope you are not distracted on watch. Is that not punishable by death in the Legions?'

The puppy jumped up at the sight of the Rat emerging from his bed and rushed over to him, little tail wagging wildly. Cosmas reached into his robes and pulled out a small piece of dried meat and fed it to the dog. Ursa lay back down and started eating his tidbit.

'Unlike humans, you can buy a dog's love,' said Rat.

'I would not be so sure,' said Theo. 'I think the dog is wiser than you credit him.'

Once he had finished the treat, Ursa left Cosmas and returned to sit by his master as Padma set water to boil. Around the campfires, others did the same as the caravan made ready for the day's travel.

'It looks like the weather will be good again, if still cold,' said Cosmas. 'We are making fine progress.'

'We made less than ten miles yesterday and the valley curved back west until we passed over and down into this bowl.' Theo waved at the mountains around them. 'From what I understand that is good going in this terrain. But at this rate it will still be another six weeks before we get out of the range, and that is only if Suraj is correct about the distances.'

'I am certain it will not take that long,' said Rat.

'I am certain that you are wrong.'

***

The brutal mountain trails were hammering at Cal's knee; the cumin potion and even the poppy juice had little effect on the inflammation with such daily punishment. Narrow ledges followed by scree slopes and precarious descents, always slipping and sliding; there was ice and snow packed down as they passed making the going even more treacherous. The air was more difficult to breathe the higher they climbed, and the trail went ever upwards. Whenever they descended into the valley floors, the next pass would be still higher again. He strapped up his knee tightly with a linen bandage, took his potions dutifully, and leaned heavily on his staff as they crawled like insects through the towering peaks. He found the mountains oppressive, always looming over him; the white tops gleaming in the spring sunlight whilst the valleys were still deep in dark shadow. The valleys themselves were mostly bare and barren now, with little vegetation other than clumps of brown grass. The fuel for their fires came from the porters packs, and the only hot food was gruel. The lower valleys had been green with crops and people, or herds of yaks grazing on the meagre grass, but few if any people lived among these high peaks.

'Thank you,' he said to Juana, taking a cup of hot butter tea. She called her sister over and pointed at Cal's leg.

'How is your knee?' asked Padma. 'My sister is concerned.'

'It is of no matter,' he said trying to brush them both away.

'Of course it is, Theo and Cosmas would have to carry you if you cannot walk,' said Padma, as Juana sat beside him. 'Have you been taking your medicine?'

He nodded. 'Of course and I can walk, I do not see the Rat helping me if I break down. Perhaps the boy; he has grown up some.'

Padma translated for her sister who giggled and then spoke to Cal, with her sister translating back for the charioteer.

'You judge the Rat too harshly, I think,' Juana said. 'Cosmas sees you as his friend. He would willingly help you, and then enjoy complaining about it for the next six months.'

Cal grunted at that. He had known the Rat for years, the man was famed for his ranting outside the hippodrome, but the charioteer had never much cared for him and would have described him as an unfortunate acquaintance rather than a friend. Cosmas had been an incessant irritant on the journey, but even Cal had to admit that the Rat had been useful. He had got them to Tashkent in the first instance, and then found Suraj to get them home.

'If he gets us home, I will declare him my friend to all in the forum of Constantinople.'

'Shhh,' said Padma with a little giggle. 'He will hear and hold you to it.'

'What of you and Theo, what will happen when you get back?'

She gave a grimace at that and glanced down at her sister tending to Cal's knee. 'I do not know. My sister is not impressed; she thinks it is a poor match.'

Cal burst out laughing, drawing looks from Cosmas and the others, and Juana who looked up from the bandage with a quizzical look on her face.

'And there was me wondering about Theo's family's reaction,' he said in a low voice.

Padma was nonplussed at that. 'Our ancestors were satraps under Alexander.'

'I did not know that,' he said.

To a Roman mother that is still a barbarian, he thought.

27

A deep blue lake, perhaps two hundred metres wide, but stretching away in the distance faced them as they came around a spur in the gorge. Sunlight glinted off the crystal blue waters and the towering mountain peaks were reflected in the water's mirror. The divine majesty of the scene stunned even Rat into silence. There were green spruce trees at the shoreline, small boats on the water, and people waving as they approached. They were the first men the caravan had seen in over a week, and they had smiling faces and rushed to welcome. The porters tramped down to the lake's edge, dropped their packs and settled down to camp even though it was only early afternoon.

'Well will you look at that,' said Cosmas with wonder in his voice at the glistening blue waters.

'It is indeed beautiful,' Cal agreed with Cosmas, leaning heavily on his staff.

The high passes had been hard going for all of them but Cal had suffered the most. He was the oldest in the party, and his knee was heavily strapped and bathed every night by the Nestorian women. They had been fortunate that the fine weather had held barring the odd flurry of snowflakes and bitter cold winds. Whilst every day had been a mix of climb and descent for almost a month, Cal had noticed that they had been going down more than up for the past week. Not that it brought him any relief: the descents were worse on his knee than the climbing.

Cosmas nudged Cal in the ribs and pointed to Theo and Padma who were already setting up the pavilion tent, watched over by Juana. The elder sister had a sour look on her face.

'Love's young dream is a nightmare for others.'

'You are sly, Rat.'

Cosmas sniffed. 'I speak only the truth.'

'It is the way you do it. If their feelings can survive this journey.' He waved his arms around them. 'If they can survive these mountains. Then they can survive a disapproving sibling.'

'Ah but can it survive an Emperor's court? Which do you think is more deadly, Charioteer, mountains in the wilderness or a palace in Constantinople?'

'That is a different proposition altogether,' said Cal with a wry grimace. 'But we shall return as heroes. Theo will be feted by the Emperor.'

'Didn't you and the Empress Theodora...' Cosmas voice tailed off as he made the horn shape with his fingers.

'No,' said Cal firmly. 'She was a beauty in her youth, mind you, and I could have once. But there were enough other ladies at court who wanted to dally with a charioteer for me to avoid Theodora. After Nika, well I got out of the city for twenty years. I raced some in Antioch and Alexandria but I was married by then, had enough coin and a family and fancied myself a farmer.'

'I was on a ship in the harbour when the Nika Riot happened, but a young boy on one of my first voyages. We had only just put in from Alexandria and the ship's master would not let us ashore. Afterwards the city was a ruin.'

'I left before the slaughter. I could see which way it was going,' said Cal.

Cosmas nodded. 'Poor Hypatias never wanted to be Emperor, but Justinian killed him anyway.'

'Hypatias was a fool.'

The campfires had started up and the smell of barley porridge and spiced rice started to waft on the air with the wood smoke. They were about as far away from Constantinople and the imperial court as a man could be. The African charioteer looked down at the little merchant.

'Damn me I am so hungry even their mush will taste good.'

Cosmas smiled. 'Wait till you reach the coast, there will be swordfish caught and grilled on coals in front of you on the beach. I can almost taste it, we are so close.'

'It is a thousand miles and more still.'

'But most of it will be by boat along the river.' Cosmas pointed to the lake. 'Water that flows from here will be at the sea before us. Once we are out of these mountains we are almost as good as home.'

They camped that night by the banks of the lake. Suraj told them that boats would take them to the far end the next day, and then they would follow the river down to the Indus.

'This is the Indus?' said Theo.

'A tributary,' said Suraj as Cosmas translated. 'We are making good progress; the worst of the terrain is behind us. We cross here and there is but one more great pass to climb and then it is downhill all the way. At Giljit there is a Buddhist monastery and good markets to resupply. Once we reach the Indus we can follow it south until the plain and then take boats to the sea.'

'You make it sound as simple as Cosmas,' said Cal. 'Why do I get the feeling that there is a but coming.'

'But, the next few days will be dangerous. Once we cross the lake we are in bandit territory. The risk of attack is greater now that there are more people.'

'There is always something. In Giljit will we be able to get different provisions? I am sick of this mush for breakfast and supper.'

'And yet you still manage to eat more than any of us,' said Cosmas, poking him in the belly. 'Whilst grumbling the most.'

After they had eaten, in the fading afternoon sun, Padma and Theo walked along the banks of the lake hand in hand with Ursa loping alongside them. The Roman aristocrat had spent the cold dark nights teaching the animal Latin commands which the beast had picked up remarkably quickly. For all his faults, Cal had to concede that the boy had a way with animals. He was a born horseman, as he had proven on the steppe, and now he had the giant puppy following him adoringly wherever he went.

Perhaps he will persuade his mother that it is a good match after all, thought the charioteer.

Suraj knew this route, even if they had not travelled it before, and it was clear that the Indian was anxious to get the next few days over with. News from the boatmen was not good. There had been attacks throughout the previous summer on caravans crossing the mountains to Giljit. A couple of small merchant convoys had been lost to them. Weapons that had remained mostly packed away in cases for the journey thus far were taken out and worn by the porters. Light hunting bows and curved swords at their waistbands. The silk and other goods that the caravan had brought from Kashgar were worth an imperial ransom. Word of their passing had spread through the mountain passes, and the first fat caravan of the season would be a rich prize for any bandit chief.

***

Theo ruffled Ursa's ears as he sat on watch and relaxed. It was almost dawn, and Padma would rise soon. The young couple looked forward to the quiet moments together before the camp rose for the morning. In two days, they would reach Giljit and the going would become easier; the mountains less cruel and the weather kinder. Suraj assured him that the passage had been remarkably easy compared to groups in the past that had crossed the range at this time of year. The dog's ears pricked up and he looked out into the darkness and started to sniff the air.

'What is it?'

Theo had his spatha to hand in an instant. He couldn't hear anything and the rest of the camp sounded undisturbed and quiet. There were other guards on watch, porters and hill men, but the whole encampment was stretched out along the valley floor instead of gathered together defensively as the Roman would prefer. Two feathered arrows thudded into the ground next to him, and Theo instinctively rolled away from the firelight and into the shadows to make less of a target.

'Alarm!' he shouted as he rolled. 'Alarm!'

There were other shouts coming along the caravan now, as the other guards were disturbed by the ambush. Ursa started howling at Theo's shouts and Cal came out of the tent with a gladius in one hand and his staff in the other.

'Get down!' Theo shouted at him. 'Archers.'

The charioteer bent down and made his way over to Theo, shielding behind some packs from the baggage dumped the night before by the porters, and crouched beside the aristocrat. More arrows flew in at the camp from the darkness, but it seemed ineffective.

'They are not very good marksmen,' said Cal.

'Thank God for that. They should have swarmed us in the darkness whilst we were unprepared, not attacked with arrows.'

The bandits came in a rush then to overwhelm the caravan, as if Theo's whispers had spurred them into action. Rough turbaned men with dark beards and faces painted red, white, and black. They looked like demons in the firelight. Four or five came at Cal and Theo, armed with curved swords and buckler shields. The puppy's hackles were raised and it snarled as he stood alongside his master.

'Three for me two for you,' said Theo, stepping forward. 'I think that is only fair, as you are getting along in years and have a crippled knee.'

'My thanks,' said Cal.

Theo did not have a shield or his mail coat on to defend him, just thick furs and spatha, but he had speed and years of training. The blonde warrior did not wait for the bandits to close to him; instead he leaped into the attack as he had been taught. The first bandit was cut down with one thrust, leaving a wide look of surprise on the man's face. Theo barged into the next with his shoulder, throwing him to the floor and stabbing down at him.

Cal battered one of his enemies around the head with his staff, and cut at another with his short sword forcing them back from the tents, but Theo, facing down two more grim faced attackers, was backing up into him.

They came at Theo from different sides in unspoken agreement, and the Roman was hard pressed to defend himself against their curved blades. He parried and dodged desperately, backing away from their swords, until Ursa sank his teeth into the ankle of the bandit to Theo's left making the man scream and look down. Theo stepped forwards and killed the other man with one blow whilst his partner was distracted by the dog. The other bandit kicked Ursa away, the puppy yowling out in agony, but Theo slashed his spatha across the bandit's belly, disembowelling him with one blow. The man looked down, dropped his sword and tried to catch his intestines as they fell out of his stomach, and then collapsed to the ground moaning.

'Don't you dare kick my dog,' said Theo to the dying bandit.

Without Theo's training or speed Cal was hard pressed, he kept the bandits at bay by swinging his staff and cutting at them if they dared to close, but he was being forced back towards the tents and campfire. He could still hear arrows whistling through the air and did not want to be silhouetted in the firelight, but the two mountain men were determined to press him. One of them suddenly collapsed to the floor with Theo standing behind him, blade dripping blood. Cal did not wait; he struck out at the other man with his staff forcing the bandit to parry the blow with his shield. Then he stepped up and smashed the hilt of his gladius into the man's face, the pommel popping his eye socket. The bandit started screaming until Cal silenced him with a thrust of his short sword to the neck.

The two of them looked about, the attack was still going on along the caravan, but the enemy numbers were less. Theo could still see some fighting going along the camp but it was clear that they were winning.

'They should have just swarmed us in the night,' he said again to Cal.

The tent flaps opened and Padma stood at the entrance in a white robe, silhouetted in the firelight.

'Is it over?' she called to Theo.

'Get back inside!' he screamed.

A black feathered arrow thudded into her throat with an audible thump, and she slumped down to the ground.

'No!'

Theo and Cal both ran to the girl. Her eyes were open but she could not speak with the arrow caught in her throat, and there was blood everywhere. Neither of them knew what to do, how to stop the bleeding and staunch the wound. Neither dared touch the arrow. Padma died gazing at Theo and him back, holding her hand as she bled out.

It was a blur for Theo after that. Juana began screaming when she saw her younger sister lying on valley floor dead. The bandit attacks had been beaten off, but the Romans were disconsolate. As the sun came up, Juana washed her sister's body. There was no time for a burial or funeral rites. Instead a small stone cairn was raised over Padma's body along with four others killed in the attack.

The despair for Juana at losing her sister was clearly evident to Cal and Cosmas, but she stoically carried on. Her mute servant ignored the others keeping his eyes on his mistress at all times. Cal wished he could talk to the woman, but without Padma communication was impossible.

Theo said nothing as they buried Padma and prepared to leave, only the dog could get a response from him, but sensing his master's distress it curled around Theo's feet and growled at anyone who came close. The caravan master got them moving by mid morning down the valley towards Giljit.

28

Taxila was little more than a broken sun-bleached ruin to Cal's eyes when he saw it from the river. Weeds grew everywhere and half of the buildings were abandoned and overgrown. It had been a thriving and prosperous town once, that was obvious, but war and pestilence had reduced it to a shadow of its former glory. He noted the marble domes, like Roman basilica that still gleamed in the sunlight and reminded the charioteer of a basket of eggs from a distance. But up close the domes were shattered and cracked and the churches and temples abandoned. They had followed the Indus down through the foothills after Giljit, before embarking on a leaking flat bottomed barge that brought them into the Indus town. Suraj came from the place; his was one of the few merchant families that still traded from the ruins.

'What happened here?' Cal asked the slender merchant with the Rat's help.

'The Huns came and the town was sacked. Afterwards there was plague and the people that were left fled south or east. My grandfather was only a boy, but the town has not recovered despite our position on the river.'

Taxila's position was certainly perfect for trade coming out of the mountains down the Indus. On the east bank of the river were stone jetties that had survived the Hunnish devastation, but south-bound boats rarely bothered to stop these days. Suraj assured the Romans that they could still find a berth on a boat, and would soon be sailing down to the sea. The Indus was a great highway for trade in the Indies, as well as the border between the Hepthalites and Kushan kingdoms of the east.

'That is Hepthalite land over there?' Cal waved at the western bank.

'Yes, but the lords and warriors are mostly over the mountains in Bactria making ready for the war with Istami. They rarely trouble our trade anyway, they value the taxes too much and we always pay on time.'

The Roman party disembarked from the barges and stood on the stone jetty with their baggage wondering what to do next. Theo sat on the chest containing his mail shirt and weapons, saying nothing to the others with Ursa dozing at his feet. The dark circles under his eyes showed how little sleep he had managed recently, but since Padma's death he had said little and slept little. Cal and Rat had both tried to talk him around, to no avail, even Juana had tried once but there was no reasoning with the aristocrat. He was inconsolable since the battle in the mountains. Without Theo's leadership, the charioteer had taken charge of the little group as they made their way out of the range. From Osh to Taxila had taken nearly three months and it was five weeks since the ambush and Padma's death, but the pain was still raw for Theo and her sister.

'Come with me,' Suraj told them.

A gaggle of small children picked up the Romans baggage and they followed the Indian through the wide streets. The heat was oppressive, as hot as a summer's day in Alexandria, but heavy and humid not burning and dry. They were all drenched in sweat by the time they reached Suraj's home – only a short distance away. The merchant had his own house overlooking the river and he was anxious to get home after so many months away. A young wife dressed in a silk robe with bared midriff and a gaggle of children all rushed out to welcome Suraj home. The Kushan trader's parents joined them, and it was a while before the Indian remembered he had houseguests. The Romans stood about uncomfortably at the weeping women and joyful shouts at the merchant's return.

'My friends, I must apologise, I have neglected my duties as a host.'

Suraj introduced them to his family, all of them bowing and smiling at the three Romans and Nestorian woman and her mute servant. Slaves picked up their bags and showed them to their quarters – a set of clean chambers with windows overlooking the river.

'This is a fine place,' said Cosmas. 'We are nearly home now.'

'You have been saying that ever since we left Tashkent.'

Rat had travelled this way before and had been pontificating about the sights, sounds and smells of the Indus cities ever since they had come out of the mountains. Juana too had sailed the Indus although her and Padma's home was further east. She assured them that there would be Nestorians in Barbarikon at the coast who would help them in their mission if there were no Roman ships. Whilst Theo was still sunk in misery and arrack, Cal was utterly amazed by the river lands. This broken dying city may have been mostly abandoned, but the Indus valley was teeming with people to the African's eye. There were farmers tending to crops and cattle, and merchants, tradesmen, and artisans in the villages and towns. Children were everywhere. The men were short in stature but all sporting manicured beards and moustaches – even the rudest and poorest of them. It was the women that entranced the African charioteer: dark haired and dark eyes like the two Nestorian girls, but made up heavy with kohl like an Egyptian queen, and barely dressed in silk with bare midriffs that would have scandalised a Roman court. The sweltering fleshpots of Alexandria and Constantinople were nothing compared to the Indies. Cal took out a rag and mopped his brow.

'Damn me it is hotter than hell.'

'In the marshlands around Barbarikon there are mosquitoes,' said Rat. 'They eat you alive if the krokadillos do not get you first.'

'What of disease?' The last thing he wanted was to catch ill now that the way home was clear. 'Malaria and marsh fever are killers.'

'Lemon oil,' said Rat. 'The Indians douse themselves in the stuff; it smells good and keeps the biters away. I am certain that Suraj will have some.'

'That is expensive.'

'There are lemon orchards all over India,' said Rat. 'It is cheap here and there is still some coin in the boy's purse.'

'Let's just leave him out of it for now.'

'He is drinking.'

'That arrack liquid makes him insensible before he gets belligerent,' said Cal. 'Then he passes out.'

'He had barely touched a drop since we left Taurica, over a year ago, and then only when he was forced to, and now he is reduced to a drunk in the space of a few weeks.'

'He is dealing with his grief, let him deal with it.'

'He is risking everything and only the dog seems to rouse him. He is a drunk,' insisted Cosmas.

'He was already a drunk, he always will be a drunk; it is how long he indulges his drunkenness that is our only concern now. The pain is still raw for him and there is no need for him to be sober yet, nor is there until we get to Barbarikon. Leave him be until then.'

Theo overheard their words and they stung him, but he poured himself another cup of the bitter arrack.

'Well at least we have until Barbarikon,' he whispered to the cup, and ruffled Ursa's ears.

***

Taxila reminded Cal of a Roman city, perhaps one of the abandoned ruins of Italia or Gaul, built on a familiar grid pattern with a great stone wall and gates. It was clear that there had been a Greek influence, and Cosmas had told Cal that Alexander had once come here. Overgrown temples that would not look out of place in Olympus or Corinth made him think of home, five thousand miles and more away.

'Greeks get everywhere,' muttered the charioteer. 'How many of Alexander's crew made it home, I wonder?'

Theo would know the answer to that, but he was still sotted with arrack. Once we get back on the riverboats I will have to put a stop to that, thought Cal. He found the crossroads where he was supposed to meet the Rat. There were men gathered around a cart selling fried food of some type. They grinned at him, and the charioteer glanced at the giant pot and the rack of crispy unidentifiable chunks of meat and vegetables. The smell was enticing enough, but Cal had learned on the streets of Constantinople that he would suffer tomorrow for a morsel today.

'Where is the Rat?'

The charioteer perched on a low wall and leaned on his staff. Finding boats to take them all the way to Barbarikon was proving more difficult than both Suraj and Cosmas had promised in the mountains. It would take at least a week before a barge would be ready to make the journey, and then it would be another month of journeying to the mouth of the Indus. It would be the end of May by the time they got to Barbarikon. There was still more than enough time to make the coast before the ships left for Rome, but they could not afford to get distracted. Theo would need to sober up soon.

'Here you are, I have been looking for you.'

The Rat was silhouetted in the sunlight and Cal shielded his eyes with his hand before replying.

'I have been waiting, and you are late.'

'You will not believe who I have met. He has news of the north.'

They had been trying to find out what had been happening in Tashkent ever since they had arrived in the Indus valley, but reports had been garbled at best. The news of the battle before the city in the winter had made it back, but the details were confused with Hepthalite advocates insisting that the Goturks had been badly defeated. Whilst the international politics were of little concern to the Romans, being so far from their own Empire, all of them felt some affinity for Tardu and his father. Cal had liked the khan's son.

'Come along, come along.'

Cosmas let Cal down some twisting alleys behind the main thoroughfare. Most of the buildings were occupied in this part of the town, but they were rude and badly maintained, filth was running down open sewers at the side of the streets.

'This way, this way.'

'Dear God you are irritating.'

Rat stepped over a stream of effluence that emptied into the river, and took Cal to a small flat roofed building painted sky blue with the chi-rho sign on the door in white. The colours were faded and stained yellow by the elements but there was no mistaking the Christian symbol.

'There are Christians here?'

'There is a Greek here,' said Rat.

He rapped on the door and a small girl dressed in a linen shift opened it and let them in.

'They are expecting us.'

The priest was not any kind of Christian that the patriarchs in Constantinople, Jerusalem, Rome, or Alexandria would recognise. He was not even a Greek, not really, his grandfather had been a Greek but apart from his piercing blue eyes the man looked like any other emaciated ascetic that were everywhere in the town.

'Here he is, Father, here is the charioteer.'

'What have you been telling them?' hissed Cal.

'I told him that I travelled with the greatest charioteer to have ever lived. He wanted to meet you.'

'Why?' said Cal as he knelt to receive the priest's blessing.

'I do speak Greek you know,' said the priest.

'My apologies, Father,' spluttered Cal. 'I am just bemused as to my irritating companion's intent.'

The little man smiled, teeth stained blood red from the betel seeds that they all the men chewed. 'But you are famous, Charioteer. You are Porphyrius the Great.'

'I am not famous in India, surely? I am just an old man.'

'I have heard of you because there have been people asking after you and your friends.'

'Who?'

'Persians,' said the priest. 'They were here three weeks ago, spending gold for word of your whereabouts. There will be those in the city who will go to them and take the money. You can be certain of that. Their leader was a trader called Naghi.'

'And why did you not go to them and claim the reward?'

'I am a Greek not one of these Indians, and I did not like the Persian. He smelled bad.'

Cal almost let out a laugh, but did not want to offend the man who had given them fair warning.

'Where are these Persians now?'

'They are in Peshawar. There are agents waiting for news in the city; it is over one hundred miles away, but a fast horse could ride it in three days.' He looked at the pair of them. 'The Persian horses looked fast.'

Both of them, Cal and Cosmas, understood the danger they were in at the priest's news. Whilst there were few if any

Hepthalites this side of the mountains, the lords of these lands paid their taxes to them and normally would not have hesitated to hand the Romans over, but whispers of the defeat of the Hepthalites in the winter was changing the politics of the Indus river. To the south was an Indian Kingdom that paid no heed to Persian or Hepthalite demands. They needed to get out of Taxila quickly and away from Naghi's pursuit. Three days to Peshawar and three days to get back; it had been nearly a week since they arrived in the Indus city. News could already have reached Naghi and he could arrive at any moment.

'We need to tell Theo,' said Cal, looking around as if he expected Persian agents to burst in and arrest them.

'We need to sober him up first.'

29

Cal and Cosmas left the strange priest in his faded church, and hurried back to Suraj's home to deliver the bad news. Their urgency was obvious to everyone except Theo, who remained lounging in the sun with a cup of arrack as Cosmas outlined what they had discovered. Juana and her servant were quick to prepare for their departure, whilst Suraj went to find a boat's master that would take them downriver to Barbarikon.

'And what of our drunken leader?' Cosmas asked Cal.

Cal glanced outside to the courtyard overlooking the river where Theo, oblivious to the news, sat supping the spirit and gazing out at the small fishing boats on the Indus.

'I think it is way past time we stopped indulging him.'

'Finally.'

Cal strode out to the courtyard to confront Theo with Rat trailing behind. Theo did not even bother to look up as the charioteer and a grinning Cosmas approached. Ursa stood up which gave Cosmas pause for thought but not Cal. The stocky African ignored the hound and slapped the cup of arrack out of Theo's hand.

'What are you doing? I was drinking that.'

'And now you are not. Do you see how quickly things can change?' Cal kicked the bottle of arrack into the river.

'I am harming nobody, just leave me alone.'

'You have a duty to the Emperor, a duty to us, and a duty to Padma's shade; along with Godda and Uba and you besmirch the memory of their sacrifice with your drunken indulgence.'

He slapped Theo a couple of times in the face as he spoke, bringing up red hand marks on the nobleman's suntanned skin.

'How dare you!' Theo stood up to face Cal. 'You're but a common slave-born pleb. I have tolerated your insolence for far too long.'

Cal knocked him down with a single punch to the solar plexus, leaving Theo gasping and on his knees for a few moments. Cosmas was surprised at the fury on the charioteer's face, and the fact that the dog was simply allowing it to happen. Ursa sat on his hindquarters, tongue lolling, as Cal berated and beat his master. Cosmas took a step forward to join in the condemnation of the officer, but the dog's head turned fixing Rat with its amber eyes and growled. Cal, it seemed, was allowed to slap Ursa's master about but not Cosmas.

'Slave-born pleb I am proud to be, because I am not an irresponsible drunk.'

Theo dragged himself to his feet at those words. 'I am no drunk.' He raised his hand to strike Cal back but the charioteer grabbed him by the tunic.

'Can you swim?' asked Cal.

Theo spluttered as the charioteer lifted him off his feet with ease. The old man was immensely strong despite his advancing years and gammy knee. He held Theo up above his head by the throat with the boy's legs dangling.

'I should throw you down to those logs in the river.'

'Cal.' Cosmas was worried at that suggestion as Theo gasped for breath.

Cosmas tugged at the charioteer's tunic but Cal ignored him. He shook Theo, dangling him over the waters and made ready to drop.

'Cal!'

He finally looked down at Rat. 'What is it?'

'Those logs are krokadillos, and whilst we all want Theo to sober up I suspect swimming with the monsters is not the best way forward.' Rat gestured to the reptiles.

'Oh.'

Now that Cosmas had pointed it out, Cal could see the impassive eyes watching, unblinking, from the river. Four large crocodiles were observing the whole scene, and just waiting for one of them to step into the waters. Theo would be spun around and chewed up in an instant if he threw the boy into the river to sober him up. It punctured the bubble of fury in the charioteer, and he lowered a gasping, still indignant, Theo to the ground.

'I will beat the arrack out of you should you indulge again on this journey, and even the Rat will not stop me throwing you to those dragons.' He waved at the reptiles still watching from the waters. 'Do you understand me?'

'You are cruel,' muttered the sullen aristocrat rubbing his neck.

'Don't you dare answer me back!' Cal took a step forward and Theo flinched. 'Go and wash and clean away the stench of the arrack, and then get your baggage together. We are leaving as soon as Suraj finds us a boat.'

The two of them watched in silence as a snivelling Theo went inside to clean himself down and get ready. Ursa made to follow his master but turned back to Cal and sniffed him, then licked his hand as if in thanks. Then the dog padded after Theo into the house.

'Do you think that a beating and threats will work?'

'For a while,' said Cal. 'The fear of me mashing him to a pulp and always watching his cup is a deterrent, but only the boy can decide if he wants to change for good or not.'

'It sounds like you have some experience in these matters?'

Cal sighed.

'Do you remember Beric the Castaway?'

'The Briton who raced in the thirties? Didn't he break his legs in a smash?'

'Aye, he drank himself to death afterwards. He would stop for a while but the grape always called him back. Complete abstinence is the only sure way to survive being a drunk.'

'Theo is no monk.'

'No,' said Cal, sadly. 'He is not, which makes it all the more difficult for the lad to resist temptation. His men drink, his family own vineyards, and the imperial court is swimming in fine vintages. Not drinking wine will mark him out as different among the courtiers and sycophants that plague Constantinople, and being different is not always a good thing in Justinian's palace.'

Cosmas understood that as well as Cal. After all, he was always being called out for challenging the foolish notion of a round earth when it was clearly flat. Being different could be difficult.

***

The boat that Suraj had found them was a small sailing dhow, large enough for the Romans but the Kushan trader insisted on his family embarking with them which put space at a premium. Theo and Ursa sat up in the bow of the boat, still sulking after his beating, gazing out over the muddy waters. He had not touched a drop of arrack since the morning's confrontation, and his hands were shaking and he felt unsteady on his feet.

Just one sip would make me feel better he thought, and then glanced over at the charioteer. Not worth it, he decided as Cal caught his eye; the man is not one to make empty threats.

'Are you seriously asking for more?' Cosmas and Suraj were bickering about the cost of the small boat. 'We have already got an agreement on the costs?'

'That was before we had word of Persian agents on the Indus,' said Suraj. 'Now I have to pay for added speed and security that is not covered in the original agreement. You would not want me to be out of pocket?'

'I think it is rather duplicitous to make a bargain and then break it at the first sign of trouble.'

Suraj sighed. 'I can always leave you here, friend Cosmas and you can wait for the next transport to come downriver.'

Cosmas bit back a snide retort. Suraj was correct that the plans had changed and speed in getting to Barbarikon was now of the utmost importance.

'What of your wife and children and father? Are we paying for them too?'

'Would you have me leave my family to be tortured by Naghi's men?'

'No, I suppose not.'

Cosmas went and sat at the bow of the boat with Theo as the last of their baggage was loaded and Suraj's wife and gaggle of children jumped on board. The two sailors and ship's master was the only crew, all dressed in dirty rags and bare feet and stinking of fish.

'It smells like an amphora of garam,' muttered Rat. 'The stench makes me gag.'

'They are fisherman,' Theo said

'Admittedly a most blessed profession, but I wager the apostles washed every night in the Jordan.'

'There are krokadillos in the Indus.' Theo gave a strange laugh. 'I am watching them watching us.'

The arrack has sent him into stupidity and it makes him a poor conversationalist, thought Cosmas.

Cal was in the stern as they pushed off and glided into the middle of the river. The current caught the small dhow taking it away from the riverbank, and Taxila was soon disappearing behind them. At the first great bend, Cal took a last glance back at the gleaming broken domes of the Indian city. They had managed to escape Naghi again but the week's wait had made the race to the sea tight. The Persians could follow them on the river or on horseback. It was like the last leg of a race in the hippodrome, he decided: we are in the lead but our team is tiring and the Bulgar's quadriga is coming up.

'I wonder what tricks Naghi will try to play before the final trumpet call,' he muttered.

The boat's master looked over from the huge tiller at his words and started chattering away unintelligibly at him. Cal shrugged and tapped his head, and the man shrugged back and fell silent.

Juana and her servant, and Suraj's family, were all huddled amidships with their bags and boxes piled high. The young wife did not look happy at being taken from her home and transported downriver, but the children all had excited grins on their faces at the sudden adventure. The Nestorian woman smiled at Cal, she had been most approving of Theo's beating when Cosmas told her. There was a part of her that blamed the Theo for her sister's death, although she recognised that as irrational, and there was a grim satisfaction at his punishment. Of the three Romans, Cal was the only one she had any real regard for.

The river was bordered by lush forests and mangrove swamps that grew more numerous the further south they travelled. Every day Cal and the other Romans were astounded at the wild animals they saw. Rhinoceros and elephants, water snakes and crocodiles, river dolphins and wild birds; it was a veritable Garden of Eden. The sailors would catch fish fresh every day as they travelled, broiling them on an open grill at the bow of the boat. Every night they would throw a heavy stone out to anchor them in the river rather than mooring up on the shore. When Cosmas asked why, the boat's master explained that the land was more dangerous with wild beasts and crocodiles than the river.

'And Persians chasing us,' Cal told Rat. 'How far to Barbarikon?'

'Three more weeks,' said Cosmas.

They had travelled for a fortnight already, passing small villages and towns. The boat's master wanted to put into one of the towns for news, but Suraj insisted on them moving further downriver before stopping. The Romans all agreed with him. They did not want word of their passing to feed back to Naghi. All of them prayed that they had finally escaped the Persian agent, but all of them had learned on the quest that the spy was like a limpet.

'Do you think that we have escaped him?' Theo asked the question on everyone's mind.

'No,' said Cal. 'Every time we think that he turns up again.'

Theo had been sullen and silent for the first week of the voyage as his body sweated out the arrack. He had endured shaking hands and body, night sweats, and bad dreams if he managed to sleep at all, but now he just felt weak, empty, and slightly ashamed of himself. The desire for a drink of arrack or cup of wine was still there, but the young noble was determined to resist his urges. Ursa gave him comfort, his constant companion, and every time that Theo thought he was weakening the dog instinctively took his attention to distract from the pangs of desire. He gave the dog a great hug.

'You are the best thing to come out of this journey,' he told the dog.

The hound just licked his face with its slobbering tongue.

***

The children all watched in silence as Ursa crept, on his belly, under the gunwales towards Cosmas at the bow. The little Alexandrian merchant was standing on his bench, pontificating about the flat world to the uncomprehending crew and uncaring passengers as they ate a supper of fresh grilled fish in the evening sun. Cosmas had placed his platter of fish on the bench to deliver his sermon, and the dog was creeping straight towards it. Suraj's wife nudged her husband as Rat talked down at them and he smiled at Ursa along with the rest. Theo and Cal watched intently from the stern.

'A solidus that the Rat does not notice,' whispered Cal.

'I would not bet against my own hound,' Theo whispered back.

They seem to be more attentive than usual to my words, thought Cosmas. It must be their experiences on the journey. They have learned that Cosmas the Truth Teller is no fool, and they have been deceived all their lives.

'We have all seen the pillars of the sky,' he said, loftily. 'We have all seen the steppe, as flat as unleavened bread. The physical evidence is clear that the whole world is also flat, and the idea that it is a globe but a foolish Greek notion from a thousand years ago.'

'Egyptian,' said Theo.

Everyone turned at that. Theo had been subdued all down the river, barely saying a word to anyone. It was the first time he had actually ventured information since the mountains. Cal smiled at the boy.

'What?' asked Cosmas.

'It was Egyptians like you that made the discovery. Eratosthenes merely calculated the circumference.'

'We Indians had also calculated the circumference a millennia ago,' Suraj pointed out. 'And we understand the meaning of nothing which you Greeks and Romans still find so complicated.'

'That is just mathematics, it is not real life,' said Cosmas.

'All life is mathematics,' Suraj told him.

Ursa's head popped up behind Cosmas. He hauled his forequarters up onto the bench, grabbed the fish in its mouth and bounded past the surprised Alexandrian. Suraj's gaggle of children burst out laughing; they all adored the dog.

'Where did that animal come from?' Cosmas looked down, 'The beast has my supper! Catch him.'

Ursa bounded across the boat to Theo in the stern as everybody fell about laughing at the Rat's protests. The dog growled but let Theo take the prize from his mouth.

'My fish?'

Theo held up a half eaten tail to show Cosmas.

'Never mind.'

Theo gave the fish back to Ursa who wagged his tail and set to gobbling it up.

'I think when a dog can beat you in real life, Cosmas; it is time to listen to the mathematicians,' said Suraj.

'Typical,' said Rat, and sat down with his empty plate.

Theo stood up to address everyone.

'No more sermons, please?' said Cal.

Juana and her servant smiled at the charioteer's words when Cosmas translated. The pair of them looked over the cane that contained the silkworm eggs every day to check for splitting or moisture, but otherwise did not interact much with Cosmas or Theo unless they had to.

'No,' said Theo. 'I think it is right that I offer my apologies to all of you.'

'There is no need for that,' said Cal.

'Thank you, friend, but there is a need. I have let you all down these last months. I wallowed in my own misery and forgot my mission and my duty. It was you who brought me back to my senses, and I owe you my gratitude. Without you taking charge, I fear we would have been lost in the mountains.'

Cosmas translated the words back to Juana and her servant. The Nestorian woman nodded in agreement at Theo's words, and smiled broadly at Cal.

'Just make sure that Narses pays us when we get back,' muttered Cal embarrassed at Theo's words.

'Oh I will make him pay.'

'That sounds threatening?' said Rat.

'We have succeeded in the mission, we deserve our rewards. They say we will get to Barbarikon tomorrow and there are Roman ships waiting for the weather to turn to get home. I will use all my family's contacts if Narses tries to weasel out.'

'He won't,' said Cal. 'He will want all the glory himself. As long as we keep our mouths shut we will be paid. I learned that of him a long time ago.'

'A toast then,' said Cosmas. 'To Barbarikon and home, and Narses paying his debts.'

All of them took a sip of kumis from their cups excepting Theo.

30

It had taken them four weeks of travel down the Indus to reach Barbarikon. They avoided any large settlements, slipping past in the early morning or as night fell. Instead, the boat stopped in small villages a couple of times to buy fresh food; the Romans hid under a dirty sail whilst Suraj and the Fishermen dealt with the locals. It would have been excruciatingly monotonous, but Cal and Cosmas watched the shoreline in wonder at the strange sights and animals. Theo was left making sure that Ursa did not jump in the waters and become Crocodile fodder. The dog was always watching the waters intently and barking whenever one of lizards appeared.

'They are smaller than the ones on the Nile,' said Cosmas.

'They will still chew him up,' said Theo with a firm grip on his hound's ruff.

Once the winter of arrack indulgence had been sweated out in the burning heat, Theo was much like the man they had known on the outward journey. As Cal observed, it was spirits and wines that was the problem for the boy. All of them had taken to wearing cloth turbans around their heads in the local fashion to deal with the heat and glare of the sun, but Theo suffered most. The blonde aristocrat's face was blistered and the skin peeling in strips, but he did not complain, considering it a penance for his failures in the mountains.

Day after day had slipped by in muted conversation and dozing. As they sailed down the river, the sun burned ever hotter and the rains steamed but passed quickly. By the time they reached the delta at the coast, all of them were just begging for the voyage to end. The boat took the central channel downriver, the others courses too muddy and infested to risk, where the city of Barbarikon was fixed on the banks close to the sea.

'There, look!' Cosmas stood up in the boat and pointed as they rounded a bend in the river.

'Barbarikon,' gasped Cal, almost overwhelmed at the sight of their destination.

'Bhanbhore,' Suraj corrected him. 'The home of the Princes of Sindh.'

The boat moored at stone jetties along the river and they quickly disembarked, all eager to see the town and hopefully find their passage back to Roman lands. Suraj accounted for the fishermen's price as promised, and the others all bade farewell to the men who had been their travelling companions for a month. Once they were all standing on the waterfront, the sailors took the boat away from the jetties so they did not have to pay a toll, leaving the Romans and Suraj's family alone. Cal looked around at the party and burst out laughing.

'What is so funny?' asked Cosmas.

'Look at the state of us: an Indian family,' he gestured at Suraj and his wife, father, and gaggle of children. 'A senator's son whose blistered face makes him look like leper from Subura with this huge puppy, and you a filthy smelly sewer rat.'

'Me?'

'You must be the dirtiest man I have ever seen, Cosmas; did you even wash whilst we were on the boat?'

'You are no pretty picture yourself, Charioteer, and there were crocodiles.'

Cal just smiled.

Suraj explained to Cosmas that he had a contact in the city where they could stay for at least a few nights, whilst they found a ship's captain or more permanent lodgings. Once Rat had informed the others in turn, they picked up their baggage and trooped after the merchant – eyes wide like children at the sights and sounds of the strange city.

There were people everywhere. The markets and stalls along the river were thronging with customers. Barbarikon was a thriving port, grown rich on the trade with Rome, and the Yemen or Ethiopia. Goods from the west flowed into the city from the ships that came every year, whilst goods from all over the Indies made the return journey: glittering topaz, rainbow coloured corals, frankincense, vessels of glass from Roman factories in Egypt, silver and gold plate, and boatloads of wine amphorae; there were spices and dyes, turquoise, lapis lazuli, ivory, cotton cloth, silk of course - there was always silk - and indigo. The markets and bazaar of Barbarikon were royal ransom.

'It is such a shame we are not buying or selling,' said Cosmas.

'I think we have more than enough trouble to go on with,' Cal told him.

The Indian trader known to Suraj lived in the eastern section of the city, in a well built flat-roofed house with a nondescript façade painted sky blue. Servants greeted them, but made them wait on the doorstep whilst one ran to fetch their master. Such a dirty crew was unexpected and unwanted as far as the doormen were concerned, but Suraj was most insistent.

'Well, well, Suraj of Taxila, what are you doing here?'

A slender man with greying black hair and beard and dressed in a flowing white cotton robe, finally appeared at the door to see what the commotion was about.

'Sidarshan, it is good to see you old friend. We find ourselves in need of hospitality.'

The man looked taken aback at first but then beckoned for them to enter.

'Come in then, come in,' he said, but then stopped talking as he saw Cosmas.

'Do I know you?'

'No, no, I do not think so,' said Rat.

'Yes, yes I do. You started the riot on the beach a few years back?'

'We Romans all look alike,' said Cosmas, keeping his eyes to the floor.

The others were all looking in askance as Rat and their host spoke. The Romans could not understand the Indian language, but Juana most certainly could.

'Did you start a riot?' she asked the Rat in a tone that would brook no prevarication.

Cosmas looked guilty, eyes flicking around at everyone nervously.

'The sailors would not believe me that the world is flat,' he said. 'They kept pointing to the horizon and laughing at me. It sort of escalated from there...'

The merchant that Suraj had called Sidarshan burst out laughing.

'The Raja had to send down his own royal guard to break it up and throw a few in a dungeon to restore peace, Lady,' Sidarshan told Juana.

Suraj looked down at the Rat. 'Really, Cosmas, we cannot take you anywhere.'

Juana started chuckling as the rest all watched uncomprehendingly on. It was the first genuine laugh the others had heard from her since the mountains. Mostly she just sat apart from the Romans with her mute servant and neither ever ventured conversation to the others. To the Romans it was strange and aloof behaviour, but to the Nestorian woman it was their prattle that was strange.

'There is no need to tell the others,' said Rat looking around at Theo.

'You are fortunate that I cannot tell them, but if I could...' Suraj left that hanging.

Sidarshan took them in and gave them a couple of large rooms to stay in whilst they found a Roman contact at the ships.

'Are there Romans in port?' Theo asked through Cosmas.

'Oh yes,' said Sidarshan. 'The fleets arrived a month ago, late this year, but we have merchants from every creed and race down at the beach. Christianity is accepted here, but make sure you do not cause trouble.' He looked directly at Cosmas as he said that. 'Buddhist, Hindi, Christian, Zoroastrian, Jew; there are temples and churches to all the gods here, and we have people from all over the Indies as well as Romans, Greeks and Africans. There are merchants from Yemen and Persia.'

'Persians?' asked Theo.

'There are always Persians,' said the merchant.

* * *

Theo took out his mail coat from the chest it had been packed since Tashkent. He had not put it away properly in the rush to leave, and the conditions in the mountains and then the rains and heat of the Indus had tarnished the metal. Links were fused together with a layer of red rust, the leather undercoat was stiff and brittle – cracking in places – and the whole suit needed polishing and greasing to be restored to battle worthy condition. He let out a big sigh, normally one of his retainers or servants would have seen to his armour.

As he lifted the coat up to survey the damage, a single dried flower fell from the folds of the metal. A pink peach blossom, fragile but still retaining its colour, fell to the floor. Theo picked it up and almost burst into tears. Padma had given it to him on one of their walks along the battlements of Tashkent. The others all looked back on their time in the citadel of stone as cursed, and whilst Theo had to admit the misery they had suffered there he had fallen in love. He would always remember the Goturk city with fondness. The Roman aristocrat picked up the flower and placed it at the bottom of his trunk, stored safely so it would not be crushed and crumble. When he got home, he would have it fixed in glass and set in gold.

'I think I should clean the armour,' Theo said to himself. 'She would approve.'

He took the mail coat and helmet out into the courtyard to sit in the sun and grease, polish and buff until he was satisfied it was perfect. Rat and Suraj were down at the beach, where the trading fleets lay at anchor, trying to find Roman ships to take them home. The Indian merchant had invested his whole fortune into the Roman contract; he had been forced to abandon his home in Taxila and was unlikely to be welcomed back in Tashkent in the near future. Everything that Suraj possessed depended on the Romans getting home and fulfilling their promises. Cal sat dozing in the sun as Theo started dabbing fat onto the mail coat and polishing it with a rag.

'We are almost home, Charioteer,' he said to Cal. 'You will see your granddaughter again soon.'

'I have learned on this journey not to count our chickens before they come home to roost.' He opened his eyes and rolled over to face Theo. 'You do not seem to be accustomed to polishing.'

Theo grimaced. 'Normally I would have a slave to deal with it all. I am beginning to realise just how spoiled I have been.'

'Well, if nothing else some good has come out of the journey. What will you do when we get home?'

'I will go wherever the Emperor sends me. Before we left there was talk of reinforcing the army in Italy. I think I would like to see Rome.'

'I never raced in the Circus Maximus,' said Cal with more than a hint of regret. 'The despot Totila sent his agents to beg me to race in his games before Narses trapped me, but I refused to race for a barbarian.'

'Perhaps you will race there one day.'

Cal laughed. 'I think I have raced my last quadriga. It is a young man's game, and the Goths still rule in Rome.'

'That is only a temporary situation.'

'It is a lifetime since the west fell.'

'Italia will be restored soon enough,' said Theo confidently. 'Hispania and your home in Africa are already returned from Vandal oppression to Roman rule. Gaul and perhaps even Britannia will be brought back to the fold one day. Llew used to say that the Britons would welcome the return of Rome.'

They had rarely talked about home or the future on the journey, but now that they had the secret of silk, now that they were on the verge of getting home, all their dreams lay heavy on the mind.

'Let us hope that Rat doesn't do anything to stall our return, then,' said Cal. 'If one of us is going to scupper the ship it will be him.'

'Oh, I do like the nautical allusion.'

As if he had been summoned by their words, Cosmas and Suraj returned from the beach. The Rat was grinning from ear to ear.

'We have found them!' He shouted excitedly at the others when he saw them. 'You will have to go down to persuade the company agent that we are on Justinian's business, Theo, but there is room for us all on board.'

'It would be well if we moved on soon, said Suraj, looking about the sundrenched courtyard. Our host's hospitality will only extend so far.'

'You are not coming back to Greece?'

'Of course not, once you have found passage and my contracts are confirmed I will take my family back home to Taxila.'

'What of Naghi?'

'It is you they want, and I will happily tell them everything if they come looking for me, but by then it will be too late.'

Theo looked down at his armour. It glinted in the sunlight as he turned the mail over in his hands looking for any breaks. Most of the rust was gone and the leather undercoat buffed and greased to give it back flexibility. It would do, he decided. He looked back to Cosmas.

'Well then, it is time I got dressed and reminded this petty mercantile administrator of the glory of Rome, and the spite of the Emperor's secretary.'

***

It was late by the time Theo, Cosmas and Suraj and the charioteer finally arrived at the beach where the Roman ships lay at anchor. The sun was just hovering over the sea in the west, as if it was beckoning the Romans home, glittering golden on the waves and drenching the beach in honey twilight. Six large corbita merchantmen sat at anchor, with round belly hulls and a great single rudder on their small stern decks, silhouetted by the fading sunlight. The masts had been unstepped whilst they lay at the river mouth in case of storms, and the crews were spread along the beach in a variety of camps carousing and drinking as they waited for the winds to turn. There were stalls with locals serving food and drinks; dancers and musicians playing strange instruments and beating out wild rhythms. To Cal and the others who had endured so much since leaving Tashkent it seemed like some wild bacchanalian festival.

'Where is this agent?' Theo looked at Rat.

'At the far end of the beach, there are stone jetties and boats that unload the cargoes.'

They trudged along the shore, their boots sinking in the soft white sands, past the drunken sailors until they found a bamboo shack serving food where the agent was eating. A fat man with receding blonde curls and blue tunic spotted with sauce stains reclined on plush cushions with plates of food and drink. When he saw Cosmas and the others on the beach, he beckoned for them to come over.

'Well, I can scarcely believe it. You were actually telling the truth for once, Cosmas.' He nodded to Cal. 'Master Porphyrius, I am indeed honoured.'

'You know me?'

'I saw you race in Antioch as a boy, I thought you were long dead and yet here you are in the Indies. It is a wonder.'

'I am hoping to get home,' said Cal beaming at the agent.

'For you, Master Charioteer, there will be no fee for the passage. You have paid me many times over at the races.'

'I like this one,' Cal told the others.

'What about the rest of us?' Theo was more than a little annoyed at being ignored by the man.

'I must apologise, Magister,' said the man, bowing. 'I am Alexander Polipidus of Antioch.' He smiled at Theo dressed up in his armour with insignia of rank displayed. 'Taking you all home can be easily arranged, however, the price is the problem.'

'You will be well rewarded.'

'Oh I am sure that is your desire now, but I find that people often forget their promises when they get home. This one.' He beckoned at Suraj. 'Has contracts issued in your name for two shiploads of glassware. That is nearly two hundred tonnes of goods; a third of what I bring on the outward voyage would have no profit if I fulfil it. The company would then have to pay in silver to fill the ships on the return journey. I want your seal on contracts and documents indemnifying the company from any loss incurred and ensuring payment from your family should you expire on the way home.'

'Do you people think of anything other than contracts and profits?'

Alexander gestured to Cal. 'Demonstrably, but you are here on this one's say so...' He looked at Rat. 'Which brings us to our final problem.'

'What problem?'

'He is not to preach any of his nonsense to the crews on the beach. He is not to badger the navigators, and he is not allowed on the stern deck of any ship he travels in.'

'Some people don't like hearing the truth, they prefer their comfortable self deceits,' muttered Cosmas, as Cal gave out a throaty chuckle.

'We happily agree,' said Theo. 'The Charioteer will tie up the Rat and gag him if needs be, and I will affix my seal to such and assure you that Narses will pay.'

'The contract is with your family, Magister. You can get the payment off of Narses, not the company's investors. They would not thank me for that.'

'As you wish,' said Theo, and fixed his seal in the soft wax. There would still be more than enough profit for his family out of the journey.

Once all the paperwork was completed, Alexander sat back in on his cushions. 'Well, will you take a cup of wine to seal the deal? It is a fine Cretan vintage that I brought myself.'

'I have taken a vow of abstinence until we return home,' said Theo. 'So I must regretfully decline. The others will of course'

Cal and Cosmas both smiled behind the young noble's back and accepted cups of wine to sip.

'It will be perhaps a week or so before the winds turn again. You have a woman with you? A Nestorian Rassaphore?'

Theo nodded.

'Well, if she is offended by coarse sailors it may be best to wait until we are ready to sail before bringing her down.'

'If we cannot wait?'

'My men are coarse but god-fearing.'

One of the coarse sailors appeared at the shack at that point.

'Boss, there is a child looking for these.'

'Send him in.'

The small dark haired child was one of Suraj's brood, who ran straight into his father's arms, babbling in their own language whilst the others watched on. When the conversation had finally finished, Suraj turned back to the others.

'Naghi.'

31

There was a Persian Immortal waiting outside Sidarshan's home. When he saw them arrive back from the beach he ducked into the merchant's house.

'Blades out?' said Theo.

'What blades?' Cosmas pointed out. 'You are the only one with a spatha.'

The guard had reappeared and opened the courtyard gates for them. They approached him slowly, warily, Theo with his hand on his sword hilt, but the Persian merely nodded and grinned at them and stepped aside to let them enter. The Immortal's short sword was sheathed and he wore no armour under his black tunic and kilt. He was not expecting trouble from the Romans.

'That one is yours, Cal,' Theo said in Latin.

The charioteer merely grunted in response.

Inside the courtyard, Naghi was waiting for them with another Immortal. The Persian spy was seated on a bench alone, with Sidarshan and his family and Suraj's wife and children huddled together in the corner of the courtyard behind him. Juana and her mute servant stood nervously with them but the relief when she saw Theo and the others was palpable. Naghi beamed widely as well when he saw the Romans step into the courtyard.

'Cosmas of Alexandria, here you are again,' he said in Greek, standing up. 'And you still have the young disgraced noble and the crippled charioteer with you.'

'What do you want, Persian?' said Theo.

'Oh I am not here to harm you, Romans. I am here to make you despair.' He grinned at them again.

'Some might say that is the worst harm,' said Theo.

'Those people are poets or fools.'

Theo noted that Cal had stayed at the back, close to the door, close to the guard by the gate. The Immortal standing outside had come into the courtyard, closing the gate behind him and the charioteer was ready with his staff.

'Will you sit and take some wine with me? I believe it is an Alban vintage.' The sneer in the Persian's tone was unmistakable.

'What do you want?' repeated Theo.

'Ah, I forget that you cannot partake of the grape without losing your wits. It has been a long time since that brawl in Chersonesus, Dagisthaeus.'

Theo pursed his lips but said nothing and made no move to sit with Naghi.

'Well, never mind,' said Naghi after a pause. 'I am merely here to inform you of your failure. To gloat at you, if you will.'

'Failure?' said Cosmas.

'Oh yes, Rat. Did you think that my emperor would let a Roman embassy ally with the Goturks? Did you truly think you could start a war in our eastern provinces and get away with it?'

He does not know, thought Cosmas. He thinks this is about politics not trade, he doesn't know about the silk. He flashed a glance at Juana, but Naghi noticed.

'Oh, my emperor's satraps will deal with your Nestorian treason. You can rest assured on that, Lady.' He turned back to Theo. 'Your boy in Tashkent told us everything. How you planned to raise an army of steppe warriors to attack Persia. How you flattered and deceived the Khan and his son merely to start a war. It is quite remarkable how talkative a little torture made the lad. Was he your catamite, Dagisthaeus?'

It was then that Theo realised just how brave Uba had been when he was captured. The lad had known all about the silk and the worms. He had known all of their secrets, yet even under torture had constructed a ruse to deceive the Persians. The boy must have known he was going to die.

I will raise a stone in honour of the boy on the estate, thought Theo. He may just have saved us all. If Naghi had realised their true mission, his men would be murdering them instead of gloating.

'Of course, I could go straight to the khan and offer more than Rome ever could' the Persian continued. 'The Goturks will rule in place of the Hepthalites and bow down to the Sassanid emperor.'

'If you think that the Goturks will bow before anyone, you are a fool,' said Theo.

'I thought you were trying to arrange silk shipments over the steppe at first, to avoid Persian officials,' said Naghi ignoring Theo. 'But then you stepped into the rebellion and saved that barbarian prince. Oh, I cursed you then, we had spent so much money starting the damned uprising and then some wandering Romans saved our main target.'

'We Romans do not like injustice.'

Naghi burst out laughing. 'Tell that to the fools in your forums. We Persians know you somewhat better.'

'So what is all this for? Just to mock us?'

'I suppose it is,' said Naghi. 'You did well though, escaped Tashkent and made us follow your men over the steppes but I had an inkling you would slip to the south. Why else would you bring this fool?' He gestured at Cosmas. 'We thought we had you in Taxila and you slipped away again, but by then it did not matter.'

'Why?' asked Cosmas.

'Because by then we had secured an alliance with the khan; the Goturks are our vassals now, as I said.' The spy beamed widely at them.

Theo laughed in his face. 'Do you want to know the real reason we came and now why we go home?'

The smile of smug superiority faltered on the Persian's face. 'What do you mean?'

Theo leaned forward, and unclipped the buckle on his spatha's scabbard.

'We stole the secret of silk from Serica and now return home with it,' he said in an almost whisper. 'We are going to bankrupt every merchant in Persia and bring your empire to ruin.'

The shock on the Persian's face gave Theo a moment of grim satisfaction, and then he drew his blade in one movement and sliced at the spy's throat. Naghi put up his hand in desperation, but Theo's blade cut through it to the bone. Blood spurted from the severed artery, but the man's screams were silenced by Theo's second thrust.

As soon as Cal saw Theo move, he lurched at the immortal by the gates. The man was fumbling for his sword, surprised at the sudden action as Cal butted him, smashing his nose sending him spinning to the floor, and then he battered him with his staff again and again until the Persian was still. Juana's mute servant had grabbed the other from behind by the throat and slowly throttled him, letting the body slump to the ground where Cosmas slit his throat with a dagger.

Sidarshan and the women and children had merely watched on in stunned silence as the three Persians were butchered. One of the children started sobbing at the blood running slick on the cobbles, and the Barbarikon merchant looked down at the three corpses in his courtyard.

'You will need to get rid of the bodies and you will leave tonight,' he told Suraj.

Theo agreed once the words were translated. They had already outstayed their welcome in Barbarikon, it would be best to get down to the beach and wait for the winds to change.

'How exactly are we to dispose of the bodies?' asked Cal. 'At home we would stuff them in the sewers, but here...' He left that hanging.

Sidarshan was already barking at one of his servants who disappeared for a moment and came back carrying a rug. The servant dumped it on the floor and then disappeared again.

They all looked at Sidarshan.

'Well?' said Suraj.

'Roll them up in the carpets. I will give you a handcart and then you take them to the river and roll them down.'

'Why us?' said Suraj. What if we are caught?

'Because it is your crime and if you are caught I will deny all knowledge of it.'

The Kushan trader explained everything to the others, as the servant reappeared with more carpets and then a small handcart.

'I expect you to pay for the replacement carpets, Suraj.'

'I would expect nothing less.'

Once the bodies were rolled up and dumped into the cart, buckets of water were drawn from a well and thrown over cobbles to swill away the blood. Theo and Cal grabbed the cart's handrails and started rolling it into the street outside. Suraj and Cosmas both led the way, keeping a watch for any more Persians, and took them down to the Indus River.

'Why the river?' asked Cal.

'Crocodiles do not eat fresh meat, they kill their prey and then store it like a squirrel saving nuts for winter,' Cosmas told him. 'A couple of corpses are a nice morsel for them to pack away.'

'How do you know this?'

'Any child who grows up on the banks of the Nile knows.'

'What about newly butchered meat?' asked Theo.

'We know not to leave it by the river at night. Are you ready?'

Theo and Cal lifted Naghi's corpse up in the rolled carpet and span him down into the river, keeping a hold of the end of the rug. Naghi's corpse tumbled down to the water and out of sight. There was a muffled splash and then silence. Then they did the same with the other two bodies. They could all feel a cool breeze coming down the river to the sea. Cosmas sniffed at the air, like a dog sniffing gravy.

'The winds are changing,' he said.

Epilogue

I stopped writing and put down my pen alongside the papyrus and looked at the three miscreants before me: the black charioteer with his white curls, the weasel faced Alexandrian and the Goth born aristocrat with an influential family and huge dog. They were perched on a marble bench like recalcitrant schoolboys in front of their pedagogue, the hound's tongue lolling in the heat. The tale they told was wondrous indeed, but the truth of their words are evident in newly hatched silkworms munching on mulberry bushes all across Greece.

'And after Barbarikon?' I asked.

'We sailed home, Master Procopius,' said the Rat. 'It was easy enough.'

'Not so easy,' said Cal. 'I was sick the whole way and so was Theo. I'll be damned if I ever get aboard another ship.'

'There was a small storm,' Rat conceded, but looked at me earnestly. 'The ship was never in danger, whatever some people might have thought...'

'We put in at the old port of Myos Hormos,' said Theo quickly, before the other two could start an argument. 'After that it was a short ride to the Nile and a boat to Alexandria.'

'Another boat and then a ship,' said Cal.

'And then a ship back to Constantinople,' said Theo. 'It was quicker than riding through Syria and Anatolia, and safer.'

'There was another storm.'

'It was just a squall,' said Cosmas.

The three of them have no real idea what they have achieved. They understand that Rome now has silk but they do not quite grasp the implications of that. At least the merchant and the charioteer do not. The aristocrat is wise enough in the ways of politics at court to see that Rome is made richer and more powerful at a stroke, whilst the Sassanid Emperor no longer gains from our profligacy.

I sat back in my chair and pondered them for a moment.

Silk from Constantinople can be sold all over the empire. Even petty barbarian kings in the lost western provinces will pay good coin for the cloth. Instead of money flowing out of Justinian's coffers it will pour in, and with it the re-conquest of the west can be paid for. I have to admit Narses is a clever snake; he will make the barbarians pay for their own demise. At the same time we will make a pauper of the Sassanid Emperor and diminish the threat in the east. Men guarding the eastern frontiers against a Sassanid at attack could be better used by Belisarius and Narses in Italia and Gaul. With such high stakes, I am surprised that the eunuch entrusted the task to these three, and yet they have succeeded where a legion would have failed.

'What of your bucellarii?' I asked.

Cal and the Rat both looked to Theo who gave me a wide grin.

'They made it back a couple of months before we did. Beremund led them over the steppe and they had some adventures of their own, but they got home. The Persians chased after them, but with Naghi following us the pursuit did not last. It was the same with us. After I killed him in Barbarikon we had no more trouble with Persians. We feared Sassanid ships taking us at sea, but we saw none on the voyage.'

'I will want to talk with the bucellarii, to hear the details of their journey.'

He nodded. 'Of course, Master Procopius. Narses told us to tell you everything that you want.'

I bit back a barb about the emperor's eunuch. He was another one to be careful of in the palace and informants were everywhere. It would only get back to him.

'The Lady Juana assists now with the new silk farms?'

They nodded.

'We have not seen much of her since our return, she has been intent on the worms, but I am told she is happy enough,' said Theo. 'Once the farms are established I believe she will return to the east. Her family is there, and they have been well rewarded by the Emperor.'

'Did Narses pay your debts to the Indian merchant?'

'With no ifs, buts, or equivocations,' said Cosmas. 'The contract for glass will be fulfilled with this year's fleets to India. Suraj will be pleased.'

I was surprised by that, but some shiploads of glassware to cultivate an agent in the east was not so great a price to pay.

'He has kept his promises to all of us,' said Cal. 'My farm is returned and my granddaughter's debts are redeemed. She had a baby son while we were gone. I am a great grandfather.'

'What will you do now?' I asked

'Retire and farm worms and mulberry bushes,' said Cal. 'No more travelling or races for me, my own hearth is enough.'

'As you sink into decrepitude,' said Rat.

I smiled and turned to the Egyptian. 'So what next for you, Cosmas of Alexandria?'

The Rat paused and looked down at the papyrus before me where the ink was drying on the words – black scribbles on yellowing sheets that told their tale. He sat back, folded his arms, and looked me straight in the eye.

'I am going to get the fish eggs from Atil, and with my fortune earned write a book,' he said, and pointed to my papyrus. 'Will you include how the world is proven flat by our travels in your own writing, Master Procopius?'

'No,' I said. 'Because it is most demonstrably not flat.'

'See,' he said triumphantly to the other two. 'I told you so; it's always authority's version of events that we are told, never the real truth.'

The others both sighed, shook their heads, and looked back to me.

'And Magister Militum Dagisthaeus?'

The officer smiled at hearing his rank aloud.

'I am away to Italia in the spring,' he said. 'The army gathers in Salona and I have been given a command under Narses. We go to take back the eternal city.'

I smiled at him. 'Your replacement in Lazica was Bessus,' I told him. 'He lost Rome but recaptured Petra. Perhaps you shall do the reverse.'

Historical Note

Procopius' enigmatic entry in his histories about the theft of silk making from China in the 6th century marks one of the first documented cases of industrial espionage in history. Whilst the entry frustratingly only contains the basic details of the mission, it must have been well planned and organised. It was also undoubtedly a success with the subsequent establishment of the Byzantine silk industry under Emperor Justinian.

The Roman Empire was in its final flourish before becoming in essence a Greek medieval empire a century later. By 550, provinces lost with the fall of the West in 476AD were being brought back into the Roman fold. North Africa had been retaken from the Vandals along with large parts of Spain, the conquest of Italy was well underway with Rome having changed hands multiple times, and Roman ships once again controlled the Mediterranean. At the same time, as the Empire's reach expanded, new products and innovations such as caviar and stirrups began to make an appearance. Justinian perhaps has the distinction of being both the last Classical Emperor as well as the first Medieval, or at least sub-Roman, monarch. His secretary Narses was central to the restoration of imperial authority along with the great general Belisarius. There appears a real sense in contemporaries that the old empire was about to be restored. It would not last and within 50 years of Justinian's death the Byzantine Empire was in crisis.

Cosmas Indicopleustes was a real sailor and traveller who wrote the medieval Christian Topology. He is the only known defender of a flat earth theory in medieval history (whatever Mark Twain might have you believe), and his ideas were scorned at the time by fellow travellers, monks, and the overwhelming majority of educated Romans. Similarly Dagisthaeus the boy general who lost Petra and ended up in Justinian's dungeons existed, and had somehow restored his reputation by 551 to be given a military rank in the Italian campaign where he helped recapture Rome for the last time.

Porphyrius the Charioteer was the greatest charioteer of the late Roman Empire – somewhat akin to Heavyweight Champion of the World mashed up with a Grand Prix champion. Born a slave in Libya in the 480s, he won every honour in the races that were fanatically followed in the Empire and beyond. Statues and tributes to his success littered the Hippodrome in Istanbul and his fame was renowned across the later Roman Empire, and a wider ancient world addicted to the sport. His involvement in imperial politics was also well documented, as was his initiating massacres of anti-imperial rioters in 515 and a vicious pogrom against a synagogue in 507. The former on behalf of the emperor, the latter because he had lost a race; he had a renowned temper in his youth. He survived the Nika Riots where Justinian's soldiers butchered thirty thousand rioters in the hippodrome, and was still known to be racing into his 60s. Like Cosmas and Theo, the character of an old charioteer sickened by his past came out of the research and I ran with it.

Grateful thanks to my beta readers and everyone at Sharpe Books in getting this one to publication. All the mistakes are mine!

Theo, Cosmas, and Cal will return in The High King

Made in the USA
Monee, IL
01 September 2022